NORTH CAROLINA
STATE BOARD OF EDUCATION
DEPT. OF COMMUNITY COLLEGES

W9-CZW-909

A CELEBRATION OF BLACK AND AFRICAN WRITING

A Celebration of Black and African Writing

edited by

BRUCE KING

and

KOLAWOLE OGUNGBESAN

AHMADU BELLO UNIVERSITY PRESS

and

OXFORD UNIVERSITY PRESS

Ahmadu Bello University Press

ZARIA

Oxford University Press

OXFORD LONDON GLASGOW

NEW YORK TORONTO MELBOURNE WELLINGTON

IBADAN NAIROBI DAR ES SALAAM LUSAKA CAPE TOWN

KUALA LUMPUR SINGAPORE JAKARTA HONG KONG TOKYO

DELHI BOMBAY CALCUTTA MADRAS KARACHI

ISBN 0 19 575280 5

ABUP ISBN 978 125 001 1

Reprinted 1977

*Printed in Great Britain at the University Press, Oxford
by Vivian Ridler, Printer to the University
Published by Ahmadu Bello University Press, Zaria and
Oxford University Press Nigeria, P.M.B. 5095
Oxford House, Iddo Gate, Ibadan, Nigeria.*

TABLE OF CONTENTS

Foreword

While it is useful to celebrate the traditions and values of the past as part of our cultural heritage it is also necessary to remember that a vital culture is alive, energetic and changing. The essays in this book, although primarily intended as literary appreciation, offer a panoramic view of part of the modern black and African cultural and intellectual heritage. The essays form a roughly chronological sequence beginning with some of the first twentieth century African writers, and show the development of black creative writing as it emerged among West Indians seeking a cultural identity and then as part of the African independence movements. Subsequent chapters study such writers as Cesaire, Senghor, Achebe, Soyinka and Ngugi, who have achieved classical status in our time. There are also welcome essays on recent developments in African writing especially in Sierra Leone and in East Africa.

Throughout these essays certain themes recur, showing the important role of the modern literary tradition in bringing our cultural past in alignment with the present. Many of the writers studied are not only concerned with the rediscovery and status of their cultural heritage, they are also concerned with how its essence may be preserved in the modern world, how local traditions and customs are related to such larger matters as the independence struggle, the building of the modern state and the subtle connections felt among black men throughout the world. In a sense the history of modern black writing is in itself an analysis of our problems and a celebration of our cultural indentity.

Celebration of Black and African Writing was initially conceived at Ahmadu Bello University as part of the Second World Black and African Arts Festival. It is, however, truly an international effort, including essays from many countries. The large number of contributors from the West Indies is a testimony to this. Many of the contributors have played an important role in bringing black and African Writing into the mainstream of modern literary studies. Within the limited space available, the book is also international in its wide coverage of black writing from many different nations and language groups.

Iya Abubakar,
Vice-Chancellor,
Ahmadu Bello University.

Introduction

The development of black writing has been closely connected with the renewal of African cultural and political consciousness after the demoralizing effects of the slave trade and colonialism. In its earlier stages, African and black written literature was a matter of racial pride, showing that black men could succeed and answer back within European cultural forms. This was followed by the gradual elevation of the African and black cultural experience to an equal dignity with the European. The period of cultural affirmation has now passed. The rise of independent African and West Indian states during the late 1950s and 60s was paralleled by a phenomenal flowering of black writing. As writers have turned from the older problems of colonialism towards the new issues resulting from political independence, some of the original Pan-African idealism and concern for a racial cultural heritage have been lost. The Second Black and African Arts Festival, therefore, seems an occasion to see black literature in its historical and intercontinental perspectives. No one book can, of course, cover everything. Many important authors have had to be neglected. It is particularly unfortunate that essays could not be included on the vernacular literatures, which will undoubtedly be found to have had a strong influence on African writing in the European languages.

Written African literature came about with the introduction of Arabic and, later, European languages and culture. Who were the first black writers? Many Africans living in Arab and European countries adopted the culture of the land; their writing became part of European or Arab literary history. Perhaps modern black writing began when the slave trade and colonialism forced Africans to think of themselves as culturally or racially distinct. By the eighteenth century the slave trade had resulted in the first black poets of Brazil, Haiti and the United States. Slavery was supported by a doctrine of racial inferiority. Early American black writing reflected this situation: while protesting against slavery it sought assimilation or accommodation within the dominant culture. Such American poets as Phillis Wheatley and Jupiter Hammon, both slaves, were educated to give thanks to Christianity and white civilization for saving them from savage Africa. In South America and the West Indies, where more of African culture survived, although often in rather confused forms, a nostalgia for Africa and an affirmation of black identity developed. Writing in Portuguese, the Brazilian mulatto Domingos Caldas Barbosa brought his African heritage into his poems and songs. In Europe, where slavery was ending, such writers as Ottobah Cugoano and Olaudah Equiano represent a new kind of African, literate, westernized and conscious of his race. Cugoano's *Thoughts and Sentiments* (1787) uses arguments based on both the Bible and Enlightenment humanitarianism to oppose the slave trade. Equiano's *Narrative* (1789), while recounting the author's memories of Africa and his adventures in various parts of the world, describes the cruelties of slavery.

By the end of the eighteenth century the first schemes had started for resettling such men in Africa. This resulted in a European-educated elite which later provided the intellectual and literary leadership of the nineteenth and early twentieth century nationalist movements. Newspapers began in Liberia (1820s), Sierra Leone and Ghana (1850s), Nigeria and Senegal (1880s). Journalism provided a place for early creative and political writing. Poetry was soon being written in Liberia and Sierra Leone. Modern African historiography, in contrast to oral history, began with Abbé Boilat's *Esquisses Sénégalaises* (1853) and Carl Reindorf's *History of the Gold Coast and Asante* (1889). Such written history contributed to the retention of traditions and the development of national self-awareness. Towards the end of the nineteenth century vigorous written literatures began in such South African languages as Sotho, Xhosa and, later, Zulu. These literatures produced several minor classics, and are among the oldest continuous traditions of African creative writing. Perhaps the first truly African poet to write in Portuguese was Costa Alegre of São Tomé, who, while studying in Lisbon during the 1880s, felt alienated and distinct.

In the New World, consciously black poetry, referring to its African heritage, developed in nineteenth century Brazil around such writers as Gonçalves Dias, Luis Gonzaga Pinto da Gama, and, most important, João da Cruz e Sousa. Poetry was written in Haiti throughout the century, and Emeric Bergeaud's *Stella*, the first Haitian novel, was published in 1859. The first black American novel, William Wells Brown's *Clotel*, appeared in 1853. Paul Lawrence Dunbar, an important black American poet, began publishing towards the end of the century. Whereas black American writing of mid-century often consisted of slave narratives published in connection with the

Abolitionist movement, Dunbar presented an idyllic view of plantation life, which enabled him to bring rural black folk-culture into the domain of American literary high culture. The beginning of American black middle-class literature is represented by the novels of Charles Chesnutt, who wrote of exemplary American black heroes caught in situations of racial prejudice. If American writers sought to become part of white society, the West Indian increasingly turned towards Africa. Edward Blyden, a West Indian who lived in Liberia, is particularly interesting for anticipating the main themes of Négritude writing. He wrote of the communality of African life, the importance of the extended African family, and of the African's communion with nature. In Africa work and play are not separate and the social order is integrated with the religious. 'Africa may yet prove to be the spiritual conservatory of the world'. Blyden's vision influenced the early African nationalists and found expression in many later writers.

In 1901 Frédéric Marcelin published a 323-page novel, *Thémistocle Epaminondas Labasterre*. In what was to become the ironic mode of Haiti it was subtitled 'petit récit haïtien'. The next decade saw the appearance of René Maran's first volumes of poetry, although it was not until 1921 that he published his prize winning novel, *Batouala*. Writers from Haiti, Guyana and Martinique are noteworthy for combining African and indigenous subject matter with sophisticated French irony. The American occupation of the long independent black nation of Haiti, in 1915, no doubt contributed to the growing militancy of the francophonic West Indian writers who later influenced the rise of the Négritude movement. Haiti became the centre of Indigenism, which glorified the folklore of the black peasantry. In 1928 Jacques Roumain of Haiti wrote the influential poem 'Appel', although it was not until 1944 that he wrote *Gouverneurs de la rosée*, one of the major novels of what is called the literature of black revolt. Roumain brought a Marxist analysis of society to the Indigenist focus on the peasantry.

Meanwhile, in Africa, Ghanaian writing had started with O. Dazi Ako's poems, *The Seductive Coast* (1909) and, most important, J. E. Casely-Hayford's novel, *Ethiopia Unbound* (1911). *Ethiopia Unbound* is a strange, dream-like work, part autobiographical, part visionary; influenced by Blyden it both affirms the value of African culture, and argues for the need to create an African university-trained elite for the future. Its Pan-Negro vision and its allegorical techniques might be said to anticipate novels written by such Ghanaians as Ayi Kwei Armah and Kofi Awoonor during the late 1960s. In South

Africa the vernacular tradition produced what was to become a well-known classic, Thomas Mofolo's *Chaka* (1925), written in Sotho. Mofolo contributed to the transition from oral, tribal traditions to a modern consciousness by showing that African history could be complex. While we now think of traditional African culture as tribal and communal, many writers of the early twentieth century recall the empires of the past as a cultural heritage equivalent to the history of European nations which was being offered to Africans as the record of civilization. An important South African writer of the period was Solomon T. Plaatje, perhaps more interesting for his *Native Life in South Africa* (1916) and his diaries, which show a clear, precise intelligence, than for his romantic novel, *Mhudi* (1918). South African writing in both the vernaculars and English was continued throughout the next decades by James Jolobe, H. I. E. and R. R. R. Dhlomo, John Dube and Benedict Vilakazi.

By the 1920s Harlem had become the international focus of black culture. Claude McKay's *Home to Harlem* (1928) perhaps sums up the mood—McKay was from Jamaica. The period saw Jean Toomer's *Cane* (1923), Langston Hughes's *The Weary Blues* (1926), James Weldon Johnson's *God's Trombones* (1927) and the poems of Countee Cullen. The tone of the era was a mixture of *avant garde* techniques, use of the rural black American heritage of spirituals and blues, and a growing interest in the new urban black culture of the northern cities. By consciously incorporating the styles of black culture into their work, the Harlem writers were pointing the way towards the development of a black aesthetic.

There was continual contact among black writers and intellectuals throughout the world during the first three decades of the twentieth century. Several international congresses were held. Partly influenced by the Harlem Renaissance, the journal *La Revue du Monde Noir* was started in Paris in 1931. It was also strongly influenced by the francophonic, West Indian Indigenism movement, of which many of its contributors were formerly members. Led by Jean Price-Mars, who had studied the folk ways of the peasantry, and who recommended the use of Haitian rather than European material, the mood of the Haitian writers was defiantly anti-bourgeois, anti-assimilationist. The 1930s also saw the appearance in Paris of the journal *L'Etudiant Noir*. Aimé Césaire from Martinique and Léon Damas from Guyana joined with Léopold Senghor from Senegal to assert a black culture and identity different from that of European civilization. The magazine was influential in establishing the concept of Négritude which was to play such an important role in giving cultural and intellectual support to the independence movements of the 50s.

The attitudes of *L'Etudiant Noir* were an expression of an emerging concern with black culture throughout Africa and the Americas. The Cuban Negrismo movement of the 1920s and 30s is an example. The great Cuban poet, Nicolas Guillén, based his lyrics on rhythms and words supposedly of African origin. In Haiti, Phlippe Thoby-Marcelin published *La Négresse Adolescente* (1932), while Léon Damas published *Pigments* (1937). Akiki Nyabongo of Uganda produced *The Story of an African Chief or Africa Answers Back* (1935). There were two Afro-Brazilian Congresses (1934, 1937) and in 1936 the Uruguayan writer, Ildefonso Pereda Valdés, published an anthology of Negro poetry in the Americas. Throughout the period there was a rejection of assimilation into European culture and a deepening study of African traditions. Ousmane Socé's novel, *Karim* (1935), contrasted traditional village life with Europeanized, urban Dakar; Paul Hazoumé's novel, *Doguicimi* (1938), reconstructed a detailed picture of the old kingdom of Dahomey in the early nineteenth century; Jomo Kenyatta's *Facing Mount Kenya* (1938) recorded the educated African's awareness of his alienation from his people and from European culture. Whereas Hazoumé continued the interest in an heroic African past, Kenyatta was moving towards the emphasis on village and tribal life which was later to become a model of African communal culture for such writers as Laye, Achebe and Ngugi.

The decade ended with the publication of Aimé Césaire's long poem, *Cahier d'un retour au pays natal* (1939) and Richard Wright's short stories, *Uncle Tom's Children* (1938) and novel, *Native Son* (1940). They may be said to have put black writing in French and English on the world literary map. Both were concerned with the situation of the black man in the Americas. A major difference between authors from Africa, where there was still a vital village and tribal culture, and black writers from many other parts of the world was that the latter had been cut off from their heritage without being accepted as Americans or Europeans. Many westernized black intellectuals either turned towards ideologies which promised to create equality or they attempted to reconstruct an African personality out of the cultural survivals still retained as part of black American folk ways. Césaire made up the expression 'Négritude'. While he felt he had to liberate himself from his educated, European self-consciousness before he could create a new black identity, he saw that it was necessary to go beyond identification with a black folk-culture if a mentality of inferiority was to be transformed into a new, aggressive, black personality. One could free oneself from habit, disrupt rationality, and create new kinds of consciousness through a psychology of violence and revolt. Césaire's work thus looks forward to the psychological and political theories of Frantz Fanon, also from Martinique. The West Indian fusion of Indigenism with French Symbolist and Surrealist literary methods also began a major tradition of black poetry. In the tradition, which stems from Damas and Césaire through Senghor to U Tam'si, the repetition of poetic images knits emotional associations together; such poetry progresses by dialectical contrasts and eruptions of new perspectives, rather than by linear thought or narrative. Verse written in this manner, while creating a feeling of revolt against European culture, approximates some of the elaborate rhetorical patterning and development by linking of associated but independent units of meaning often found in African oral poetry.

Richard Wright was the first black American novelist to deal seriously with ghetto life in the northern cities. While *Native Son*, like much protest literature of the period, emphasizes physical details and strong sensations to show how man is conditioned by his environment, Wright's instinctive use of images and symbols makes his novel superior to most 'naturalistic' fiction. He portrays racial discrimination as an aspect of the exploitation of the weak by the strong within capitalism. Injustice creates frustration which breeds revolutionary violence. Violence, however, is only a first liberating step towards the creation of a proletarian class consciousness which will unite the downtrodden whites and blacks to bring about a Communist society. Living during the Depression, McKay, Wright and many other black intellectuals of the 30s, were influenced by Marxist thought. This influence continued during the next two decades, when leading writers accepted the Marxist position that racism and colonization were a product of capitalism. They often concluded, however, that the situation of the black man was not the same as that of the urban white proletariat.

Major events of the 1940s included the founding of influential magazines and the editing of important anthologies. *BIM* was started in Barbados in 1942. In 1943 Roger Bastide edited *A poesia afro-brasileira;* in 1947 *Présence Africaine* began. 1948 saw the establishment of the East African Literature Bureau, to encourage African authorship, and, most important, Senghor's *Anthologie de la nouvelle poésie nègre et malgache de langue française.* Senghor's anthology, with an introduction by Jean-Paul Sartre, brought the variety and richness of the developing tradition of francophonic black writing to world attention.

In 1953 the journal *Bingo* was started in Senegal. The appearance of local sources of publication helped create a more direct sense of community between authors and readers.

The period 1945 to 1956 saw the publication of most of the classics of the Négritude movement. Although the poems of Damas and Césaire had previously set the mood, its first major African works were *Chants d'Ombre* (1945), *Hosties Noires* (1948) and *Chants pour Naëtt* (1949), in which Senghor combined a sophisticated use of the techniques of modern French lyric poetry with African images and rhythms. While using the idiom and style of *avant garde* literature, the poems created a sense of Africa's heroic past and the warmth of communal life. Birago Diop followed with *Les Contes d'Amadou Koumba* (1947), an attempt to recreate the manner of the traditional story tellers. Bernard Dadié's poems, *Afrique Debout* (1950), and *Légendes Africaines* (1955) contributed to the movement. Camara Laye's *L'Enfant Noir* (1953) portrayed the harmonious life of an African village and the growing tension the African child feels when he goes to school and is caught between two cultures.

For black men whose ways of life have changed rapidly and who have often moved between two cultures, autobiography is a natural literary form of self-assertion. Laye's genius was to turn the autobiographical novel into a consciously representative genre for the modern African whose education would uproot him from family and tribal values. Laye's attempt at being representative may be said to be part of the desire to create a communal aesthetic in contrast to European individualism. Thus modern African writing, which developed as a result of detribalization, now aspired to recreate communal archetypes and values. Négritude writing of the period was influenced by such anthropologists as Placide Tempels, who in *Philosophie bantoue* (1945) claimed that the African had a direct, intuitive, harmonious relation to life and the cosmos which was different from the cold conceptual logic of European civilization. Senghor spoke of himself as a cultural mulatto who wanted to create a new humanism combining European rationality with African intuitiveness. The period of affirming a separate African psychology and cosmology was followed by a literature of direct protest against colonialism: Mongo Béti's *Ville Cruelle* (1954), F. L. Oyono's *Une Vie de Boy* (1956), David Diop's *Coups de Pilon* (1956), and the early novels of Sembène Ousmane. The literature which later developed in the Cameroons, from Béti onwards, became progressively ironic and satirical, as writers became aware of a discrepancy between rhetoric of communal, tribal life and the cultural chaos and materialism of contemporary Africa.

Basically the Négritude movement began by asserting a black identity. It then created modern literary reconstructions of traditional African society, philosophy and customs; having made its point about the existence of a valid African culture, it moved into protest themes as the momentum towards African political independence gathered force. Many of the writers of the period believed that the communal life of the tribal village would lead naturally to the emergence of socialist African nations. Perhaps the most successful ideological novel is Sembène Ousmane's *Les Bouts de Bois de Dieu* (1960), which avoids most of the clichés of earlier 'left' literature. The novel shows the importance of the labour unions in the independence movement. The workers are Africans and their fight against exploitation and growth of political awareness are part of the West African anti-colonial struggle.

If Négritude was ignored in English-speaking Africa, as less relevant to conditions under British indirect rule, its influence was beneficial in the Portuguese colonies, where Africans had to become 'assimilated' before they could gain political and economic rights. Until recently, writing in Portuguese by Africans was sporadic and only a few names achieved reputation outside their own areas. The Angolan novelist Oscar Ribas and the Cape Verdean poet Jorges Barbosa are perhaps the best known. In the early 1950s the situation changed when a group of African students in Lisbon known as the 'Casa dos Estudantes do Império' began to publish short stories, poetry and political works, until the authorities moved against them. With such writers as Césaire and Senghor in mind, they were a catalyst for emerging literary, intellectual and political energies. Négritude influenced Mario de Andrade and Francisco José Tenreiro's collection, *Caderno da Poesia Negra de Expressão Portuguesa* (1953) and the 'Vamos Descobrir Angola' writers, including Antônio Agostinho Neto, whose *Colectânea de poemas* was published in 1961.

When Victor Reid of Jamaica published *New Day* in 1949, the title, subject matter and style of the novel were usually taken as symbolic of the hopes of the West Indies at the time, when a new constitution was being introduced. Reid's attempt to construct a mid-nineteenth century rural Jamaican dialect for his narrator in *New Day* might be considered a cultural manifesto showing that the West Indies has a useable history and past. A major period of West Indian writing in English followed: Derek Walcott's 25 *Poems* (1949), Samuel Selvon's *A Brighter Sun* (1952), George Lamming's *In the Castle of My Skin*

(1953), and the first novels of John Hearne. As a result of the confused history of the West Indies, and the many races and cultures within the area, most of the writers have made use of personal or regional identity as their theme or even directly as their subject matter. This produced a literature of great sensitivity and awareness in which the educated imagination could explore, meditate upon and respond to the varied aspects of West Indian society. During the 1960s there was a change in mood, as many intellectuals began to see the economically under-privileged, culturally dispossessed black peasant as the authentic West Indian. The current militant mood is perhaps best represented by Edward Brathwaite's Césairean-influenced poetry.

The sporadic development of black South African literature in recent years has been directly influenced by the nation's rapid social and political changes. South African writing came to international attention in the early 40s with the first novels of Peter Abrahams, especially *Mine Boy* (1946). At the time the black South African had become largely urbanized, or, if living in a rural area, worked on a white farm. There was a strong trade union movement backed by Marxist intellec-tuals, to which the African writer was attracted in seeking equality within an increasingly industrialized multi-racial society. *Mine Boy*, a protest novel, portrays a typical modern African who has left the impoverished tribal areas to work in a city. He is brought to political consciousness through an act of revolt against the harsh conditions in the mine. The African townships which grew up around white urban centres produced many writers, who were later forced into exile by the repressive measures instituted by the Nationalist government from 1948 onwards. No doubt because of such urbanization, South African writing is often marked by a strong sense of the individual rather than of the village, tribe, nation or race. The vitality of this black urban culture is reflected in such autobiographies as Peter Abrahams's *Tell Freedom* (1954), Ezekiel Mphalele's *Down Second Avenue* (1959) and Bloke Modisane's *Blame Me on History* (1963), and in the lively articles and short stories published in *Drum*, which was founded in Johannesburg in 1951. The Marxist-influenced tradition of the 40s continues in the novels and short stories of Alex La Guma; realistic descriptions of filth and squalor show a harsh urban environ-ment where the poor are conditioned to a life of petty crime and violence.

While some writers—James Baldwin is particularly notable—have tried to avoid being limited to protest themes, most recent black American literature focuses on the problems arising from the discrimination against blacks in the United States. The narrator of Ralph Ellison's *The Invisible Man* (1953), perhaps the finest novel written by a black American, might be said to live through the intellectual history of the modern black American: Booker T. Washingtonism, Garveyism and Marxism. The novel concludes with the narrator celebrating modern, hip, urban black culture, with its role-playing and irony; he is, however, still seeking means of organizing black America into a political movement. Whereas Ellison has written with sympathy of the dignity and culture of the rural southern Negro, most contemporary writers have preferred to write about life in the northern cities. Lorraine Hansberry's popular play, *A Raisin in the Sun* (1959), portrayed the difficulties of blacks aspiring to leave the urban slums for a middle-class life. Beginning with LeRoi Jones's plays of the early 60s, many writers scorned such aspirations, and tried to articulate the angry alienation felt by most black Americans.

The development of African writing was somewhat slower in English-speaking than in francophonic countries. Although there had been a thin but continuous tradition of poems and short stories in English by such authors as E. H. Appah, Roland Dempster and Michael Dei-Anang, the poets were still largely wedded to sentimental themes and an old-fashioned style, while the novel was still in its infancy. Amos Tutuola's *The Palm-Wine Drinkard* (1952) retold in English the kind of material found in D. O. Fagunwa's Yoruba tales. Another Nigerian, Cyprian Ekwensi, used the temptations and problems of urban life for his novels, but he was less successful in mastering such technical matters as form, characterization and dialogue. The situation changed towards the end of the decade. The Nigerian Gabriel Okara and the Ghanaian Kwesi Brew were more modern and accomplished in style than previous poets; their work also showed more awareness of the cultural problems of modern Africa. 1958 saw the publication of Chinua Achebe's *Things Fall Apart*, perhaps the classic novel of traditional village and tribal life. *Things Fall Apart*, while highly technically accomplished, africanized the novel by its use of Ibo idioms and a narrator who, like the story tellers, represented the communal point of view. Achebe's novels and those of many Nigerian writers who soon followed him were part of the cultural nationalism which paralleled political independence. The novels showed that Africans have a past not recorded in most history books and a rich culture which was fragmented by colonialism.

Those whom we have come to think of as the main Nigerian writers appeared soon after Achebe. By 1960, the year of Nigerian independence, Wole Soyinka was already known as a promising dramatist, although *A Dance of the Forests* and *The Lion and the Jewel* were not published until 1963. Christopher Okigbo's *Heavensgate* (1962) is the first really modern sequence of African poems in English. It was by mastering the modern poetic idiom that such writers as Okigbo and J. P. Clark were able to bring the resources of oral poetry into their writing. Much of the literary production of the period centred upon *Black Orpheus*, founded in 1957, and Mbari, a literary club located in Ibadan, which published many of the new writers from other parts of Africa, including Alex La Guma, Dennis Brutus, and Kofi Awoonor. Whereas the francophonic authors affirmed the dignity of African civilization against the political and cultural effects of colonialism, the Nigerians wrote freely about the problems of tribal life and modern Africa. Literature had become de-colonialized in the sense that it was now written for Africans and not as part of an independence movement.

In East Africa creative writing in English began later than in West Africa; it was influenced by the remembrance of the Mau-Mau uprising in Kenya and the presence of a foreign settler caste which had dispossessed many Africans of their tribal lands. The magazine *Transition*, started in Uganda (1961), was more politically and intellectually oriented than the Nigerian *Black Orpheus*. Ngugi wa Thiong'o's first novels, *Weep Not Child* (1964) and *The River Between* (1965, but written earlier), show the influence of Achebe's communal point of view, his portrayal of traditional life and his awareness of the dynamics of social change. Ngugi's writing, while aiming for objectivity of presentation, has a didactic contemporary political function. Africa's cultural traditions must be preserved to bind society together, and the various wounds caused by the struggle for independence must be healed if a modern nation is to succeed. Similarly, the appearance of an English version of Okot p'Bitek's *Song of Lawino* (1966) showed the direction East African writing would take with its use of the techniques of oral literature and its attack on Africans who had lost their cultural traditions.

The latter part of the 1960s witnessed a literature of disillusionment in which Africans took stock of the period since independence. Writing increasingly focused on why independence did not bring individual freedom and social equality. Achebe's *A Man of the People* (1966) satirized the corruption and materialism of independent Africa; Laye's *Dramouss* (1966) lamented the turning away from Senghorian humanism and cooperation with the French towards the single party state; Soyinka's *Kongi's Harvest* (1967) satirized the growth of dictatorships and ideologies. One of the most significant passages in the literature of the period occurs at the end of *A Man of the People*, where we are told that the sayings of the past, which epitomized tribal values, are no longer relevant in a modern Africa obsessed by material wealth.

Disillusionment was followed by works which analyzed the earlier dream of African unity and continuity with past traditions. The title of Kwei Armah's *The Beautyful Ones Are Not Yet Born* (1968) is symbolic. The novel shows the hopes and disillusionments of the African intellectual from the period after World War II, when there was an upsurge of feeling that colonialism must end, until after Nkrumah's downfall. A dream has been betrayed. An obsession for acquiring European luxuries has replaced the ideals of the independence movements. Yambo Ouologuem's *Le Devoir de Violence* (1968) attempts a 'demystification' of African legends, customs and history. For centuries African rulers have sold or exploited the masses; Africa must liberate itself from its past before it can be really free. Daniel Ewandé's satire, *Vive le Président* (1968), continues a francophonic African tradition of seeking a new humanism rather than a specific African identity. For such writers Africa and the Third World are still in the grips of an economic and spiritual neo-colonialism; the rhetoric of independence and traditional values sustains the elite and prevents the development of an authentic modern culture. Such criticism should be seen as an attempt to feel one's way towards relevant values in a rapidly changing society. The desire for an authentic modern African culture has been paralleled by the increasing use of traditional oral literature as a model for modern writing. The Ghanaians Kofi Awoonor in *This Earth My Brother* (1971) and Kwei Armah in *Two Thousand Seasons* (1973) have followed Okot and recent East African writers in using the structures and stylistic features of traditional laments and dirges in their books.

A will to authenticity has been a major force behind twentieth century African and black writing. Although writers, by education or achievement, are part of an elite, black writers have continually attempted to define or express the culture of the people. The desire for authenticity can be seen in the attempt to create a black style based upon oral literature, black urban culture, or traditional African symbols. The black writer still speaks as a representative voice of problems which concern the nation, continent or race. Indeed one of the strengths of black writing has been its refusal to demarcate sharply the boundary between the artist and his community. The commitment remains the same although, as a result of new political and social conditions, the perception has changed with each generation.

From the vantage point of the mid-70s it can be said that black and African writing reveals both an intercontinental tradition and the growth of national literary traditions. If writers continue to remind us of the Pan-African ideal and its history, we are also conscious that many of the nations of Africa and the West Indies now have long traditions of written literature and have started to assemble a canon of significant national authors.

B. King
K. Ogungbesan
Ahmadu Bello University 1975

1

Early South African Black Writing

by

T. J. COUZENS

Just as an economy at a certain stage 'takes off' (and the South African economy 'took off' in the 1930s) so South African literature reached its turning-point in the 1950s and writers such as Peter Abrahams, Ezekiel Mphahlele, Can Themba and Lewis Nkosi came to the fore. Many of these writers were associated with *Drum* magazine, which first saw print in March 1951. But such an abundance required a long prior history of the slow accumulation of literary capital and the application of much imaginative industry. The writers after 1950 owe much to their often unsung predecessors whose labour over a period of more than a hundred years before laid the foundations for what modern black South African literature has achieved. The production of oral literature in South Africa goes back into the unrecorded years of history and its successes are undisputed. Written literature is a much younger sibling, only a hundred and fifty years old.

In June 1953 an anonymous writer in the Zulu-English newspaper *Ilanga Lase Natal* wrote a series of articles on the evolution of black literature, music and the press in celebration of the newspaper's fiftieth anniversary. It was, in retrospect, a symbolic event. The writer was undoubtedly H. I. E. Dhlomo, who will in future be seen as one of the most significant early writers who laid the foundations for modern South African literature. The newspaper (and, indeed, the institution of journalism in general) was one of the major influences and breeding grounds for black literature. And the time was just about the beginning of the new era for black South African literature. What follows is a brief and necessarily sketchy survey of some of the elements which made possible the post–1950 'Renaissance'.

In the beginning the written word was with the missionaries. In the first of the above-mentioned articles H. I. E. Dhlomo acknowledges their achievements:

As in several other spheres of African progress, the missionaries were the pioneers in the field of written Bantu literature. We say 'Written' because there was already a vast and rich body of living oral literature, not only handed down from generation to generation but constantly and persistently being created—folklore stories from history, animal and tales of nature, sagas and even epics of heroes, kings, battles and tribes. These types of epic narration took the form of mystical and moving 'izibongo'—a kind of Zulu poetry that students of art-forms have found intriguing and about which much has been written in the three past decades. So that when the missionaries came they found a rich mine of ready if not recorded material. The works of missionaries were, therefore, mostly religious, linguistic, historical, anthropological and about folk tales and customs.

As well as helping to produce the first written literature the missionaries were the first to inspire the recording of black music and were the initiators of the black press. Very soon after the first large-scale contact between black and white took place on the 'Eastern Frontier' in the Cape, the Glasgow Missionary Society established itself in the Tyumie valley where, in 1824, they founded a mission and the first printing press. In 1826 the mission was named Lovedale and it was from here that the first black writing appeared. Under the influence of the missionaries the first productions were grammars of the vernacular languages, translations of the Bible, and collections of oral stories, as well as, in the field of music and language, the introduction of hymns. In 1837, under the Wesleyan missionaries, the first Xhosa newspaper was printed, appearing off and on for the next five years. This was a crucial event. Journalism has played a vital, but largely underestimated, part in the development of black South African literature.[1]

In the late 1850s a young man, Tiyo Soga, began the translation into his own language of *Pilgrim's Progress*, a task he completed in 1886. Translation was a form of literary art for which Sol Plaatje was to become well known in the Tswana language, and Bunyan's allegorical work (partly, perhaps, because it fitted in so well with fable forms and concerns) was to be the model for or chief influence on some of the works of the first two major vernacular novelists, the Xhosa writer S. E. K. Mqhayi, and the Sotho writer Thomas Mofolo. In 1914 Mqhayi published his *Ityala lama-wele*, a novel which was concerned with the defence of the traditional law of black society.

2

His second novel, *U-DonJadu*, published in 1929, is a utopian novel dealing with his envisaged ideal Xhosa independent state.

But acknowledged as greatest of the earliest vernacular writers is Thomas Mofolo. His first book, published in 1907, entitled *Moeti oa Bochabela* (*The Traveller of the East*[2]) is a fascinating production. It is a novel in the form of a long fable. A young black man, sickened by the evils and hypocrisy of his society, decides to leave it in order to seek God (whose existence he has already inferred from the harmony and beauty of nature). The influence of both Bunyan and the Romantics is clear. He travels east, meets the newly-arrived whites who tell him about Christ and he finally crosses the sea to reach the home of God. But apart from this heavy Europeanization of belief the real interest of the book lies in its technique, its inclusion of Sotho myths within the larger form of the novel. He accepts Christianity without rejecting the customs of his people and the essential truth lying at the heart of the Sotho mythology.

As the people realised that Fekisi was an unusual person, they told him the whole truth as they knew it, they added nothing, they left out nothing, they told him as they knew. They told him the things of long ago, of old time, which they had heard told them. They told him about Kholumolumo.

Long ago, they said, there appeared a marvellous monster, with a long tongue, which ate all the people, which ate all the animals. This monster would pick up a man at a distance or a thing at a distance by means of its long tongue, and swallow it. It swallowed people alive, and an ox and any animal the same, all things indeed which walked. It roamed about the earth thus, until it finished human beings and animals. Because of the weight of its belly, it sat down, and gathered in by its tongue only. When all the people were finished up and the animals likewise, a single pregnant woman escaped, and hid herself. She was confined whilst still in hiding, and delivered of a male child. That child puzzled his mother much, even when he was still young. He was hardly born before he had teeth. He quickly asked his mother where the people had gone, and his mother told him. Then he fashioned a bow, he fashioned arrows broad like a razor and sharp and said "Mother, lead me to that monster, that I may kill it." His mother refused, but at length her son overcame her, and she took him.

When they were still a long way off, Kholumolumo saw them. It stretched out its tongue and tried to lick them up but the boy

3

stabbed its tongue and cut it; it tried to lick them up, he stabbed its tongue and cut it; it tried to lick them up, the boy stabbed its tongue and cut it; it tried to lick them up, he stabbed its tongue and cut it, and so he went on cutting it; it grew shorter and shorter, and they came nearer and nearer. Kholumolumo nearly went mad with pain and with desire to swallow a human being. It was in a furious rage, its eyes became red, they were as blood, but the weight of its belly overcame it, it could not stand, it could not fight. The boy kept on coming nearer and nearer, and at length he killed it. And then he took a knife and plunged it into its belly.

The greatness of that monster's belly was more than Basutoland of those times, that is to say, that boy could not see the other side of it. He saw only the side he was on. When he pierced its belly a person screamed from inside and said: "Do not pierce me, make a hole over there." When he tried to pierce there, a dog howled; when he wanted to pierce in a different place an ox bellowed. In the end he just made a tear without listening to the cries of those in the belly. Out came people, cattle, dogs—everything living took the opportunity to come out. Then all the people thanked that boy, and they even made him their chief. But soon jealousy arose among the men who had been saved by the boy, at being governed by a boy, and finally they murdered him. My readers know this fable and its ending. I will not relate too many details.[3]

The parallels to Christianity are obvious. The use of near repetition is close to oral style. In a sense this short fable represents in miniature the whole novel which has the form of an extended fable. This kind of experimentation, where the novel is consciously seen as an extension of the fable form, was equalled by Mofolo's third and most famous work, *Chaka*. His second novel, *Pitseng*, deals with the confusion created by the introduction of Christianity into traditional society—particularly on the level of love and marriage. *Chaka* is really the first psychological novel by a black South African. Finished in 1910, published in 1925, *Chaka* is a blend of European models (the influence, for instance, of *Macbeth* and *Doctor Faustus* is clear) and African forms, for example, praise songs. Though partly critical of Chaka from the moral standpoint of a Christian, the book nevertheless recognizes Chaka as an early African nationalist who sacrificed personal happiness (he kills his lover Noliwe) to unite his people against the coming threat of the whites. Particularly effective is Mofolo's creation of the character Isanusi, a Mephistopheles-like witchdoctor, who, in return for a

4

promise of final payment when Chaka reaches the height of his power, helps Chaka to that power. In an aesthetically satisfying ending, Chaka discovers that the final payment is Chaka's final sacrifice—his own death. This novel acknowledging Chaka as a great nationalist hero was completed two years before the founding, in 1912, of the African National Congress, one of the oldest of African nationalist movements.

Although many of the early works by black writers are overwhelmed by missionary, Christian and European influence, modern black literature nevertheless owes a big debt to these early, often apparently staid grammarians, translators, hymn-writers, educators and experimenters with form. They represent a continuity of black writing almost from the first moment of contact with literacy, an early, not always totally recognized but perhaps intuitively perceived, perception that future resistance by the blacks would depend on their development of this vital medium. Oral literature and written literature fused into a single continuous strain of literature. Some of the above productions are not normally considered to be literature in the pure sense, but they were the necessary precursors of such literature.

But although black literature for a long time went overboard for western influences, the continuity of political resistance within the medium, over and above the continuity of written literature, should not be underestimated. Many blacks, once perceiving that 'primary resistance' on the battlefield was no longer viable, took to forms of 'secondary resistance', for example, separatist religions, as a sublimated means of expressing political and social grievances. This orientation of consciousness, perceived as political necessity, is beautifully expressed in a poem written in the 1880s, by I. Citashe.

> Your cattle are gone, my countrymen!
> Go rescue them! Go rescue them!
> Leave the breechloader alone
> And turn to the pen.
> Take paper and ink,
> For that is your shield,
> Your rights are going!
> So pick up your pen.
> Load it, load it with ink.
> Sit on a chair.
> Repair not to Hoho,
> But fire with your pen.[4]

Resistance then has never been suppressed. It has merely altered its form. As in the above example literature itself became a means of expressing 'secondary resistance'. Another such poem was written by Mboza Matshiwulwana to Miss Harrietta Colenso, in 1895.

The sons of our people were scattered and slain on the hillside,
 Their women were borne
To the bed of the foe-men–our strong men were given as cattle
 Whom the lion hath torn.
We were hunted and slain—We were dead—yes, the worms devoured
 us,—
 An end of strife!—
When lo! no men, but a woman, came forth to save us,—
 And brought us back to life.
O tender hands! Oh heart of a sister! O mother,
 Whose child is our race!
O sing her praises, Usutu! There is not such another
 On the whole earth's face.
Alone she stood before the face of the mighty—
 She said—Ye do wrong!
No weapon had she but the word of her lips to smite them,
 But lo! she was strong.
We lay as men doomed to death, fast bound in a cavern,
 No light was to see,
Save a hole that a man might span with his thumb and finger.
 No hope,—then came she,—
And with only her two bare hands, she clave us an opening,
 And bade us go free.
What shall the children of Shaka say, when they praise her!
 Whose tongue hath the skill!—
O the brave, the wary—who flew on swift wings of pity,
 To save us from ill:
Mandiza Matotobha, thou child of the Just One,—
 Who loved us,
 Our hearts love thee still.[5]

Of this poem H. I. E. Dhlomo wrote in the late thirties:

(a) It gives the lie to the contention that Africans are ungrateful. In my opinion they are too docile and ready to pay thanks. Here, a tribal poet sings of a white person.

(b) It proves that Africans fully appreciated and honoured womanhood.

(c) For its poetic value. And remember it was composed by what was called a savage, a raw man, a child—by a member of that group which was the army of domestic servants, mine workers, farm labourers and other classes of unskilled workers who suffer so many disabilities, the chief of which is to regard them as unfeeling, unable to think, sub-humans.[6]

Obviously, one of the most direct methods of articulating grievances was through political organizations, such as the A. N. C. from 1912 onwards, and through such institutions as newspapers, which from 1880 onwards began to replace the missions as the main institutional bases for black literature. The first fifty years of the twentieth century were characterized by the efforts of the black educated elite to reach a wider audience of black people, to understand their own history, to get closer to native literary forms.

Because of political factors and the relative smallness of the black reading public, publication presented a difficult problem for black writers during this period. Sol Plaatje, for instance, who wrote the first novel in English by a black South African, *Mhudi*,[7] about 1917, had to wait until 1930 before the book was published despite the fact that he submitted it to many publishers. Newspapers provided the one consistent outlet for expression. Consequently, the medium had a great influence on the kind of writing which appeared. It probably encouraged the forms of poetry, the short story and the essay rather than longer forms like the novel. Writers tended to orientate themselves towards public concerns rather than private and psychological worries. The frequent appearance of short biographies in newspapers may have helped lead to that characteristic form of South African black writing, the autobiography. Although there were also obvious disadvantages in many of the black newspapers being largely white-owned, the institution led to other phenomena. The period 1900-1950 is characterized by the close connection between journalism, literature and politics. John Dube founded *Ilanga Lase Natal* in 1903, was the first president of the African National Congress in 1912 and published the first Zulu novel, *Insila ka Shaka*,[8] in the 1920s. Sol Plaatje edited two Tswana-English newspapers, was the first secretary of the African National Congress, and wrote a famous political book, *Native Life in South Africa*,[9] a slashing attack on the Native Land Act of 1913, and his novel, *Mhudi*. I have argued elsewhere that *Mhudi* is not only a work with a new historical bias for that period but was also a deeply political, and revolutionary, book.[10] R. R. R. Dhlomo, who wrote a short novel in English, *An African Tragedy* (1928)[11], which deals with the terrors of urban life for the country man, and who then turned to writing novels in Zulu, was an assistant editor of *Bantu World* in the thirties (and also edited the women's page), and editor of *Ilanga Lase Natal* from 1943 onwards. Perhaps the greatest of the Zulu poets, B. W. Vilakazi[12], consistently wrote for the newspapers. Both of these, together with lesser-known writers, were invariably strong supporters of the A. N. C.

The same interests can be found in the life and works of H. I. E. Dhlomo. Dr. N. W. Visser and I recently rediscovered the unpublished manuscripts of Herbert Dhlomo. These writings are a unique achievement for a black African in the thirties. The sheer bulk of the writing is staggering. We have discovered thirteen unpublished plays (over and above his single published play[13]), several short stories, many essays and a book on *Zulu Life and Thought*. At present best known for his published 40-page poem, *Valley of a Thousand Hills*, Herbert Dhlomo will be seen in the future as one of the more important figures and writers in the black South Africa of the thirties and forties. For, in addition to the above manuscripts, we have discovered hundreds of pages of his journalism, often written under a pseudonym. Amongst all this great volume of writing he touches on most subjects which preoccupy all the other better-known writers of the time—writers like Dube, Plaatje, Mqhayi, Mofolo, R. R. R. Dhlomo, Vilakazi and A. C. Jordan, writer in Xhosa of one of the greatest South African novels, *Ingqumbo yeminyanya* (The Wrath of the Ancestors).[14] H. I. E. Dhlomo's writings can therefore be seen as largely representative of other writers of the period and to some extent as a culmination of the preceding literary history of blacks in South Africa.

His range of subject matter is wide. He wrote in English five historical plays which ignore tribal boundaries. Although a Zulu, he takes a largely nationalist viewpoint. He has two plays, *Ntsikana* and *The Girl Who Killed To Save*, which deal with Xhosa history; his play *Moshesh* concerns the founding of the Basuto nation and *Dingana* and *Cetywayo* deal with events concerning the Zulus. The remainder of his plays are set in contemporary South Africa and range over such issues as the relationships between 'Africans' and 'Coloureds', the conditions of workers in factories, the role of the artist in his society, the nature of marriage, the (for him) hypocritical stance of white liberals, education, ancestor communion, doctors and nurses.

8

Like Vilakazi he was heavily influenced by the Romantic writers and by Shakespeare, often to the superficial detriment of his writing. But below the surface there is a persistent strong undertone of political resistance. This is frequently expressed explicitly, as in such poems as 'Because I'm Black', which begins:

Because I'm black
You think I lack
The talents, feelings and ambitions
That others have;
I do not think I crave positions
That others crave.

Other poems, though, are more subtle, more implicit. 'The Harlot', for instance, is a poem concerned with the desperate lot of the *Lumpenproletariat*, a poem of which Frantz Fanon would surely have approved.

I have no love for you,
You to whom my flower I give. ·
I need your aid . . . I don't care who . . .
For, though poor, I too must live.

You call me harlot,
Forget my cursed lot.
'Tis you, yes you
Proud Christian, greedy Boss, you apathetic citizen,
Didst me undo,
Though now my company you eschew . . .
For you retain a system that breeds me—despised denizen.

Yet I am Queen
I choose whom I would choose!
'Tis you, not I, who lose,
I form a chaining breeding link between
The black and white;
And in my way I fight
For racial harmony;
For in dire poverty
We are the same,
Play one grim game,
And when colour counts for nought
When men in stark realities are caught;

Their eyes are open and they see
They are alike. For poverty,
Like Capital (or truth and works of art)
Reveals the naked aching human heart.

Call me unclean
Yet I am Queen
Your daughters, sons, wives, husbands, sweethearts know
I reign! With tears and bleeding hearts they crown my brow!
For I am Queen
Although unclean![15]

But Dhlomo's great achievement is that there is in the expanse of his
writing an implicit attempt at a synthesis of the historical, religious,
political, social and literary life of his people. He tries to encompass
the past and the present, the elite and the illiterate, the rural and
urban. He tries to preserve and he tries to incorporate change.

In *A Girl Who Killed To Save* he puts forward the at-first startling
theory that the Xhosa Suicide was, in the long term, a beneficial occur-
rence. He justifies this in terms of his belief that rapid modernization
was necessary for a successful nationalist movement and the attaining
of political equality between black and white. Yet without contradiction
he can defend aspects of the past. In 1954 his play *Dingana* was produced in the Durban City Hall. (Its original version was written
before 1941). In the same year he wrote an article on Dingana.

In discussing the subject with some Europeans I was amazed
with their unquestioning and childlike reliance on what they call
'authorities' on the subject. Most of the 'authorities' are the well-
known South African European historians, missionaries and tra-
veller-traders of olden times. It is surprising that intelligent,
educated persons regard these 'authorities' as correct and final
in these matters. First, as even a cursory reading of the records
concerned will show, the supposedly infallible 'authorities' con-
tradict each other and give different versions of and impute
conflicting reasons for the same historical incidents .... It only
goes to prove the old observation that a history of a people is
never written until it is written from two or more sides. So far,
South African history is written by Europeans from their point
of view.

He goes on, for instance, to dispute the usual idea that Dingana sold
Piet Retief land before he had the Trekker murdered.

10

At once we find a clash in meanings, customs and interpretations. According to Zulu customs land is never bought or given. It is allocated or 'lent'. It is impossible to think of Dingana 'giving' land to Europeans in the sense of purchase and ownership.[16]

He finally sees Dingana not merely in the normal interpretation as a bloodthirtsty and treacherous savage but as a partly tragic nationalist hero.

Was not Dingana (according to his own light and tactics of the times) defending his country against what he regarded as an invasion?

Dhlomo had integrated these ideas in the original version of the play. Recalling Shaka's dying prophecy that the white birds would come and conquer the Zulu nation, he probes Dingana's fears of and reactions to the whites.

BONGOZA: The Boers have one aim only—land and cattle, the very things that are the soul of our race. They have also come in great numbers like invaders, I smell dust, sister of my father!

DINGANA: You speak weight and depth, Zulus. The bowl.

BONGOZA: Thou of heaven!

NDLELA: The beer speaks worlds to me. (Drinks)

BONGOZA: They say that is their chief! That eagle can be leader of devouring birds only!

DINGANA: (Aside, concealing his fear) Did he say birds? (Aloud) I will do what any other king would do. I mean that if the Boers are after land and power, I will resist them.[17]

In his historical play *Cetywayo*, too, Dhlomo examines the historical origins of present-day 'separate development' in the policies of Sir Theophilus Shepstone. These are only two small examples of Dhlomo's unifying vision: the present is determined by the past, yet there is not too much sentimentalizing of the past. There can be no return.

Finally, Herbert Dhlomo, as Professor Gérard has pointed out,[18] wrote, in about 1939, the first essay in literary theory by a black South African. He was to write several such essays. In one he advocates the incorporation of such native forms as the 'ingoma' and 'Izibongo' into modern literary works. To some extent, he did this within his own drama. His critical stance is perhaps best summed up in a paragraph in an essay on *Zulu Tribal Poetry*.

Every one will agree, I think, that the modern African poets should give us, as far as it is possible, poetry that is distinctly and truly African. Like our music, it should not be a mere imitation, an adulterated copy, of European poetry. It must be original and African in content, form and spirit. This is important. If our literature is to hold its own among the literatures of the world, if it is to offer something distinct and unique, if it is to reflect the Soul of Africa, it must spring from indigenous, tribal culture. When men seek for first, fundamental, original, principles, they go back to the beginning, to the years of ancient times, to the work of their primitive forefathers. We cannot build by forsaking our origin. We must go back to go forward, and employ the process of literary necromancy. The primitive is the embodiment of the fundamental. Originality is not the quality of being ahead of the times, but the capacity to discover a simple, fundamental law that others in their march forward, have missed. The problem is thoroughly to explore and excavate the great field of our culture elements, and give an intelligent and searching analysis of the rich remains we unearth . . . . The izibongo and other tribal artistic compositions are, as it were, an extensive dense forest where we can go and gather sticks to fight our literary and cultural battles, timber to build our literary genius, wood to make our poetic fires, leaves and flowers to decorate and to give perfume to our achievements. They give us contact with the culture, the life, the heart of our forebears. They are a sacred inheritance. They are the essence of our being, the meaning of our name. They can only live through us, and we through them. In them the old and the new meet and unite and flower forth into a birth miraculous. . . . They touch the very spring of African life and thought and ought, therefore, to appeal instinctively to us all. They reveal the common origin, the spiritual unity, the essential Oneness, the single destiny of all our tribes. Today, when the theories of certain scholars, the work of literary fanatics, the tactics of some politicians, and the poverty, exploitation and disintegration of our people, all combine to threaten Bantu unity, it is most important that this essential Oneness of the African people should be broadcast from the hilltops on the most powerful horns. These cultured elements will help the African writer not to vacillate between two points—the false foreign and the unenduring indigenous—but give him something substantial upon which to hold.[19]

It is thus symbolic that H. I. E. Dhlomo's article, quoted at the beginning of this essay, appeared in the fiftieth anniversary edition of

Ilanga Lase Natal. From the early difficult beginnings of the introduction of writing, through all the integration of technical forms and establishment of historical, political and social themes, through the development of such institutions as the newspapers to the critical detachment of literary theory, the process had been a slow and painful but necessary one. The sureness of touch of such writers as Can Themba, Alex La Guma and others owes an implicit debt to the struggles of their predecessors. Lewis Nkosi acknowledged this in a poem dedicated to H. I. E. Dhlomo, which appeared in *Ilanga Lase Natal* in 1955.

H. I. E., H. I. E.

Me and all my brothers dark,
Those that mumble in the dust,
Without a hope, without a joy,
Streaked with tears for ravaged Africa
Have, with thy silence, ceased to live.

* * * * * *

In vain we seek the lost dream to regain,
In vain the vision yet to capture:
The Destiny of a Thousand, million dark folk
Who seek, who yearn
Alas! A fruitless toil.

H.I.E.,H.I.E.

Speak to us again;
Whisper thoughts yet to impower us
To live the Dream, to live the Vision
Of a free Africa over again.

Drum and *Classic* magazines would achieve their masterpieces of integrated consciousness and protest partly because of the slow but courageous development which could finally allow H. I. E. Dhlomo to assert, about 1940, with a modern unselfconscious confidence:

Lord, I am proud, that I am fully black.

NOTES

1. For two valuable and fuller accounts of black South African literature (particularly in the vernacular) in the nineteenth century, see Albert S. Gérard, *Four African Literatures* (Berkeley: University of California Press, 1971), and

13

A. C. Jordan, *Towards An African Literature: The Emergence of Literary Form in Xhosa* (Berkeley: University of California Press, 1973).

2. S. Mqhayi's works have not, as yet, been translated into English. Mofolo's first novel was translated into English by H. Ashton as *The Traveller of the East* (London: Society for Promoting Christian Knowledge, 1934).

3. *Ibid.*, pp. 35-36.

4. Albert S. Gérard, *Four African Literatures*, p. 41.

5. Quoted in H. I. E. Dhlomo's unpublished manuscript, *Zulu Life and Thought*.

6. Unpublished manuscript, *Zulu Life and Thought*.

7. Sol T. Plaatje, *Mhudi* (Lovedale: Lovedale Press, 1930).

8. *Insila ka Shaka* was translated into English by J. Boxwell with the title of *Jeqe The Bodyservant of King Tshaka* (Lovedale: Lovedale Press, 1951).

9. *Native Life in South Africa*, (Kimberley, Tsala Ea Batho, 1917).

10. 'Sol Plaatje's *Mhudi*', in *Journal of Commonwealth Literature*, VIII, 1, (June 1973), pp. 1-19.

11. *An African Tragedy* (Lovedale: Lovedale Press, 1928).

12. For examples of the poetry of B. W. Vilakazi see *Zulu Horizons*, translated by E. L. Friedman (Johannesburg: Witwatersrand University Press, 1973).

13. *The Girl Who Killed to Save* (Lovedale: Lovedale Press, 1936).

14. *Inggumbo yeminyanya* (Lovedale: Lovedale Press, 1940).

15. *The Democrat*, 4 August 1945, p. 14.

16. *Ilanga Lase Natal*, 24 April 1954.

17. Unpublished manuscript.

18. Albert S. Gérard, *Four African Literatures*, p. 227.

19. Unpublished manuscript, *Zulu Life and Thought*.

2

Claude McKay: Individualism and Group Consciousness

by

HELEN PYNE TIMOTHY

The work of Claude McKay (1889-1948) may be seen as the formal output of those formative influences which shaped his life. Born and educated in Jamaica, his early experiences were those of the black man nurtured within the British colonial system. At the age of twenty-three he migrated to the United States. There he became deeply immersed in the Afro-American experience, especially within that area which contained perhaps its most quixotic and volatile manifestations, Harlem. These dual influences, perhaps the most important to which any black man in the modern world, outside of Africa, can be exposed, provide the basis for all McKay's work. But the interpretations which he imposes on the events which inform his life are highly individual and separate his work from those of other black writers of the period.

McKay, under the influence of his older brother, a school teacher, could easily have dedicated his life to the pursuit of a formal academic education for himself. The achievement of such a goal would surely have meant a comfortable middle-class existence, in which his concern for the black working class might have been expressed by his involvement in the great task of the 'uplift' of his race, within the framework of colonialism and education. Instead, McKay chose to become a poet, a university dropout, a labourer and immigrant, radical socialist, novelist and essayist, finally, a Roman Catholic.

The concern for his race could only be expressed through his writings: and throughout these we are presented with themes which reveal McKay's responses to many facets of black life. Bernard Shaw when he met Claude McKay in 1919 remarked 'it must be tragic for a sensitive Negro to be an artist'. Indeed, McKay's life and work portray to a painful degree just this sensitivity to some of the problems which

15

contributed to the appalling dilemma which life itself presented for the black man, whether he was based in colonial Africa, in America or in Europe. Some of the issues to which he repeatedly responded were those of Jamaican nationalism, the maltreatment of the Afro-American, the viability of communism as a solution to the race problem, the values of miscegenation and segregation. But these public issues were always seen from the viewpoint of the individual. The great issue for McKay was simply the survival of the individual black in western civilization.

It is customary to counterpoise the Jamaican period of McKay's life against the later American and European years of hardship, bitterness and loneliness. Within this dichotomy, the Jamaican years are seen as representing a structured pattern of peasant values within which McKay, demonstrating the security of total understanding, found a sense of peace which informed both the artist and his output. This coherency and wholeness gave him the capability of producing literary works which had the serenity of art. The bitter and fragmented American experiences are thought to have engendered the militancy which made his work propagandistic.

But a careful study of McKay's work reveals that even in his earliest dialect poetry, written as a young man in Jamaica, there is some intent which could be called propagandistic. His two volumes of dialect poetry appeared in 1912 when McKay was just twenty-three years old. At this time he was under the definitive influence of Dr. Walter Jekyll, the eccentric Englishman who encouraged his reading and his poetic instinct. But Jekyll was 'unconsciously biased against what he felt was propaganda'. Hence it is likely that McKay in writing his early poetry would have eschewed the use of propaganda in his verse. Yet in McKay's dialect poetry there is an intention at the deep level which is not merely sentimental and romantic, but which is clearly social and political. Such a meaning emerges in the poem 'Quashie to Buccra' for example, where a peasant speaking to the white man says:

> You tase'e petater an' you say it sweet,
> But you no' know how hard we wuk fe' it;
> You want a basketful fe quattiewut,
> 'Cause you no know how 'tiff de bush fe cut.[1]

The militant tone here is masked by the stanzaic form of the poem and by the lyrical movement which is imparted both by the form and by the informal rhythm of the Jamaican dialect: and the young McKay

16

vitiates his social militancy when at the end he succumbs to romanticism:

> Yet still de hardship always melt away
> Wheneber it come roun' to reapin' day.[2]

But it is true that the political tone of these works is far less apparent
than the author's interest in the basic concerns of the life of the ordinary
Jamaican peasant. Through McKay, and in his own authentic speaking
voice, the Jamaican creole, the peasant parades the rhythm of his
day-to-day life. All aspects of his attitudes and beliefs, his cultural
habits are represented: 'Little Jim' has his sore toe healed with a blue
stone, and the little girl in 'Fetchin' Water' is memorable as she struggles
uphill with her gourd.

These vignettes of rural life are interesting and authentic. Atmosphere is created by the actual natural beauty of the Clarendon hills.
Here is the rich, unchanging tapestry of nature which had such a powerful influence on McKay's imagination and which seemed to have
represented the fertility of all life on the island. Yet inescapably, some
of the special qualities which characterized the later McKay are there.
He always asserted the importance of authenticity of setting for his
literary works and attempted to maintain the expression of black life
in the different levels of language which were appropriate to different
characters.

These linguistic attempts ratify the notion of McKay's iconoclasm.
It is in fact remarkable that McKay should have published a book of
dialect poetry in 1912. The spoken language of the peasants in Jamaica
was then and still is considered by the intelligentsia as ignorant,
broken English. It has never been considered a proper vehicle for
serious, intelligent or learned conversation and is rarely written except
with humorous intent or for the provision of local colour. McKay,
the son of peasants, saw that his environment could be seriously treated
in the formal mode of poetry using the language of blacks. This apprehension demonstrated qualities he never lost: the tremendous sense
of poise and confidence which he had in himself and in the black race
in general, and his determination to advocate the preservation of their
culture and their diversity.

The later stances of McKay on other public issues are further
apparent in the dialect poetry. In *A Long Way From Home* and, fiction-
ally, in *Banjo* McKay articulates his intense dislike for the effects of
colonialism as seen in France and Morocco, and especially for the

individual who was the petty British official, that type who was 'over-bearing to common persons and crawling to superiors'. The colonial British subject was always a common person, always exposed to the unsympathetic, often cruel and brutal arm of government. Certainly McKay seems to have thought that the colonial situation put the government out of touch with the true aims, desires, and beliefs of the common man. In a poem like 'My Native Land, My Home' nationalistic ideas about the place of the blacks in the world are interwoven with complaints of the everlasting petty irritations of the colonial government:

> Jamaica is de nigger's place
> No mind whe' some declare!
> Although dem call we "no-land race,"
> I know we home is here.[3]

He goes on:

> You hab all t'ings fe mek life bles',
> But buccra 'poil de whole
> Wid gove'mint an' all de res',
> Fe worry naygur soul.[4]

McKay's basic sympathy with the peasants and his antipathy towards officialdom, the arm of colonial administration as represented in his island, made him unable to remain in the Police Force of Jamaica. Some of his poetry, published in *Constab Ballads* (1912) while he was a policeman, is amusing in that he interprets the common people's complaints against the police: their interference in the peasant's attempts to obtain a livelihood, their use of their position to exploit women.[5] But what made McKay most unhappy as a policeman seemed to have been the realization that he could not serve the government and also serve his people. This dilemma is movingly expressed in 'The Heart of a Constab'[6] where he reveals that his position has estranged him from his people and has engendered hatred between him as the official, and them the peasants. Here it is clear that McKay, unlike most educated colonial blacks who consciously sought to distance themselves from the illiterate mass, deliberately set out to reimmerse himself in the ordinary mainstream of black endeavour.

It is interesting to note that once McKay had emigrated, his loneliness and nostalgia reduced the social intent of those examples of his poetry which dealt with Jamaica. The tropical riot of nature, the freshness and serenity of his beloved 'Sukee River' provided oases of pleasure when, in memory, he revisited them while living in the greyness, harshness, the concrete and steel of New York City. Having left Jamaica he abandoned dialect poetry. As he told Frank Harris, he had come to America not merely to educate himself but also to find a bigger audience. Hence those poems which he wrote about Jamaica from the American scene were written in standard English. They proved more interesting to literate Jamaica, and in fact his poem 'Flame Heart' is perhaps the best-known example of his work there. The social and political ambivalence of life in Jamaica have been distilled by the loneliness of the years of exile. Only the happiness, the meaningful rhythms of rural life remain forever and with love imprinted on his memory.

But the American experience brought into McKay's poetry all the anger and frustration, the boiling emotionalism with which his sensitive spirit continually responded to his position as a black man. He said that as a writer he carried 'a poem in his heart, and a story in his head' and he clearly used his poetry to express the spectrum of all the emotional responses which American life pulled out of him. In general terms it may be said that, apart from the lovely, lyrical, warm poems of the 'Songs for Jamaica', many of the other poems are militant, concerned with the place of the black man in white society, overwhelmed by the burning necessity of a response to the social situation in which McKay finds himself. In 'To the White Fiends'[7] for example, McKay begins:

> Think you I am not fiend and savage too?
> Think you I could not arm me with a gun
> And shoot down ten of you for every one
> Of my black brothers murdered, burnt by you?[8]

Poems like the above, the famous 'If We Must Die' and 'The Lynching' all express McKay's rage, particularly in response to the post-World War I lynching of blacks in the Southern United States, and the general brutality white society directed against blacks.

Sometimes, however, McKay's response to America showed not militancy, but a delicate tenderness and melancholy for the plight of 'the Negro' in America. 'Outcast' expresses this mood. Its final couplet declares:

> For I was born, far from my native clime,
> Under the white man's menace, out of time.

19

Occasionally, also, the poet seems burdened by the responsibility of expressing these powerful emotions, not merely for himself, but also for his race. He poignantly reveals this in 'O Word I Love to Sing' where he seems to consider the medium of poetry 'too slender/Too fragile like a globe of crystal glass' to '. . . render/My hatred for the foe of me and mine.'

Poems like the above demonstrate that it would be a mistake to think of the Afro-American McKay only as the poet of militancy and turbulent emotion. He also expresses his joy in the vigorous, stimulating struggle for existence which occurs in New York, his admiration for the beauty of some member of his race whose sudden vision has perhaps pierced his imagination, or his celebration of some meaningful romantic entanglement. All of these aspects of his poetry are interesting, and all bear the stamp of the identity of the author as a black man.

The dates of McKay's poetic expression in the post-Jamaican period are not readily established. Apparently he wrote poetry throughout his life. But much of the material in the *Selected Poems* belongs to the early years in Harlem (and the period to 1928). His association with Frank Harris and Max Eastman between the years 1919 and 1922 is well known. Harris, as editor of *Pearson's Magazine*, the radical publication, and Eastman, then in charge of the Communist *Liberator*, both encouraged McKay's writing of poetry and gave him the opportunity to publish his work. During this period the literary circles in the U. S. were aware of him as a good (if militant) poet and an effective columnist who always used his pen to write on 'the Negro question'. His commitment to the expression of what he considered the 'true position of the Negro in America' led to a quarrel with his co-editor on the *Liberator* and McKay resigned. During this period he also went to England where he worked with Sylvia Pankhurst on the communist paper, *Workers Dreadnought*. At this time McKay considered himself an 'international socialist' because he apparently felt that communism represented a path through which the black worker could make significant social progress.

In 1919 it was obvious to McKay that something had to be done for the black man. McKay's Harlem was in ferment. The demand for cheap labour in the industrialized North created by the First World War and continuing into the post-war years was just beginning to slow down. This demand had drawn Negroes in great numbers from the South. Their attempts to leave the South were resented by Southerners unwilling to lose their cheap source of labour. Their arrival in the

North creating larger slums, an ever more desperate housing situation, also caused trouble in New York City. The arrival of more blacks than could be quickly absorbed into the working force resulted in widespread unemployment among them, a hardening of the attitude of the white working class who feared displacement by a cheaper source of labour, and the barring of Negro members from most trade unions. These problems set the stage for an extremely difficult period for the Negroes trapped in the slums of New York. In 1919-20 an orgy of violence was perpetrated against blacks.

McKay apparently thought that international socialism could provide an answer to these problems. But it was clear even in 1922 that McKay as a socialist was something of a maverick. He seems to have cherished a highly romantic notion in which he saw 'communism liberating millions of city folk to go back to the land'. In 1922 Garvey and the United Negro Improvement Association were the most powerful organizers of blacks in the United States, but already the Communist Party had seen that Garvey would not bring the thousands of blacks he led within the party structure. Hence all true international socialists should have been willing to denounce the Garvey movement. But McKay wrote:

> I am supporting the movement for I believe that for subject people at least, Nationalism is the open door to Communism. Further more I will try to bring this great army of awakened workers over to the finer system of Socialism.[9]

As his poetry had revealed, McKay was interested in nationalism and socialism but only from the viewpoint of progress for the black man. Communism was not an abstract concept equally applicable to all workers and in which he fully believed.

McKay found himself unhappy in England, totally at variance with the British temperament and viewpoint. He was depressed by what he later called the 'ignorant snobbishness' among the educated classes toward the black, an attitude clearly seen in the *Spectator*'s review of his book of poetry, *Spring in New Hampshire*, published in England in 1920. The reviewer merely treated the idea of the production of poetry by a Negro as an amusing novelty and said, 'the ordinary reader's first impulse in realizing that the book is by an American Negro is to inquire into its good taste'.[10] McKay's reaction to England and in fact to all of Western Europe was conditioned by the Europeans' attitude towards the black which he described as 'misinformation, indifference and levity'. It was impossible for him, as a sensitive man, to view with equanimity an attitude which was essentially a denial of his individuality and his humanity.

McKay's experiences in Western Europe were firmly contrasted with the attitude of the Russian intellectual and peasant when, in 1922, he attended the Fourth Congress of the Third Communist International in Moscow. McKay, although thinking himself a socialist, was not then a member of the American Communist Party, and seemed to have viewed Russian communism from a highly individualist perspective. While being feted by the officials of the party, he spent most of his spare time among writers who were anti-Bolshevist. While he was discussing 'the Negro problem' and attempting to persuade the leaders to include 'the Negro worker' as a special group within the international workers' movement, he was writing to Max Eastman:

> Do you think any fool could think that with the revolutionary overturn in Russia all class, national and racial differences would disappear as if by magic?[11]

It is clear that even as early as 1922 McKay would not see communism as providing a salvation for 'the Negro' in any quick or easy way. And he would not, he thought, totally embrace a revolutionary political system unless it could offer to the whole of the black race, trapped within the system of the United States and Western Europe, a way through which their social and economic positions could be improved.

Although relatively cold towards the Communist Party, McKay was extremely moved by the attitude of the ordinary Russian towards him; in the euphoria which the prosperity of the post-revolutionary era brought, he could empathize with their joy and to them he was like 'a black ikon in the flesh'. He saw nothing of the boorishness of the average European in their attitude. Indeed, he described their response as 'beautifully naive; for them I was only a black member of the world of humanity'. Their admiration and respect spurred him on to attempt to produce more literary works; and from 1923 to 1934 he exiled himself in France, Spain and Morocco, becoming one of the first of a long line of black expatriate writers, distancing himself for the production of his prose works.

McKay's first full-length prose work, *Home to Harlem*, appeared in 1928. Within the more spacious boundaries of prose McKay began a fuller expression of his social, political and racial attitudes. But he did not allow these issues to obscure the intimate understanding of the rhythm of black relationships to which he felt so clearly allied. In *Home to Harlem* he tried to capture all facets of the life of the ordinary working-class black in Harlem, a life in which he had participated. He wished to render the experience faithfully and with realism. It might be thought that such an aim, aside from the normal vicissitudes of artistic creation, would be relatively easy to accomplish. But McKay was a black writer before the era of Richard Wright; and the Afro-American intelligentsia was against the presentation of 'the Negro' in any manner except that which was 'decorous and decorative'. McKay stoutly stated that it was 'an illusion that an Aframerican literature and art may be created out of evasion and insincerity'.

The viewpoint of *Home to Harlem* may be described as trenchantly realistic. Jake, the main character, is a homeless wanderer like McKay. He is the kind of sensitive, likeable, apparently easy-going black man who takes life as it comes. He dwells in an environment of extreme depression, even misery. But he does not succumb to despair or pessimism. In the harsh reality of crowded rooming houses, dirt, disease, inadequate medical care, drugs, booze, crime, fights, sex, certain human qualities make life bearable for the black and enable him to survive. One of these, according to McKay, is the sincere friendship, loyalty and humanity which exist between the men at this lowest level of existence. Thus Teddy, Jake and Ray help and support each other through the most difficult times, although each has only a modicum of material things. Another is the ability to love, warmly and completely, to raise relationships from a purely mechanical and business level even when one is a pimp or a prostitute. Finally, there is the ability to enjoy with the completeness of the moment the pleasures of the body. McKay's characters have a vitality, a pleasure in movement, in the fusing of their music and the dance, of achieving harmony of mood and movement.

Yet these qualities are shown by McKay as being only the minute devices which ease the daily harshness of their lives. And in fact such moments of relief are not available to everyone in Harlem. The Chief on the train, for example, is excluded from the solace which the camaraderie among men offers. His strictness and total honesty are at variance with the prevailing value system among the other workers. Hence he is isolated and eventually humiliated. His mean spirit and lack of joy may be seen as the result of this isolation. Similarly, the desire for a warm and simple human contact, when expressed in purely sexual terms, can lead to great humiliation and suffering. Indeed at many points in the story McKay seems to suggest that sexuality is a trap, a cage into which poignant figures, like the ladies of Myrtle Avenue, fall joylessly again and again. He also shows through Ray, the aimlessness, bitterness, pain of the educated black forced to do menial jobs, to live among the unlettered in the same squalor, unable to choose either his friends or his entertainment. Yet, in spite of all, there is joy. There is the will to survive, there is optimism amidst all the aimlessness, there is acceptance of individual by individual, there is love and understanding miraculously appearing like flowers blooming on the garbage; and there is laughter, be it profound, gleeful, or ironic.

Many of these ideas also appear in *Banjo*, McKay's second prose work. Whereas *Home to Harlem* was set in New York and dealt basically with the Afro-American in his own environment, and included one or two West Indians, *Banjo* is set in Marseilles and its scope has been widened to include blacks from all over the world. There are black men from the French and British islands in the West Indies, from America and from all parts of Africa. McKay is here impelled to reveal that the mass of black men and women are simply the flotsam and jetsam of European civilization and that, as he reiterated in his poetry, and indeed in all his work, the progress of an individual black man is insignificant, totally meaningless, while the mass of the black race remains at the very bottom of the civilized world, dispossessed and lacking the barest necessities for life. In *Banjo* the blacks are literally starving. Here is a naturalism which practically assaults the senses when, for example, McKay portrays the Senegalese and other blacks feasting from the garbage after having tossed away a dead rat, while the white passengers on the luxurious ocean liner cry, 'look at the niggers!' and take photographs of the scene for their friends back home.

McKay, however, has very cleverly contrasted the blacks who inhabit this world with the whites who also dwell at that level, the outcasts churned out by the inexorable march of civilized social systems. The quarter in which the black men from all nations find themselves belongs to the white world after all. The blacks are merely a small portion of the thickly teeming, exploited, crime-infested population, the pimps and the whores, the corrupt policemen and the blind and deaf, but obstructive officialdom. McKay treats the array of white characters with the same naturalistic searchlight which he turns on the blacks. But he seems to invest the blacks with a warm romanticism, a capacity for spontaneity and joy, a basic enjoyment of rhythm and life. Beside them, the whites are in the main treated as rather soulless, grey, mechanical, greedy and grasping. But the author could be accused of being unrealistic if this treatment were entirely pervasive. Fortunately, McKay does refer to many instances of individual moments of understanding and generosity which unite the white groups and the blacks, just as he delineates much disunity, lack of understanding and moments of betrayal among the black group.

But among these vagabonds, Banjo is the catalyst. McKay apparently meant him to be a kind of picaresque hero, taking life as it comes, squeezing from its harsh exterior moments of spiritual satisfaction. He carries with him the music of Afro-America with his banjo, and it is a music which unites all blacks in moments of complete abandonment and joy. He has his own code of behaviour, his own life-sustaining spirit, which prevents him from succumbing to the very lowest and coldest depths of vice.

Banjo was published in 1929, apparently at a time when many complex facets of the dilemma of the position of African-descended peoples settled in the Western European system seemed to have troubled McKay most deeply. Hence *Banjo* is more heavily used as a vehicle for the expression of many of the author's thoughts than the previous work had been. Ray is used as the mouthpiece for these somewhat random discussions. McKay through Ray expresses his dislike of the development of the machine age with its emphasis on money and consequent distortion of human relationships, the cruelty of sex within the confines of civilization, the problems of miscegenation. But the discussions of these topics do not seriously overwhelm the work. One serious aspect which comes through is McKay's clear desire to remind black people everywhere that they are united by more than colour, that their music, their stories, their attitudes can still appeal across national boundaries. He also seems to warn Africans against the surrender of their sustaining cultural values for the depravity which characterizes the sewers of civilization.

Banjo and *Home to Harlem* were not well received by the American black middle class. The continuing debate centred upon McKay's contempt for the concern of the black middle class that the black race should be represented in art by its decent and cultured members. McKay stingingly replied 'I could write about the society of Negroes . . . if I wrote a farce'. Black newspaper columnists, with the exception of James Weldon Johnson, were united in condemning both prose works as 'filth'. Ironically they also accused McKay of contributing to the white stereotype of knuckleheaded, laughing, whoring and boozing blacks. Such a comment must have been especially painful to McKay, a black most concerned with highly individual responses to every situation. He meant in these two books to celebrate the miracle of the irrepressible survival of the Jakes and the Banjos of the black race.

It is well known that *Home to Harlem* represented the expansion of a short story. And in fact, within the novel there is included a complete short story, 'He Also Loved', narrated by Ray. It appears that the short story form was a natural literary mode for McKay. In 1932 he published a collection which apparently represented the output of the period 1928-1932. This collection, *Gingertown*, actually reveals McKay as a much more skilful fiction writer than either *Banjo* or *Home to Harlem* leads one to expect. The collection considerably extends his scope, showing his deep-rooted understanding of people and situations. Again, as in McKay's poetry, we have a difference in treatment between the Harlem environment and the Jamaican background. Yet McKay shows that in spite of many differences there is a community of feelings and attitudes at a very basic level which black people everywhere can understand in each other.

In the six stories set in Harlem life is difficult, even tragic. In nearly every one there is a search for understanding and yearning for companionship, for social intercourse, for love. Yet these needs seem almost despairingly difficult to satisfy. Nevertheless, all the major characters keep struggling, and they choose separate paths as a means of escape from the trap of the pushing, crowded, teeming, but too lonely city. 'Mattie and Her Sweetman' is pathetic; old, ugly Mattie cannot buy love and she realizes it. 'Near-white' and 'Highball' express the grief and frustration of blacks who attempt to escape by merging with the white world and the terror of their rejection. 'Truant' examines the black man who chafes against routine and domestic ties, longs silently for something better, and is motivated to desert his family to realize a vague 'something' within himself.

The next four stories are realistic portrayals of the rhythm of Jamaican peasant life. The focus here is on community, not isolation. But even in this setting there are the outcasts who are inexplicable to the peasants but whom their wisdom will accept as a part of the mystery of life. Crazy Mary with her sensational end is such a character. Sue's conduct and her relationships also preclude attempts at rational analysis, but the peasants merely accept her behaviour as 'her way' and relate to her humanity, her friendliness, her niche in the complex daily round of their lives. Even in the simple environment there is complexity, tragedy, but there is, above all, human understanding. Little 'Sheik' and 'Nigger Lover' are McKay's attempts to represent white people as his main characters. 'Nigger Lover' is an interesting and moving vignette of the lower-class white woman who has received the hand of generosity, humanity from an anonymous black in a moment of need, while 'Little Sheik' is a delicately ironic little fantasy highlighting the innocent, romantic naïveté with which the young, fresh American girl approaches her adventures abroad.

Banana Bottom is McKay's West Indian novel. It appeared in 1933, a lovely, well integrated piece of work, a fusion of the struggle between realism and romanticism which had characterized so much of his work. It is almost totally without the bitterness of the Harlem period. Yet for all that, it is clear-minded about the baffling diversity of life, as well as the lack of communication and essential loneliness which all human beings must try so hard to escape.

McKay's chief character is Bita, initiated into the life of the peasantry by an illegal sexual act, but who escapes the trap and cruelty of the uncontrolled sexual urge into which many of her friends fall, by being educated away from home in the foreign environment of England. But like McKay himself, Bita stubbornly fights the barriers thrown up by intellect and training. She realizes that her education must not separate her from her environment and her people and, even more important, that there must be no struggle within herself for a separation of the needs of the body and the needs of the mind. She is a totally integrated and poised personality at the end of *Banana Bottom* because she is the black woman who has totally fulfilled herself, intellectually, through her reading and music, and, emotionally and physically, through her husband and baby. But most of all she is true to herself.

In *Banana Bottom* Bita is unusual. Many of her contemporaries do not understand their situation so well. Herald Newton Day, for example, 'descended from the dizzy heights of holiness to the very bottom of the beast'. Mrs. Craig is too reserved to understand herself or anyone. And in the idyllic setting of *Banana Bottom* there are all sorts of human feelings, cheatings, meanness, malice, and betrayals. But McKay seems to say that for those who truly understand themselves and their environment, there is hope.

McKay died in 1948. In *A Long Way From Home*, published in 1939, he gives the outline of his literary development, and discusses in detail his attitude to many of the events of his time, especially the Bolshevist Revolution, and most particularly, to the place of the black man in western civilization. *Harlem: Negro Metropolis*, published in 1940, contains a valuable set of essays giving a contemporary view of the development of Harlem, focusing on the religious and occult movements among the blacks, especially that of Father Divine. McKay also goes into very detailed discussions of the development of the labour movement in Harlem. Always a radical thinker, in this work he is explicitly and mordantly anti-communist, moving towards a segregationist position, where he stipulates that black people alone by writing and organizing will be able to help themselves. He also gives an extremely penetrating contemporary view of the Marcus Garvey movement.

The last years of McKay's life, 1934-48, spent in the United States, were years of deprivation and searing hardship. He had always remained a member of the black working class and now, having been out of the United States for so many years, older and ill, he found it nearly impossible to live except by doing the most menial jobs. But to the end he was concerned with the problems of the races. His personal problems seemed to him merely the result of the awful dilemma created in white civilization by the advent of the black man. He had always pursued an iconoclastic, even solitary, way of life. Yet this personal isolation did not dull his understanding of the importance of group interaction among blacks. He saw clearly that only within the group could the black personality truly flower; that only the black man's understanding of himself and of his people could lead to a thorough integration of the black personality. He was concerned that the divisiveness caused by the minority status of blacks in Europe and in America would seriously scatter individuals, warp values, divide the group, and lead to the loss of human understanding, spirituality and warmth, those redeeming qualities which had contributed to the survival of blacks as a race.

As a man and as an artist, therefore, he had remained faithful to the task which he had set himself, to mirror and express his individual conscience, and the consciousness of his race.

NOTES

1. Claude McKay, *The Dialect Poetry* (Freeport, N.Y.: Books for Libraries Press, 1972), 'Quashie to Buccra' p. 13. Roughly rendered in standard English this would read:
    You'll taste potato and you'll think it's sweet
    But you don't know how hard we work for it

You want a basketful for two pence
Because you don't know how tough is the bush we cut.
2. *Ibid.*, p. 7, Again roughly rendered in standard English:
But all hardship melts away
When the reaping day comes.
3. Claude McKay, *op. cit.*, p. 84, 'My Native Land, My Home'. In standard English:
Jamaica is the Negroes' place
Never mind what some declare
Although they call us no-land-race
I know our home is here.
4. *Ibid.*, p. 85. In standard English:
You have everything to make life blessed.
But the white man spoils it all
With government and all the rest.
Which worry the negroes' soul.
5. Claude McKay, *op. cit.*, p. 51, 'The Apple Woman's Complaint'; p. 43 'Dis-illusionment'.
6. Claude McKay, *op. cit.*, p. 62.
7. All poems mentioned in this section are cited from Claude McKay, *The Selected Poems* (New York: Bookman Associates, 1953).
8. Claude McKay, *op. cit.*, p. 38.
9. Wayne F. Cooper (ed.). *The Passion of Claude McKay* (New York: Schocken Books, 1973), p. 54.
10. As quoted in Claude McKay, *A Long Way from Home* (New York: Harcourt, Brace and World Inc., 1970).
11. Wayne F. Cooper, *op. cit.*, 'Letter to Max Eastman', 18 May 1923, p. 89.

3

Nicolás Guillén and Afrocubanismo

by

LLOYD KING

Nicolás Guillén is Cuba's most honoured poet. There is little doubt that most of his aspirations as a political activist and 'social protest' poet have been realized since the Cuban Revolution. Within Cuba itself his most popular collection of poems is his *Songs for Soldiers and Ballads for Tourists* (*Cantos para soldados y sones para turistas*) which he originally published in 1937. These poems are anticipatory blueprints of the relationship between the people's militia, formed since the Revolution as part of Cuba's embattled response to U.S. aggression, and the Cuban people. Written at a time when the soldier seemed rather to be the tool and guardian of U.S. interests and the power hunger of Fulgencio Batista, they yet called on the soldier to recognize his links with the ordinary folk who were the victims of exploitation and political gimcrackery, and the need to forge fraternity with the oppressed masses. The *sones para turistas* expressed the repugnance felt by many Cubans towards the insensitive American tourist, and sought to dramatize the resentment and bitterness towards him as an insane but all too visible symbol of the rigorous and painful grip on Cuba's monoculture economy by American imperialist-capitalist interests.

As is well known, the Cuban Revolutionary leadership ran out the tourists and the capitalists and aligned itself with the Cuban Communist Party, of which Guillén had been a member since the thirties. The Revolution also acted swiftly to eliminate a feature of Cuban life against which Guillén had campaigned both in verse and prose, namely racial discrimination; it desegregated the schools and the beaches and provided equal educational opportunity for all. Guillén has expressed his recognition of this reality in a poem 'Tengo' (All is mine):

> Nadie me puede detener
> a la puerta de un dancing

o de un bar
o bien en la carpeta de un hotel
gritarme que no hay pieza,
una mínima pieza y no una pieza colosal
una pequena pieza donde yo pueda descansar.[2]

(They can't stop me now
at the door of a dance hall
or a bar
or at a hotel desk
and shout at me
that the rooms are all taken
both the small rooms and the large
so that I don't have
a pillow to rest my head on.)

When Guillén wrote 'Tengo' in the post-revolutionary period, it must have seemed to him that he and other militant Cubans—artists, trade unionists, ordinary folk—had reached the end of a long process of struggle and desperate affirmation during a dark night of dictatorship and violence, to bring in the dawn of a socialist state in the Americas. For Guillén it was a process which had always had to do with the achievement of an integrated national personality, based on a discovery of the common Cubanness of whites and blacks in Cuban society. But equally Guillén realized that this objective could not possibly take shape until external capitalist interests were tamed along with their capacity for disruptive activity. Thus the two constants of his verse were related to internal racial integration and socialist militancy. His verse therefore came to be prophetic of some of the main objectives of the Cuban Revolution itself.

Guillén's chief contribution to the dialogue about Cuban identity has been his unchanging insistence that Cuba's culture is mulatto or mestizo, a precipitate of the Latin-Hispanic and the African, now neither one nor the other. In an article in the newspaper *Hoy*, organ of the Cuban Communist Party, in 1959 Guillén wrote the following:

The Spaniards contributed their genius—already so complex and varied—their language, their culture. But the blacks also contributed, and not less either, in addition to their labour on the plantation and in the factory while in a merciless state of servitude. Thus the national meltingpot is not only the result of the

31

easy coupling of master and slave woman, which shows up in the most exclusive families, but another more deeply rooted cross fertilization which comes from our mixed roots. For this reason, in Cuba the white is mestizo, the black is mestizo and the mestizo is mestizo.[2]

From the thirties, when he wrote his first group of 'Afrocuban' verses, Guillén always maintained this 'mulatto' position as a way of dealing with the particular kind of racial tension which has informed Cuban society from the days of slavery onwards.

First of all, for the greater part of the nineteenth century, the white slave-owning bourgeoisie were haunted by a nightmarish vision that the coloured population, both slave and free, would join to turn Cuba into 'a black military Republic', a vision which led to one of the worst racist incidents in Cuban history, known as the Ladder conspiracy, 'la conspiración de la Escalera'. Secondly, although Cuban blacks made such a significant contribution to the achievement of independence, the ruling classes which took power in the new Republic at the turn of the century, associating themselves with the imperialist American forces of occupation, were systematically hostile to blacks. The great Cuban ethnologist, Fernando Ortiz, in a speech in 1942, pointed out that when he published his first study *Los negros brujos* (The Black Witch Doctors, 1906) 'even to speak of the black man in public was dangerous, and had to be done on the sly as it were and in whispers, as if one were speaking about syphilis or some nefarious skeleton in the family cupboard'.[3] More than this, according to Ortiz, was the fact that blacks and more especially mulattos seemed to wish to deny their race in much the way that the leper might wish to hide some of the terrible aspects of the leprosarium from the public eye. Ortiz, himself, under positivist influence, did not exactly help by declaring early in his book that 'when the blacks landed in Cuba, they automatically became criminals, not in the sense of falling from a plane of higher morality, but simply as people incapable, for the moment at least, of comprehending moral notions'.

It is easy from the above to gain some idea of the tremendous psychic and social pressures to which black men in Cuba were exposed. And, in effect, there were two kinds of responses, both emphasizing the question of civil rights, rather more than the issue of the cultural identity of the black man in Cuba, although the two things were obviously connected. Thus in the story 'La piel' by the white Cuban, Alfonso Hernández Catá, the mulatto anti-hero Eulogio Valdés sees himself as a man with a 'white' sensitivity hopelessly trapped in the barracoon of a black skin, a totally alienated being, not accepted by whites and rejecting his black brothers.

The slaves had been manumitted, but their moral enslavement was even more visible, more vexatious than before. The soul of the race had not taken a single step towards redemption, the African heritage survived, the barbarous, bloody instincts, the frenzied dances to the sound of guttural shouts.[4]

In 1907, Evaristo Estenoz founded the Independent Coloured Party (Partido Independiente de Color), a Black Power movement which in 1912 was the object of the most extreme white racist repression. The alternative procedure was one of organization and campaigning to persuade the dominant society to accept coloureds. The grand organizer was Juan Gualberto Gómez, mulatto hero of the struggle for independence who formed 'Sociedades de color'. It is obvious that at times he lost heart for on at least one occasion he even exhorted his followers to accept second class citizenship, not even opening themselves to the accusation of originality.[5] Gualberto Gómez nevertheless started the tradition of a campaign for civil rights which was carried on by Lino Dou, a friend of Guillén's father, and then by Guillén himself writing in the conservative newspaper *Diario de la Marina*, an interesting contradiction for that period in the twenties.

But the stimulus for 'negroid' verse in Cuba was the post-war interest of European artists and intellectuals in 'primitive' African art, and as far as music is concerned, the interest of 'art-music' composers such as Stravinsky in musical folk forms. An example is Stravinsky's 'Rag Time for Eleven Instruments'. The 'Afrocuban moment', that magical period in the twenties and thirties when Afrocuban folk forms excited the imaginations of young rebellious Cuban artists, was the Cuban result. The social history abstract we have offered accounts for the primary fact that in the first manifestations of Afrocubanism only white Cuban intellectuals were involved. Guillén belongs to a second phase. From the very first poem of the Afrocuban vogue, 'La rumba' (1928) by the white Cuban José Zacharias Tallet, the problematic nature of the Afrocuban experiment is made clear. Tallet, like those who follow him, was a bourgeois radical and cultural nationalist who, in seeking to enter the folk sensibility and speak its language, only managed to register some of the external characteristics of its 'culture of poverty' and the neo-African folk associated with it. In

33

general their efforts were superficial and ought to have sunk into oblivion, except that from a sociological point of view, they contributed to reaffirming certain racial stereotypes. This quotation from Professsor G. R. C. Coulthard captures in a nutshell some of the primary characteristics of the poems: 'We find Negro figures, male and female, caught in the frantic contortions of Afro-Cuban dancing. These are music, drums, *maracas, güiros*, guitars, rum-drinking, voodoo possession, and sometimes crimes of violence; the maddening rhythms of the drums shake the dancers in an atmosphere of rum and sweat as they writhe in distorted arabesques[6]'. In Tallet's 'Rumba', the atmosphere of sweat, vulgar gesture and insistent drumming achieves a particular texture from the smells evoked:

Y niña Tomasa se desarticula
Y hay olor a selva
Y hay olor a grajo
Y hay olor a hembra
Y hay olor a macho.[7]

(Madame Tomasa twists herself up
And there is jungle smell
And the smell of john crow
the smell of the female in heat
and of the rutting male.)

The titillated sexual fantasies of the white bourgeois poet alas do not correspond to Fernando Ortiz's conception of the rumba as a complex cultural phenomenon. In an essay in 1936, 'More about Mulatto Poetry', he saw the rumba as 'the release of an overabundant life force in a frenzy of all the muscles; it is the hypnosis of music which embraces with the magic of its rhythms'.

The fundamental ambiguity of perspective of the white cultural nationalists is particularly well exemplified in a poem by Emilio Ballagas, 'María Belén Chacón'. Ballagas had a genuine interest in the possibilities of Afrocuban verse, which led him to prepare two anthologies of 'black' verse in the thirties. On the appearance of Guillén's collection of poems, *Sóngoro Cosongo* in 1951, he hailed it as the point of departure for an authentic Cuban poetry, although after publishing a collection of Afrocuban verse, he turned back to the writing of 'pure' poetry. In 'María Belén Chacón', Ballagas claimed, he set out to capture the root anguish of the exploited, downtrodden Negro woman.

34

María Belén Chacón is a woman who dies of a pulmonary infection as a result of brutally overworking herself as a washer and ironer of clothes. The poet therefore intends to suggest pathos, except that the elegiac intent is contradicted by a sprightly refrain:

> con tus nalgas en vaivén
> de Camagüey a Santiago . . .
> de Santiago a Camagüey . . . .
> María Belén Chacón

> (María Belén Chacón
> With your buttocks on the swing
> From Camaguey to Santiago
> From Santiago to Camaguey.)

More than this, the poet reveals that he had exploited her sexually as well:

> Ya no veré mis instintos
> en los espejos redondos y alegres de tus nalgas
> Tu constelación de curvas
> ya no alumbrará jamás el cielo de la sandunga.[8]

> (Nevermore will my instincts behold
> In the round and jolly mirror of your arse
> The constellation of your charms
> Will no longer now light up our fleshpot firmament.)

Even when motivated by the best of intentions, the white bourgeois poet could not help revealing his alienation from the folk.

In 1930, approximately two years after Tallet started the Afrocuban vogue, Nicolás Guillén published eight 'negrista' poems in the newspaper *Diario de la Marina* with the general title 'Son Motifs' (*Motivos de son*) and in 1931 included them again with others in book form, with the title, *Sóngoro Cosongo*. Guillén was immediately recognized as a writer who had his finger on the pulse of folk sensibility. Thus Fernando Ortiz writing in the journal *Archivos del Folklore Cubano* in 1930 hailed his achievement: 'Guillén's verse is not folklore in the original sense of the word, but it is in so far as it captures perfectly the spirit, the rhythm, the piquancy and the sensuality of anonymous compositions.'[9] Guillén seemed instinctively to realize the opportunity to blend the scribal and oral traditions and derived the rhythms of his verse from a popular musical form, the 'son', which had been born of the contact between African rhythms and the creole environment, a form which had long been frowned on by polite Cuban society. In one long magical moment Guillén came to prefigure some of the obsessions of future Caribbean writing. Cuba's two best known composers of the time, who had been experimenting with Afrocuban rhythms, immediately showed an interest in setting Guillén's poems to music. Eliseo Grenet and his brother Emilio, more popular composers, also wrote music for some of the poems: 'Negro Bembón', 'Sóngoro Cosongo', 'Tu no sabes inglés'; and a later poem 'Sensemayá' was the subject of musical ballet arranged by the noted Mexican composer Silvestre Revueltas and performed in Mexico and Peru.

The poems of 'Son Motifs' explored a variety of folk urban situations. Two of the poems 'Ay negra, si tu supiera', (Aye, black lover, if you only knew) and 'Búscate plata' (Go and look for bread) deal with women abandoning their lovers because they have no money, a situation related to the effects of the Depression. Two others 'Ayer me dijeron negro' (Yesterday I was called nigger) and 'Mulata' refer to the antagonism between mulatto and black. In 'Yesterday I was called nigger', Guillén strikes what was to be a recurring note of his verse suggesting to some person who passed for white that he has African/black blood:

Tan blanco como te bé,
y tu abuela sé quién é.
Sácala de la cocina,
Sácala de la cocina,
Mamá Iné.[10]

(As white as you look
I know your grandma (the cook)
Bring her out of the kitchen
Bring her out of the kitchen
Mamma Inés.)

This Caribbean picong uses the sharp-edged social barb to puncture the pride along the colour and class line. The most disturbingly ironic of the poems is 'Negro Bembón' (Thick-lipped Nigger). The speaker, Caridad, is presented telling her Negro boyfriend with thick lips not to allow himself to be wounded by the mocking intent of those who call him 'negro bembón', and seeking to turn the epithet into a term of

36

endearment. Hers is in a certain sense a Négritude position, for she urges the man to assume freely a term which the society uses in a 'denigratory' manner:

> Por qué te pones tan bravo
> cuando te dicen negro bembón
> si tienes la boca santa
> negro bembón.[11]

> (Why do you get so vexed
> When people call you big-lipped nigger
> Since your mouth is very attractive
> You thick-lipped nigger, you?)

However the poem cannot sustain a Négritude interpretation because in the last two lines we learn that the 'negro bembón' is really living off his mistress's earnings, whatever her line of work may be.

When he widened the collection of poems in *Sóngoro Cosongo*, it was noticeable that may of the poems dealt with the self-contained violence of the low-life of Havana. 'Velorio de Papá Montero', (Wake for Papa Montero) was inspired by a popular 'son' of the time, and evokes with a mix of irony and sadness the death in a drunken brawl of a folk character. 'Chévere' (sweetman) is a short dense image of concentrated violence, orchestrating the movement of a man's rage till he slices his unfaithful woman to death.

> pica tajadas de sombra
> mas la sombra se le acaba
> y entonces pica que pica
> carne de su negra mala.[12]

> (he slashes strips of shadow
> till he runs out of shadows
> and then he slashes to pieces
> the flesh of his bad black mamma.)

Guillén's ghetto images were not calculated to win the approval of coloureds who were seeking to project an image of respectability, and in an interview with Antonio Fernández de Castro in the newspaper *La semana*, we find him denouncing those who were unwilling to acknowledge the 'son' as a part of their culture. These attitudes of shame and self-contempt were particularly striking, Guillén noted, since the 'son' was popular in Paris and even in Cuba was now accepted in the most exclusive society, and yet many Negroes demonstrated public hostility to this popular art form because it was lower-class and 'incompatible with their spiritual delicacy and their grade of culture'.[13] Angel Augier in his irreplaceable literary biography of Guillén also gathers up some of the remarks of white critics on the poems. In 1930, Juan Marinello had grandiloquently proclaimed that Cuban poets had a great responsibility to give to the continent the song of the Negro with its present anguish and in bright anticipation of its destiny. 'No country as much as ours', he wrote, 'possesses the possibility of this work of art and humanity. Here the negro is marrow and root, the breath of the people.'[14] But as Augier shows, there were critics who warned Guillén that art has no colour and cannot be racial. Jorge Manach hoped that Guillén had written his racial obsessions out of his system and would now get on with writing poetry which was more universal in reference.

One of the most hostile critics of the influence of Afrocuban folk forms on the wider Cuban sensibility was Ràmon Vasconcelos, a Cuban journalist resident in Paris. A self-styled watchdog of Cuban culture, he wrote from Paris to discourage Guillén from the idea that the Cuban 'son' could be used and become popular in the way that the American 'blues' had been, since it was not at all suitable for social commentary or serious purposes. He also reproached García Caturla, one of the white Cuban composers already referred to, for using Afrocuban rhythms in his 'art-music' compositions, on the grounds that the neo-African folk forms contaminated the Hispanic integrity of Cuban life, and urged him to look into the possibilities of the folk music of the white Cuban peasant. Vasconcelos's attitude was so outrageous that one would have expected a stinging reply, but Guillén's answer was quite mild. He explained that his use of the 'son' was simply in line with the world-wide interest in popular forms, and that the 'son' poems were not in the majority in *Sóngoro Cosongo*. He even went on to lament that it was a pity that to use the speech rhythms of the folk seemed to require heroism.

This moderate reply to Vasconcelos exposes the weakness in Guillén's mulatto position. One senses that he has always been a little afraid of being called a black racist. Thus in an interview with Keith Ellis, published in the *Jamaica Journal* in 1973, Guillén when asked about his attitude to Négritude, at first dismissed it contemptuously, then went on to admit that the assertion of blackness and of neo-African values was certainly necessary in a colonial situation. But he sees it as above all 'one of the manifestations of the class struggle'.[15] In other words, he felt that 'black assertiveness' in post-revolutionary Cuba was wrong, but even before this he always rejected the use of the term 'Afrocuban'. One need not be a black racist in order to question Guillén's attitude. In an essay in 1959 in *Hoy*, Guillén felt constrained to call for the re-writing of Cuban history so that the black contribution in the struggle for independence and national identity might be taught in schools. In 1961, in an essay called 'Cómo surgió la cultura nacional' (The origins of our national culture), which has since been withdrawn from circulation, Walterio Carbonell, a black Cuban communist, angrily accused white Marxist critics of treating the black contribution contemptuously and refusing to recognize that neo-African religious organizations had played a progressive role not only in preserving African culture but in the political sphere.[16] Since that time, there has been the case of a play *María Antonia* by Eugenio Hermández Espinosa which after being performed in 1968 has been quietly suppressed. Andrew Salkey, who in his *Havana Journal* noted that his young white guide was discomfited by the play, wrote of it with considerable enthusiasm, seeing María Antonia as 'an Afro-cuban ghetto goddess, young enough to attract all the men black and white in the ghetto to her, and maternal in the manner of the West Indian black woman who has had, historically, to be ill-used love object and mother to her irresponsible lovers.'[17] Somehow what we miss in Guillén and his involvement in the Cuban Communist Party is an equivalent to Aimé Césaire's *Letter to Maurice Thorez*, in which Césaire rejected the simple Marxist view that the race problem is only a manifestation of the class struggle.

It is not a little amazing that Guillén was never tempted to adopt a Négritude position, particularly as even sympathetic white Cuban critics were not persuaded by his claim that Cuba's was mulatto. Juan Marinello in an essay in 1933, 'Negrismo y mulatismo', frankly contradicted the thesis that Cuba was mestizo in spirit. He denied that the subterranean link between the races existed and suggested that the truth was rather unpleasant: 'To the average middle class white even if he pretends to accept the educated black—a black skin immediately brings to mind the slave-gang, the slave household, the galley slave, enduring black clay, basis of the black's triumph.'[18] The white Cuban remembers only slavery and a race's fantastic endurance when he sees his black brother's tremendous contribution in the liberation of his country from Spanish colonialism. In reviewing the poems in *Sóngoro Cosongo*, Marinello went on to state that the best poem in the collection was one called 'Llegada' (Arrival), the one poem which had no reference to coloureds.

Curiously, it was a small group of white Cuban intellectuals who showed a determination to validate the Afrocuban contribution to the island's culture: Fernando Ortiz, the great ethnologist, and the now-famous novelist Alejo Carpentier. In 1928, Carpentier collaborated with Amadeo Roldán to produce an Afrocuban ballet, *La rebambaramba*. In 1929, they put out *El milagro de Anaquillé*. His first novel *Ecúe Yamba O*, published in Spain in 1933, explored and sought to establish the validity of the neo-African aspects of Cuban life, for he felt that, in the hot-house atmosphere of knavery, violence and brutality which characterized Cuban society in the twenties, the marginalized Afrocuban folk, clinging to an age-old lore, had preserved a kind of integrity. Some years later, he put on the mask of a 'white nigger', and wrote a novel *El reino de este mundo* (The kingdom of this world, 1949), truly a Négritude novel. For in this novel Carpentier focused on Haiti's independence struggle, and assigned the voodoo cult a primary significance as an ideological weapon of liberation from the yoke of French colonialism. An appreciation of what he calls the 'maroon' experience of the Negro in the Caribbean has not got in the way of Carpentier's projecting Cuban-Caribbean experience as an integral part of a 'Latin' experience, as part of the history of a neo-Mediterranean diaspora.

In *Sóngoro Cosongo*, Guillén had captured something of the down-beat of ghetto life, a sense of its cynicism and violence, the rhythms of its speech. His next collection of poems, *West Indies Ltd.* (1934) shows that his political awareness had sharpened, for these were the years of the Depression and of the inept and brutal dictatorship of General Machado who finally fell from power in 1933. Behind him, there was already the example of another mulatto poet, Regino Pedroso, who had been converted to Marxism and the Communist Party in the twenties. In one of his better known poems, 'Hermano Negro' (Brother Black), Pedroso called upon his black brothers to acquire a right consciousness and to recognize that race prejudice was secondary to economic exploitation. They ought to reconsider their role as entertainers for the western world and understand that they were a part of the exploited proletariat. He also urged them to remember Scottsboro, a town in Alabama which became the scene of a *cause célèbre* when eight out of nine Negro boys, accused of having raped two white girls, were sentenced to death. The racist American South helped to recruit blacks to the Communist Party. In Cuba black men were prominent in the Party, and formed a solid part of its rank and file. Once Guillén got the message, his folk characters assume the elemental posture of exploited men. The poet's own posture is that of a member of the revolutionary vanguard, sharpening the consciousness of the masses. The movement in tone and perspective anticipates the classical transferral of aggression which Fanon analysed in *The Wretched of the Earth*, whereby that violence which the sub-culture practised against itself, as exemplified in poems such as 'Chévere' and 'Velorio de Papá Montero', must now be directed outwards against the colonialist exploiter and the bourgeoisie. Such poems as 'Caminando' and 'Sabás' reflect this new mood and show Guillén undertaking the task of political education. In 'Sabás', the poet calls upon Sabás, servile because reduced to penury in the Depression days, to recognize his moral and economic rights and to understand that when the society will not allow him the dignity to survive as a human being, he must be prepared to claim his rights violently if necessary The irony is both sharp and bitter:

Porqué Sabás la mano abierta?
(Este Sabás es un negro bruto)
Coge tu pan pero no lo pidas;
Coge tu luz, coge tu esperanza cierta
como a un caballo por las bridas.[19]

Why Sabás do you hold out your hand?
(This Sabás is really a foolish nigger)
Take your bread, don't beg for it
Take hold of your senses, take firm hold of your hopes
As of a horse under sure command.

In 1937, Guillén published his *Cantos para soldados y sones para turistas*, and although his earlier collection *West Indies Ltd.* (1934) and later *El son entero* (1943) have a better selection of poems, they were not greeted with as good a press as the *Songs for soldiers*. Guillén's Party colleague Juan Marinello in a review, 'Hazaña y triunfo americano de Nicolás Guillén' (The achievement and American triumph of Nicolás Guillén) hailed the *Songs for soldiers* as a definitive triumph of the American melting pot. What strikes one about this claim in relation to the poems is the fact that Guillén here abandoned the Afrocuban stance which is so easily picked up in the other collections.

One must therefore conjecture that there was possibly some pressure on the poet to move away from his 'negrista' image, perhaps to come closer to Marti's dictum that 'Cuban was more than black, more than white'. Perhaps also a bland poem like 'Balada de los dos abuelos' (Ballad of the two grandfathers) in which slave-owning conquistador grandfather and enslaved African grandfather are reconciled in the poet's dream, has been played up by some critics for the same kind of reason. There was a lot of truth in Cintio Vitier's judgment on Guillén that 'the new theme is not just a fashion, a subject for literature, but the living heart of his creative activity'.[20] But because he has always been sensitive to the charge of black racism and to the ideological posture of the Party in Cuba, he has also had to react to the association of his name with Négritude.

This is confirmed by a poem 'Brindis' (Cheers!) which he wrote in 1952 but which has never appeared in book form till the recent publication of his *Obra poética*. 'Brindis' is addressed to the famous black American singer Josephine Baker who in her day was the toast of Paris and who met with racial discrimination on returning to the United States. In disgust and anger, the poet tells la Baker that she might well have been lynched and he introduces a mood of violence which again anticipates one response of black militants which eventually came to pass:

> Después? Afuera
> la calle, ardiendo, espera.
> Volveremos después.
> Oh yes!
> Very well!
> OK![21]

> (And afterwards? Outside
> the pavements, burning, crouch.
> We shall come back, afterwards
> Oh yes!
> Very well!
> OK!)

In a few lines, Guillén evokes the long hot summer, the incendiary fury which would take place in ghettos like Watts years later. What is equally interesting, however, is that Josephine Baker had also visited Cuba, and there had also been refused a hotel room by a racist management. But the Cuban incident had drawn from Guillén an article written in sadness rather than in anger. It can be argued, and quite rightly, that Cuba did not have a Ku Klux Klan and that white Cuban racism was milder; but it is also clear that it was felt to be 'politic' to focus on the more extreme brutalities which occurred in the United States. The poet could both deliver a blow against racism and associate it with imperialistic capitalism.

One way in which Guillén tried to hit at the Cuban bourgeoisie was by insisting that most of its members had some concealed African ancestry, for example in the poem 'Canción del bongó' (Bongo song):

Y hay títulos de Castilla
con parientes en Bondó.[22]

(There are those with patents of nobility from Castille,
Who yet have relatives in Bondó.)

Guillén in such poems was striking an embarrassing note for whereas in Latin countries those who can pass for white are considered white, in the United States a drop of African blood makes a man black. The Cuban bourgeoisie who identified their interests so closely with American capitalists and American standards would therefore not particularly appreciate what the poet was taking pains to advertise.

In 1943, Guillén published *El son entero* with a number of negrista poems, 'Sudor y látigo' (Sweat and the whip), 'Ebano real' (Royal ebony), 'Son número 6' (Son No. 6), 'Acana', and even a rather embarrassing poem which calls upon Shango and Ochun to guard Stalin whom 'free men accompany singing, "Una canción a Stalin" '. These poems do not add anything new to his output although they show once again how strongly influenced by the oral tradition Guillén was. A much more interesting later poem is 'El apellido' (The surname) in which Guillén again worries about the way in which the African connection is vulnerable to the Hispanic mould, even in such things as names:

Seré Yelofe?
Nicolás Yelofe acaso?
O Nicolás Bakongo?
Tal vez Guillén Banguila?[23]

(Am I Yelofe?
Nicolás Yelofe perhaps?
Or Nicolás Bakongo?
What about Guillén Banguila?)

43

It is obvious that the poet is charmed by the sonorous quality of his possible African names. Finally one must mention a not-too-good poem 'Qué color' which was provoked by a comment of the Russian poet Yevtushenko on the death of Martin Luther King that his soul was white as snow. Guillén insists rather that Luther King's soul was as black as coal, 'negro como el carbón'. 'Qué color' shows the way in which Guillén and the Cuban Revolution are solid supporters of men who struggle against oppression and imperialism everywhere. Amílcar Cabral and Angela Davis are very popular in Cuba. Nevertheless, Guillén would never write of a *Cuban* that his soul was black as coal, on the basis that the Revolution has abolished the emotive connotations of colour.

The Marxist attitude to colour, which is Guillén's own attitude, is that it is irrelevant in a socialist state. It counts upon Revolutionary policy of equal opportunity to reverse a variety of instinctive attitudes about race, bred during more than one hundred and fifty years of Cuban history in the context of the white racist attitudes of western civilization. At the primary level of what we accept as the basic human needs and rights, the right to a balanced diet, educational development, etc. no one can disagree with the Cuban perspective. However, at a second level of reference, that of cultural formation and a variety of subtle attitudes, this writer, whose experience is that of the English-speaking Caribbean (where black men have attained the highest offices) and who has seen how readily a Euro-oriented environment can twist and confuse men of African ancestry, must express some reservations about the Cuban Revolution's desire to straighten out the kinks and achieve a determined uniformity in Cuban cultural life.

NOTES

1. Nicolás Guillén, *Obra poética Vol.* 2 (La Habana: Instituto Cubano Del Libro, 1973), p. 79.
2. Nicolás Guillén, *Prosa de prisa* (Buenos Aires: Editorial Hernández, 1968), p. 181.
3. Fernando Ortiz, *Los negros brujos* (Miami: Ediciones Universal, 1973), p. xvii.
4. Alfonso Hernández Catá, *Los Frutos ácidos y otros cuentos* (Madrid: Aguilar, 1953), p. 127.
5. See Angelina Edreira de Caballero, *Vida y obra de Juan Gualberto Gómez* (La Habana Edreira de Caballero 1955), p. 118.
6. G. R. C. Coulthard, *Race and Colour in Caribbean Literature* (London: Oxford University Press, 1962), p. 31.

7. Rosa E. Valdés Cruz, *La poesía negroide en América* (New York: Las Américas Pnblishing Co., 1972), p. 95.
8. Rosa Valdés Cruz, *La poesía negroide*, p. 127.
9. Angel Augier, *Nicolás Guillén* (La Habana: Universidad Central de Las Villas, 1962), p. 131.
10. *Ibid.*, p. 112.
11. *Obra poética*, I, p. 103.
12. *Ibid.*, p. 124.
13. Augier, *Nicolás Guillén*, p. 116.
14. Coulthard, *Race and Colour*, p. 29.
15. *Jamaica Journal*, vol. 7, No. 1-2 (1973), p. 131.
16. Carlos More, 'Le peuple noir a-t-il sa place dans la révolution cubaine?', *Présence Africaine*, No. 52 (1964)), p. 112.
17. *Havana Journal* (Harmondsworth: Penguin, 1971), p. 143.
18. *Órbita de Juan Marinello* (La Habana: UNEAC, 1968), p. 74.
19. *Obra poética*, I, pp. 140-41.
20. Coulthard, *Race and Colour*, p. 34.
21. *Obra poética*, II, p. 277.
22. *Obra poética*, I, p. 117.
23. *Ibid.*, p. 397.

4

Haiti and Martinique

by

VERE W. KNIGHT

The birthplace of Négritude was Haiti and not the Paris of the 1930s as one is likely to conclude from reading most histories of modern French literature. If Négritude is interpreted as an awareness of blackness and an assertion of black values, then history had forced Haiti long before the 1930s to adopt a Négritude stance. The War of Haitian Independence had developed into a struggle between on the one hand blacks and mulattos, and on the other white plantation owners and administrators sent out from metropolitan France. When independence had been achieved, the Constitution debarred whites from owning property on the island. The effects of this defensive reaction were aggravated by the refusal of European countries and the United States of America to acknowledge the independence of the country. Haiti found herself isolated and this isolation sharpened the hostility towards whites which was the natural legacy of the pre-independence period. Race was the most important factor determining the attitude of other countries, most of whom were still slave-owning, towards the new republic.

Soon after independence civil strife broke out and once again race was an important factor since the conflict pitted mulattos against blacks. Thus in both the external and internal life of the country, race and colour were paramount. Literature did not stand aside from either of these conflicts, although its activity in the defence of Haiti against what was seen as a largely hostile white world was greater than that resulting from its taking sides in the internal conflict. Interpreting literally the doctrine that the pen is mightier than the sword, Haiti used literature as its principal means of defence and aggression against hostile outsiders. Haitian literature therefore has an established tradition for being polemical and political. Its contribution to Négritude is a part of this tradition.

The circumstances of the years immediately following independence continued to exist for a long time with Haiti forced, as the only black republic in the hemisphere, to remain on the defensive. Inside the country, in spite of an early end to the civil strife, conditions did not materially improve; in fact, they became worse. As the price of recognition of her independence Haiti agreed to pay a substantial indemnity to France; this weakened the finances of the country. The splitting up of large plantations into small plots capable of maintaining only subsistence farming did little to improve the situation. It widened the gap, made apparent by the civil war, between the mulatto elite and the former black slaves, driving the latter further into poverty but not seriously affecting the former who either held substantial property, in many cases from before independence,[1] or filled administrative posts which could only go to those who were educated. Which in fact meant to the mulatto elite, since they held a monopoly on education. The Haitian black, it is not unfair to say, benefited as little from independence as did his fellow blacks in the islands from Emancipation. For generations Haiti presented the ridiculous paradox of an elite. mainly mulatto, defending black values against a supposedly hostile white world, but doing nothing to improve materially the situation of those in the country who illustrated those values.

Haiti's history was masked by recurrent bouts of unrest. The situation worsened in the period 1911-1915 when the head of state changed no less than six times. The United States of America used the circumstances of the last change of head of government as a pretext for intervention and landed its marines in Port-au-Prince on 28 July 1915 to begin the American occupation. The occupation was the single most important factor in the spiritual renaissance which took place in Haiti in the 1920s and 1930s and the effects of which were felt in Paris by the first generation of Négritude writers. Not the least important fact about the occupiers was that they were white; their attitudes to the Haitians in the circumstances were frequently unfortunate.[2] The ban on whites holding property in the country had been lifted but the dominating presence of whites on Haitian soil was bitterly resented, especially by those who were literate enough to be familiar with the history of pre-independence. The presence of the Americans pointed up the divisions within the society and underlined its colonialist structure. The relationships between the occupiers and the Haitians were not much different from those in a colonial situation.[3] Négritude is in effect the reaction to a colonial experience; the occupation placed

Haiti on the same level as Martinique, Guadeloupe, Guyane and the former French colonies in Africa.

Many members of the elite may have been disposed by the situation immediately preceding the intervention to welcome the Americans, but the chaos in the functioning of the society which resulted from the American presence soon made them change their minds. Americans seized the top administrative posts, previously the exclusive preserves of the mulattos; in their social dealings with the locals, they treated all Haitians as inferior; their prejudice led them to select light-skinned individuals for the desirable positions that they themselves could not fill. The elite did not share the first rung of the social ladder with the foreigners but found themselves relegated to second position.[4] The situation of the peasant remained the same. The Americans showed as little concern for the welfare of the peasants as did the elite themselves, whose general attitude is illustrated by the following excerpt from the political column of one of the leading weeklies:

> The truth of the matter is that the masses like the elite, the peasants like the city-dweller, have needs. Theirs are different from ours, that's all. The peasant does not feel the need for electricity in his home, nor does he want record-players and radios like the city-dweller. But he does like, when he has the means, comfortable furniture and a cool, shady hut to rest in in the evenings, and he does enjoy his country dancing under the thatched roof. But let him go away to Cuba or to the Dominican Republic.... They come back with the vices of the city-dwellers... their needs have changed and become more like ours.[5]

The gap between the mulattos and the blacks remained and another gap was added between the former and the white foreigners: the two-tiered social structure was replaced by one with three tiers. The life of the elite bore little resemblance to that of the majority of the population and little relation to the needs of the situation. It was a reproduction of fashionable life in metropolitan France where most of them had received some part of their education and to which they went for holidays. Culture for this class meant metropolitan French culture. The literature of this group was as frivolous and superficial as the remaining aspects of their lives. Commitment was entirely lacking, literature a dilettante pastime. Up to the start of the occupation only two attempts had been made to bring literature closer to the people. In 1836 Ignace Nau had published in *L'Union*, a journal that he founded,

48

a number of short stories which showed the importance of traditional religious belief in the life of the peasant. At the beginning of the twentieth century, as a kind of moral-stocktaking at the end of a hundred years of independence, Frédéric Marcelin and Justin Lhérisson had depicted the routine of life in the 'bas-quartiers' of the capital to which the uprooted peasants flocked, and Antoine Innocent had plunged his readers into the strange world of cause and effect peopled by the peasant and his voodoo divinities. The 'crise de conscience' provoked by the occupation had the effect of focusing the attention of the elite on the peasants. The movement which resulted was, in a sense, more national than any previous movement.

After an unsuccessful attempt by the peasants to repulse the occupiers[6]—sticks and cutlasses being no match for bullets—the struggle was taken up by the elite and conducted at a level less fraught with personal danger. The struggle was to be conducted at the cultural level. If the Americans effectively controlled the finances and the politics of the country they should at least not be permitted to influence its culture. Two sources existed for this cultural resistance and both were drawn on, although one more heavily than the other. French culture with its tradition of sophistication, elegance and courtesy offered an alternative to the brash crassness of the Americans; the French classical education provided a means of combating American attempts to influence the educational system. African culture, whether survivals in Haiti or from the corpus at the place of origin, provided answers to the racial slurs and prejudices of the white occupiers. The elite now acknowledged the existence of an African-based culture in Haiti and pointed to it with pride.

Literary journals, usually short-lived, were the points around which patriots grouped themselves and resistance coalesced. The first of these groups was the Union Patriotique founded by Georges Sylvain in 1920.[7] He had been attacking the Americans in other journals like La Patrie, which he founded in 1915 and which was dedicated, like other journals of its period and kind, to showing the injustices of the occupation and to attempting to revive the national spirit. Sylvain was a member of an older generation but it was the succeeding generation, who grew up during the occupation, that brought opposition to a head and forced the Americans to review their situation. In 1929 students at the School of Agriculture at Damien revolted and precipitated a general strike.

The lead for this generation was provided by Dr. Jean Price-Mars, whom Senghor has called the father of Négritude:

As a student at the Sorbonne, I had begun to reflect on the problem of a cultural renaissance in Black Africa and I was seeking—we were seeking—patronage that would ensure the success of this enterprise.

At the end of my search, I had the good fortune to come upon Alain Locke and Jean Price-Mars. And I read *Ainsi parla l'oncle* at one go like one drinks water from the well in the evening after a long stay in the desert. *L'Oncle* gave legitimacy to the reasons for my search, confirmed what I had felt. For by showing me the treasures of Négritude that he had discovered in and on the land in Haiti, he taught me to find the same values, but purer and stronger, on and in the land of Africa.[8]

Ainsi parla l'oncle was the principal medium through which Price-Mars influenced the Indigenist Movement, as it came to be called, initially because its members were grouped around the journal called *La Revue Indigène*. Representing his country in the United States in 1903 he had observed the attitude of Americans to their own blacks, established contact with leaders of movements for improving the conditions of blacks and tried to see the problem of the situation of the peasants in Haiti in terms of that of blacks in general. While he spent some time with Booker T. Washington, his attitude towards the black problem in the States, as can be seen from his *La Renaissance nègre aux Etats-Unis*,[9] was not the gradualism of his host; his views were closer to those of W. E. DuBois, the leader of the opposition among blacks to the theories of Washington. In fact, some of Price-Mars's ideas in *La Vocation de l'élite* seemed to have been influenced by DuBois's theories on the 'talented tenth'.

The effects of Price-Mars's reading of Gustave Le Bon[10] and his contact with black movements really became evident after 1917 when, after spending some time as his country's representative in Paris, he returned to Haiti to find the Americans in occupation. His intention in *Ainsi parla l'oncle* was first of all to show Haitians the value of their culture, but in the circumstances the implications of his actions were much wider. He underlined the links between the culture of the peasant and African culture, giving the latter, and consequently the former, a dignity which previously seemed lacking. He idealized the picture of the peasant and his culture, especially his religion, which was understandable in the circumstances, but his analysis of the situation was conducted from the viewpoint of a trained ethnographer. His encouragement to writers to exploit the resources of Haitian folklore was answered because it provided a means of combating American influence and domination. He urged the elite to stop seeing themselves as 'coloured Frenchmen', to come to terms with being 'black', 'des conditions historiques déterminées'. The case had been stated, but never so clearly, and the time was opportune. Folklore provided inspiration for artists of all kinds, and creole was given an opportunity to show its resources.

Journals like *La Revue Indigène*, *La Trouée* and in the later 1930s *Les Griots* focused attention on survivals of African culture among the peasants in Haiti. The peasants kept the African traditions strongest and were suddenly given prominence as representative of what was most typically Haitian. The attention given to the peasant was in fact a spiritual journey back to Africa:

> We restored to their place of honour the 'drum' and the 'gourd'.
> Nostalgically we look towards grief-stricken Mother Africa.
> The vanished splendours of the civilizations of the Sudan caused us intense anguish . . . .
> But where could we find this original civilization if not in the people?
> And so our uneasy spirits became passionately interested in folklore. At that time a whole world was slowly dying inside of us.[11]

While the American occupation was a colonial experience which decisively influenced the elite, the winds of change were blowing elsewhere. Europe was sufficiently shaken by the experience of the First World War to indulge in a serious reassessment of itself. Young members of the Haitian elite in Europe for their education, or for other reasons, would have encountered a wave of disillusionment which rocked the basis of the cultural values to which their parents were so attached. The climate which favoured the birth and development of Dadaism and Surrealism permitted a more open-minded examination of non-European cultures, especially that of Africa. Marxism, increasing in popularity after the success of the Russian Revolution, provided a new framework in which to study social and political problems. Haiti was linked with black movements not only because of its unique status as a black republic, but in a more direct way through the role played by Haitians in foreign movements.[12] It figured in the Pan-African Congress organized by W. E. DuBois in Paris in 1919, when it was hoped that some advantage could be taken of the new democratic, anti-imperialist, anti-colonialist mood which followed the war, for a sympathetic hearing to be given to the case for putting an end to the exploitation of blacks, not only in America but everywhere. As shown by a recommendation put by DuBois to the Board of Directors of the NAACP, DuBois saw the movement as universal in scope.[13] Haiti's awareness of its role in the movement is shown by translations of American authors·that appeared in the country in the 1930s, most noticeably those by René Piquion of the work of Langston Hughes and Countee Cullen.

Philippe Thoby-Marcelin was one of the first young members of the elite to respond to the situation. Even before establishing himself as one of the leaders of the Indigenist Movement by collaborating with Jacques Roumain, Carl Brouard, Emile Roumer, Normil Sylvain, Daniel Heurtelou, André Léautaud and Antonio Vieux to found *La Revue Indigène* in 1926, he had expressed in violent imagery his contempt for white culture and western civilization.

> ... Swearing an eternal disdain for European refinement
> Henceforth I sing of you, revolution, shootings, massacres
> of the blows of the 'coco-macque' on black shoulders.[14]

His rejection and rage are translated into the irony of *Fox-trots* which depicts the effect of American imperialism on Haitian culture and the manner in which traditional values are being eroded:

> The trumpets are dead
> >   The drums have been burst
> The lead toy-soldiers have been demoralized
> The performance of Cator
> >   and Theart
> Are just as good as
> >   fairy-tales
> You have been to the cinema
> The *Mysteries of New York* make you dream a lot
> >   Pearl White—Elaine Dodge
> >   Clarel
> >   The hand-that-claps
> Papa's car does up to one hundred an hour
> Coutou-coutou
> Your older sister for a lullaby
> hums you
> The current fox-trot.[15]

Marcelin dedicated a number of the poems he published in *La Revue Indigène* to Jacques Roumain, who was effectively the leader and the most famous member of the Movement. In spite of the objectives of the group to which they belonged, their poems in the *Revue* frequently give the impression of an apprenticeship being served, of experiments being conducted without any serious commitment. The differences between them can mostly be attributed to Roumain's commitment to Marxism which becomes more evident in his mature work, especially his novels. Their backgrounds were similar: urban, middle-class. Roumain had completed his education in Europe but when he returned home he jettisoned all the intellectual baggage that members of the elite usually picked up. He retained his Marxist ideology because it provided him with a method of analysing Haiti's problem, both internal and external: the fact that Haiti had a basic colonial structure was only made more obvious by the American occupation; Haiti's position as a pawn in the international power game also became clearer. His recipe for national redemption was dictated by political views.

These same views placed him in a somewhat paradoxical situation, in addition to distinguishing his work from that of Marcelin and other members of the group. Apparent from his novels is the fact that he was influenced by Price-Mars to use folk material, but his view of the Haitian situation, determined by his ideology, showed him that more than a national culture based on the African element in Haiti was required for a true solution to the country's problems. The search for a cultural identity offered a temporary palliative for the effects of the occupation but no long-term solution to problems which demanded a political and economic solution. For this reason the attempts suggested by *La Revue Indigène* to defend and illustrate the national culture, if they absorbed all the energies of the people, could only lead to further disillusionment. Roumain was much too aware of the harsh realities of the life of the Haitian peasant to follow Price-Mars's suggestions unquestioningly as did many of his contemporaries.

Roumain depicts the life of the peasant in his novels but he cannot bring himself to accept that unhealthy and harsh practices should be sanctioned because they form part of a secular tradition. The misery of peasant life is too closely tied to some traditional practices for him not to advocate the disappearance of the latter if it means also the disappearance of the former. Convinced as he is that much peasant belief is the direct product of ignorance and fear, he shows in *La Montagne Ensorcelée*[16] how the stoning of an old woman and her daughter, intended by the villagers as a sacrificial ritual to appease angry divinities, is nothing more than a brutal, inhuman act born of the inability to understand that drought is a natural phenomenon, resulting possibly from such actions of the peasants as deforestation of the surrounding countryside.

Roumain's rejection of traditional beliefs and practices is even more obvious in *Les Gouverneurs de la rosée*.[17]   Again there is a ritual sacrifice but this time the author approves since it is in the interest of human solidarity, serving as it does to unite two warring factions of a village, and promote progress, symbolized here by artificial irrigation. It seems that although Roumain came under Price-Mars's influence to the extent that he depicts peasant life, he was prevented by his political beliefs from accepting what the peasant sees as the motivating forces of his world. For the peasant these were the desires and moods of the divinities of Voodoo; for Roumain they were fear, superstition, insecurity and ignorance.   The attitude of Roumain differs from that of other authors of the same period who did not share his political views and followed Price-Mars more to the letter.   It differs also from that of Marcelin who in his novels (written in collaboration with his brother Pierre) purports to adopt an objective stance but shows a disagreeable penchant for the bizarre and the sensational. *Canapé Vert* and *La Bête de Museau*[18] read too much like a compilation of unusual happenings, like exotic horror stories. It seems paradoxical that Marcelin should produce this type of novel, for the evidence shows that he possessed a wealth of documentation on the life of the peasant. His choice was too one-sided.

Other art-forms participated in the revival, for example music and the theatre. The elite showed themselves confident enough to believe that America and Europe might be interested in Haitian music and introduced audiences in Paris and New York to *La Musique Haïtienne*.[19] The theatre was suited by its nature to play an important role in the national renaissance for it could have an immediate popular appeal which other genres lacked. It not only presented patriotic dramas, mounting productions which alluded in quite obvious fashion to the situation in the country, but also acted as a link between groups opposed to the occupation. The Haitian theatre 'made use of their tours around the provinces to establish bases for joining the efforts of the Haitian nationalist groups and the Patriotic Union against the American Occupation'.[20]

A number of works of a more general nature, usually by those attached to *Les Griots*, the successor to *La Revue Indigène*, were also published about the life of the peasants, especially about their religion. Religion was the aspect on which *Les Griots* primarily focused their attention, for it was there that African survivals were most apparent. With the slogan 'Haitianism and Africanism', this group took the ideas of Price-Mars to extremes; their eventual position could be described as fascist. The leading figures of this movement, Lorimer Denis, Authur Bonhomme and François Duvalier, did not belong to the mulatto elite, and within the national front certain fissures began to appear; these were the traditional race and class barriers resurfacing.

Haiti's contribution to Négritude was made, however, not only by movements like these at home but also through the role played by Haitians in similar movements abroad, especially in Paris. Paris provided Haitians with the chance to mix with blacks from the French colonies in Africa and the Caribbean and with black American intellectuals. Paris was the point of confluence of a number of currents. The end of the First World War merely served to quicken the interest that the capital had taken in African art and culture as early as 1909 through the efforts of Vlaminck, Derain and Apollinaire. Blacks from the colonies were caught in the intellectual ferment of the 1920s and 30s. Marxism and Surrealism threatened to bring down the foundations on which French society was built, and Lenin in 1922 indicated that blacks were to be classified among exploited colonial people. Not surprisingly blacks were attracted to both Surrealism and Marxism.

Out of the meetings of blacks one group emerged, formed around *La Revue du Monde Noir*. Of that group Dr. Price-Mars and Dr. Sajous were Haitian, Claude MacKay was American, Paulette Nardal and the Achille brothers from the islands, while René Maran, although Negro, was a little more difficult to classify. Dr. Sajous had earlier joined with an African called Mayoute to form the Comité Universel de l'Institut Nègre de Paris which was intended for blacks from Africa, the Caribbean and America, living in Paris. Dr. Price-Mars's presence in the group established a link between the national movement in Haiti and movements more universal in scope.

The islands had a different history from Haiti and were *de facto* and *de jure* colonies. Roumain's *Analyse Schématique* was more readily applicable to Martinique and Guadeloupe than to Haiti. Emancipation had done little to change the social structure of the islands. In Martinique, the majority of slaves remained on the same land they had previously worked, with the single difference that they now received a pittance for their energies. Guadeloupe differed slightly in that after Emancipation a number of former slaves moved towards

55

those mountainous areas which had escaped European colonization; but they settled on tiny plots and carried on subsistence farming. Daniel Guerin tells how in Martinique in 1936, five per cent of the population owned seventy-five per cent of all the cultivable land while the vast majority of the population either had minuscule plots or worked as labourers for others. Land in Martinique was monopolized by a small number of whites. They not only controlled the sugar industry, but all the other aspects of commerce such as banks and could easily bring pressure to bear on the administration of the island. The story in Guadeloupe was little different except that it showed that owning land could engender the same poverty as having to work other people's land.

To their economic domination the monopolistic clique of whites added social snobbery. Beneath this group lay the mulattos, the middle class, and they duplicated the gap between themselves and the white elite with that which they established between themselves and the peasants. The social status of the middle class was so precarious that they felt that only by emphasizing the gap between themselves and the black population could they establish their identity. Spurning all forms of manual labour or even technical work and giving themselves only the most classical of French educations, they ignored the peasants and fixed their attention on metropolitan ideals. Thus the economic gap was reinforced by a cultural gap. For in Martinique and Guadeloupe, the peasants retained many of the beliefs and practices that were African in origin.

The colonial status of the islands explains why pressure for change had to be articulated in the metropolis. Here, more so than in Haiti, change depended on the currents of ideas that were sweeping across Europe. Young members of the middle class found themselves following contemporary metropolitan intellectuals in questioning values, and were forced to go beyond this to examine their relationship to France and to the islands. A 'crise de conscience' was observed also in the islands and was marked by the appearance of journals like *Lucioles* (1927) which was directed by Gilbert Gratiant in collaboration with Auguste Joyau, a local white, and Octave Mannoni, a foreign white, and which did valuable pioneering work in bringing literature close to the people by seeking inspiration in the land around and eschewing the slavish imitation of European fashions. Publications like *La Revue des Antilles* (1900-1901), the *Bulletin pour servir à l'histoire de la Martinique* (1915-1917) and the *Revue Martiniquaise* which later became the *Revue de la Martinique*, edited by Jules Monnerot senior, were not sufficiently radical for the succeeding generation but helped to prepare the spiritual awakening which developed in the late 1930s by dealing primarily with matters relating to the islands.

All of the members of the group around *Légitime Défense*[21] with the exception of Etienne Léro, the leader, were mulatto and, as such, members of the middle class. Their attitudes were partly a revolt against the values for which their parents stood, hence the note of petulance in some of their affirmations—a conflict caused by the generation gap—and partly a genuine concern about the conditions in the islands seen in the light of those ideas to which they were exposed in Paris. Those who signed the manifesto along with Etienne Léro were Thelus Léro, Jules-Marcel Monnerot, René Ménil, Maurice-Sabat Quitman, Michel Pilotin, Pierre Yoyotte and Auguste Thésée. Although the group proclaimed itself Marxist, it made no real attempt to analyse the conditions in the islands in Marxist terms. Even less did it seem aware of the importance of the colonial structure in determining these conditions. They make it quite clear early in the manifesto that they see themsevles as traitors in revolt against their own class whose ideals they reject: 'We spit on all that they love and hold dear, on everything that provides them with pleasure and sustenance'.[22]

Their desire for self-flagellation is evident in the manner in which they denigrate their origins and their values while making only passing reference to the white plutocracy and similarly glossing over the conditions of the peasants. They save their sharpest barbs for the attitudes of the mulatto middle class but show little bitterness or even irony in speaking about 'la plutocratie blanche héréditaire'. In *Généralités sur "l'écrivain" de couleur antillais* Léro does have sufficient insight to make the observation: 'It is true that the books on which West Indians are brought up have been written in other countries for other readers'.[23] But he stops short of getting to the root of the problem, the colonial structure of the society which causes the education and the culture in the islands to be oriented towards the outside. The literature could not come to terms with the problems that perplexed the group because they had no commitment either to art or to social change.

Légitime Défense shows that Léro and his colleagues were familiar with the movement in Haiti and with the Harlem Renaissance in the United States:

> The wind that blows from black America will soon, we hope, have swept away from the Antilles the aborted fruit of an empty, worn-out culture. Langston Hughes and Claude MacKay,

the two black revolutionary poets, have brought us, marinated in red alcohol the African love of life, the African pleasure of love, the African dream of death. And then too some young Haitian poets are producing for us poetry rich in future dynamism.[24]

References to injustices against blacks and to institutions and organizations like the NAACP and the black press indicate that they saw themselves in the broader context of a universal movement to put an end to the exploitation of blacks. The salon of Paulette Nardal not only ensured contact between West Indian and African students, black American writers MacKay, Hughes, Jean Toomer and Countee Cullen and others like Price-Mars, Félix Eboué and Alain Locke, but established a link between the pioneers of the Négritude movement and the writers Césaire, Senghor and Damas. Although the members of the group of *Légitime Défense* did not produce any original work of literature, their place in the history of the movement rests on the fact that they not only proposed a cultural renaissance but, serving as a point of convergence of a number of ideological currents, provided a clear starting point for Damas, Senghor and Césaire.

NOTES

1. Many mulattos were in fact 'affranchis'—freedmen—and as such would have had rights, including the right to property, which the slaves did not have.
2. The Americans made the mistake of sending in a majority of white Southerners on the assumption that they would best know how to deal with blacks.
3. See Robert Rotberg, *The Politics of Squalor* (Boston: Houghton Mifflin, 1971), p. 158.
4. Not even the Haitian head-of-state was permitted to enter the American Club which was reserved exclusively for white Americans.
5. *Le Temps*, 2e année no 54 (15 juillet 1933), *La Semaine Politique*. In turning its back on the traditional way of life the elite was, of course, turning its back on the experience of slavery which was still sufficiently recent to be painful. What is regrettable is that at the same time they turned their backs on the tradition, they had to turn their backs on those who lived it.
6. Resistance to the occupation came first from the 'cacos' a group of dispossessed peasants whose traditional role was to provide would-be revolutionary leaders with a ready-made corps of recruits. At the time of the occupation they became patriots and under their leader Charlemagne Peralte and his lieutenant Baltravile harassed the Marines in a guerilla-style campaign. This resistance came to an end when the location of their camp was betrayed and penetrated by the Marines, and Peralte was shot. It was objection to the re-introduction of the 'corvée' (forced labour) that gained this movement widespread support.

7. L'Union Patriotique had links with the NAACP which had been founded in 1909. Haiti thus had early contact with Negro movements outside the country.

8. *Témoignages sur la vie et l'oeuvre du Dr. Price-Mars* (Port-au-Prince: Imprimerie de l'Etat, 1956), p. 3.

9. *La Renaissance Nègre aux Etats-Unis* (Port-au-Prince, 1923).

10. Prince-Mars attributes his own vocation to the reading of a book entitled *Les lois psychologiques de l'évolution* by Gustave Le Bon, 1900. This book divided up the races into four categories and placed Negroes in the category 'inferior'. Prince-Mars is here following a tradition established by Anterior Firmin and Hannibal Price, who had reacted similarly to Gobineau's book, *L'Inégalité des races humaines*, and come to the defence not only of blacks in Haiti but of the whole black race.

11. Carl Brouard, *Les Griots*, Vol. I, No. 1 (July-September 1938).

12. Not only Price-Mars, as already shown, but Benito Sylvain, for example, who was at the first Pan-African Congress organized in Paris in 1915. Antoine Berin, *Benito Sylvain* (Port-au-Prince: La Phalange, 1969).

13. Memorandum—Future of Africa, 9 September 1918, NAACP Papers.

14. *La Trouée*, No. 1 (July 1927), p. 21. The poem was written earlier but was unpublished until growing opposition to the Americans made it more opportune. Marcelin's poems in *La Revue Indigène* are more mocking than violent.

15. *Anthologie de la poésie 'haïtienne indigène'* (Port-au-Prince, 1928; in Kraus Reprint, Nendeln, 1971, pp. 60-61).

16. Jacques Roumain, *La Montagne Ensorcelée* (Port-au-Prince: Collection Indigène, 1931).

17. *Les Gouverneurs de la rosée* (Paris: Les Editeurs Francais Réunis, 1944).

18. Philippe Thoby & Pierre Marcelin: *Canapé-Vert* (New York: Farrar and Rinehart, 1944). Philippe Thoby & Pierre Marcelin: *La Bête de Museau* (New York: Rinehart, 1946).

19. The title of a lecture given in Nancy and later in Paris to the Société française de Musicologie in 1928 by Franck Lassegue.

20. R. Cornevin, *Le Théâtre haïtien* Quebec: Lemac, 1973).

21. *Légitime Défense* appeared in one issue in 1932. It took its name from the manifesto of the Surrealist movement written by André Breton.

22. *Légitime Défense*, p. 2.

23. *Ibid.*, p. 7.

24. *Ibid.*, p. 12.

5

Léon Damas

by

BRIDGET JONES

Léon Damas has received less attention than Senghor and Césaire. Out of a less abundant literary output, a few protest poems from *Pigments* (1937)[1] are too often all that he is known by. Since his brief parliamentary career which ended in 1951, he has avoided the controversies of active politics and remained an exile whose main commitment is to the cause of international black consciousness. However, the complex personality of Damas cannot be reduced to the simplified image of Négritude's poet of hate, and there is much to celebrate both in his writing and in a teaching and publishing career devoted to promoting the liberation of black poets from the constraints of 'segregation, a slavishly imitative culture, colonization, spiritual assimilation'.[2]

Born in Cayenne, French Guyana, in 1912,[3] he shared philosophy classes with Aimé Césaire at the Lycée Schoelcher in Martinique, and moved on to Paris to study law in accordance with the ambitions of his middle-class family. He concentrates in his fragile person a racial sample of the Caribbean: there was Negro and Amerindian blood on his mother's side, and his father was a mulatto of partly European origin. He has expressed very forcibly his pain at being moulded into an *assimilé* by his upbringing as a child; the constant pressure from home and school to speak, behave and if possible think like a white Frenchman. Once a student he rebelled and affirmed himself a 'poète nègre', trying also by contacts and studies in ethnology to develop understanding of the African within him. It is later in life that he writes more calmly of the three rivers that run in his veins and stands 'upright in the triple pride of my mixed blood',[4] though never embracing Senghor's comfortable gospel of cultural synthesis.

Damas's first group of writings—the poems of *Pigments*, the French Guyanese folklore retold under the title *Veillées noires* (1935-43),[5] and the report on his *Retour de Guyane* (1938)[6]—combine to chart the same passionate self-discovery and rediscovery of the native land that we find in Césaire's *Cahier d'un retour au pays natal*. However, even a brief comparison highlights some of Damas's specific quality. He burst into print more quickly and fiercely; the poems 'Solde' and 'La complainte du nègre' for example, appeared in *Esprit* in 1934. Putting great emphasis on communicating his message, Damas prefers to use lucidly sarcastic prose to expose the failures of French colonialism and the assimilation policy. His deceptively naïve animal tales present a local folk culture in which African values triumphantly survive. The directness of his poetry is far closer in spirit and technique to an oral tradition than Césaire's subtle and erudite codes. His is an analytical intelligence gifted with a wickedly destructive wit, but unsuited to the sustained effort of will and imagination demanded by an epic poem. His work betrays the more radical self-doubt of the privileged colonial of mixed racial background and that indelible *rancune* he sees as specific to French Guyana.

Among a number of other factors, two influences seem especially strong in shaping Damas's attitudes and techniques.[7] Firstly, he figures as the main heir to the spirit of *Légitime Défense*, an ephemeral little magazine produced in the margins of Surrealism in 1932 by Etienne Léro and other Martiniquan students.[8] Their manner follows the Surrealist fashion for uninhibited abuse of the older generation, but their comments on the cultural situation are solidly founded on a Marxist analysis of their society. The pallidly imitative literature of the assimilated bourgeoisie is seen as a symptom of alienation. The Creole-speaking masses have no real access to education, and authentic local culture cannot flourish in a divided and exploited colonial society. René Ménil in particular uses the Surrealist conception of poetry for a very lucid critique of the 'écrivain antillais'. Damas responded deeply to these fighting words, re-using a number of the images[9] and even syntactical tricks. However, he was not prepared to follow Léro and company in composing poetic exercises in the style of Breton or Dali.

A second major influence was Negro America. *Légitime Défense* had cited admiringly Afro-American poets, and included a key discussion from *Banjo*. As the researches of Michel Fabre have corroborated,[10] Damas extended his knowledge of the New Negro movement through the *Revue du Monde Noir* (1929-32) and took advantage of personal contacts. With astute literary judgment he looked to Langston Hughes (later a personal friend) for a renewal based on the popular negro modes: blues, spirituals and the wealth of ballad and work songs. In McKay's novels he could find a heightened folk speech which caught something of the triumph of jazz rhythms in a sad white world. Hughes belonged to a loose fraternity of left-wing poets, Roumain, Guillén etc., often compulsive travellers, who were developing a new simplified rhetoric of black awareness, sharing key images and emotive proper names across language barriers. Damas responded to this outlook, adopting something of the footloose life-style of Hughes and McKay as well as the poetic conventions. The Afro-American writers and musicians also served him as a valuable argument against assimilation.

The themes of *Pigments* have become so much part of the Négritude heritage that most of them are now taken for granted and more interest attaches to Damas's poetic technique. It is a deliberately organized and militant collection, 'the manifesto of the negritude movement' as he called it in a 1972 interview.[11] It begins where the old order of African life was shattered by the arrival of the oppressor: 'Ils sont venus . . .' and ends on a call to armed revolt. The theme of the black man's stolen African homeland is there: 'mon Afrique qu'ils ont cambriolée' ('Blanchi'), a secure ancestral community mapped out by the enumeration in 'Limbé'. and still precariously surviving in the 'ancestrale foi conique' ('Shine') which shapes his hut roof in the New World. We notice how Damas dramatizes the traumatic experience directly, speaking in the first person role of the victim and inciting the audience to identify with him against THEM. The image of Africa remains tenuous enough to mark very clearly his distance from it, but since the oppressors are rarely specified Damas can canalize very powerfully a collective anguish of persecution by the white man.

This 'tribal' voice draws with more detail and immediacy on the experience of plantation slavery in the New World. The 'cargaisons fétides' of the Middle Passage, the whip and the red-hot iron, the hounds tracking the runaway, these memories seem to well up compulsively as the movement of a poem generates emotional intensity. Damas is particularly concerned with the persistence of psychic shock, the morbidly reduced vitality of a race whose blood has drained away to fertilize the cane-crop. The sluggish impotence of the present, hinted at in many *spleen* poems, is explicitly ascribed to the brutality and tortures of the slave master in 'La complainte du nègre'. 'En file indienne' comments obsessively on the strange resignation of the peasant women bearing burdens. In 'Rappel' Damas features ironically 'the good nigger (who) stretches out ten or fifteen hours in the sugar factory on his hard bed' and he returns to this theme more extensively in the first movement of *Black-Label*.[12] It is the docility of his compatriots 'Morts pour la France' or the 'indéfectible attachement' of the Tirailleurs Sénégalais which provoke the infuriated call to arms in the last two *Pigments*, but he would not react with such violence if he did not recognize this same debilitated inertia within himself (cf. 'Réalité'). When he does envisage revolt it is in dreams of cathartic violence, like the image of the cane-cutter's cutlass raised in bloody revenge ('Si souvent', developed also in *Black-Label*).

Damas identifies the slave with the slavish cult of French culture. Most of his best poems evoke his own divided self, lifting the mask of exquisite Parisian manners to reveal the rebellious urges of natural Caribbean man underneath, or to expose the 'credibility gap' in French civilization itself. For *Pigments* has the self-awareness of Damas in France, giving voice to the loneliness and alienation of the colonial betrayed by the hollow *théories* on which he had been nurtured. It is this 'wind' no doubt which comes hiccuping up in 'Hoquet', just as he spits back 'Blanchi', or suffers 'l'indigestion/de tout morceau d'histoire de France'. He has been drilled to speak only 'le français de France'. His education has been French, including the favourite preposterous example of reciting 'mes ancêtres les Gaulois' ('Nuit blanche'). The poet ridicules the white behavioural model by using the trivial niceties of table manners or the high civility of taking tea in a Parisian salon, though he cunningly confuses distinctions of body language which relate to class as well as race. The image of European culture is similarly satirical: the Viennese waltz, a piano tinkling out 'un clair de lune à soupirs/ tout format'.

Christianity is also placed among the irrelevant manifestations of the colonizer's culture. Several poems which begin with deceptive flippancy grow harsher in tone, as in 'Solde' which culminates in a hysterical feeling of complicity in a vicious and bloodthirsty 'ci-vi-li-sa-tion'. Though he has been compelled to assimilate French culture, the eyes of the Frenchman will brand him irretrievably as other, as *nègre* (cf. 'Un clochard m'a demandé dix sous'). He feels it his duty to warn of the link between mild racist mockery and violent persecution. His waltz conjures up as partners 'tonton Gobineau' and 'cousin Hitler', while 'S. O. S.' warns of the fascist threat in terms designed to shock high-minded Francophiles.

The shared language and culture make more bitter the exclusion. Damas in blues mood paints sound pictures of night and darkness using physical malaise, especially cold, to convey inner solitude (see the rueful 'Pareille à la légende' or sobbing melodies of 'Il est des nuits'). His body remembers the warm *mornes*, his spirit is numbed by the chill *boulevards*.

One final theme has a specially close link with the Harlem-based protests against the artificial role that the white public imposes on the black artist: the musician, boxer, etc. allowed to perform but not develop independence. The image of the muted trumpet expresses this stifling in a minor key, but Damas also protests forcibly in 'Trêve' and threatens in 'Bientôt' some stronger action. Apart from a few earlier poems, *Pigments* has great internal coherence, allowing Damas to charge an individual pronoun or Creole term with the accumulated emotion of a whole racial experience.

Damas's poetic technique can be most positively assessed in terms of his own remarks on African poetry with its essentially sung nature and use of everyday language:

> (The African) does not compose for scholars. He composes so that the people can listen to him. This explains the jests, the puns, the word-play, the simplicity of expression.
>
> It is poetry where rhyme and syllable counts have no necessary role to play. Poetry which relies wholly on cadence and melody. On repetition which creates the rhythm. On effects of antithesis and parallelism in the ideas and images.[13]

Thus, unlike the more scholarly poets, Damas chose a medium to fit his message of solidarity with the black community. 'Et caetera' was chanted in Baoulé as a call to rebellion in 1939, and there is an immediate audience response to Damas even across a degree of language unfamiliarity. Coming from a speech community where standard French was the language of the colonizers, and associated with formal and official situations, Damas is exceptionally sensitive to the choice of register. His slangy conversational idiom is a *prise de position* similar to the choice of Creole by contemporary Caribbean poets, but has the notable advantage of international currency. Damas was able to draw also on the poetic experiments with metropolitan spoken French being undertaken by Prévert, Queneau and others. In all his writing that 'décalage léger et constant' which Sartre mentions in *Orphée noir* is perceptible in the juggling with a range of spoken and written styles.

Most of what can be said about the techniques of *Pigments* holds .good for all of Damas's poetry. Apart from *Black Label*, he works exclusively with the short or medium-length poem, at its best often a succint dramatic monologue or expression of mood. He has the two indispensable virtues which allow protest poetry to endure: a sense of humour and knowing when to stop.

His best poems are very skilfully constructed with a musical sense of the balance of pace and tone. Characteristically they have a forceful opening and end on a calculated dramatic shock ('S.O.S.', 'Hoquet') or occasional diminuendo ('Pour sûr', 'Position'). His use of repetition, one of the structural features which govern folk literature, is very marked and would repay precise linguistic description.[14] Typical protest poems are organised on an anaphora 'Trêve de . . . . . ' 'Passe pour . . . . ' or a repeated plain assertion of the central idea:

J'ai l'impression d'être ridicule
Rendez-les moi mes poupées noires
Ma mère voulant d'un fils . . . .

followed by a set of variations or paradigmatic substitutions which are often in a subordinate relation. 'Solde', despite its air of a folk-song stringing together improvised items by call and response (shoes on toes to bowler hat on top), shows a careful blend of easily understood phrases with more complex puns and metaphors (verses 2-3, 5-6), while developing the series: 'dans leurs (twice)/ de leurs/ parmi eux' essential to the meaning and rhythm (the pronoun allowing greater vocal emphasis than the possessive adjective). Repetition and refrains in a live speech event invite audience participation and are less quickly monotonous where the voice can add new units of meaning by ironical pauses, a higher pitch, etc. and vary pace and volume. The lulling repetition of past participles in 'Et caetera' prepares the dramatic surprise of the bold expletive. The three printed versions of 'Un clochard m'a demandé dix sous' offer a useful illustration of Damas at work: after the 1934 version he found 'hardes' to echo the stressed vowel of the key word 'clochard', then for the definitive version added three further emphatic 'Moi aussi' as well as a repetition to point the change in intonation contour from beggarly whine 'les yeux/le ventre/creux' to indignant revival of black pride. Many revisions also show increasing use of the rest for prosodic effects (typographical spacing and lines broken into shorter units), and heightened dramatization, especially of the climax to a poem; a last *noires* on 'Limbé', for example. Everything points to a poet progressively more conscious of constructing patterns for the spoken voice.

When using rhythm, password of the New Negro art, Damas delights in extravagant effects, preferring two feet for the 'poème à danser'

65

to the twelve of the Alexandrine, as he jokes in *Black-Label*. In defiant poems his repetitions often suggest a strong 'drum-beat' by the use of duple time with frequent syncopation. An apparently slight piece like 'Bientôt' (revised version) shows very dexterous stresses and patterning of oral [ɔ] [o] and nasal vowels with rapid consonants to give the key word onomatopoeic force as an urgent warning drum. The suspended high note of the unfinished sentence, and even the hint of the Creole: '(mó) pa ké dãsé', reinforce the message. *Pigments* suggested to Senghor 'un rythme de tam-tam instinctivement re-trouvé'[15] and this point could well be explored systematically in terms of the persistence of African speech rhythms in Creolized French and the analysis of Damas readings by modern experimental phonetics.[16]

Though he writes in a relaxed standard French, Damas often seems as close to Creole as to Mallarmé when he uses the concision of a pre-dicate without copula or allows the voice to punctuate the ambiguities of his syntax. Details like the high frequency of *foutre*, play on an opposition between *moi* (Creole *mó*) and *ils ont* (malicious echo of Creole *zòt*?), with the carefully selected lexical allusions, give Damas the flavour of a local entertainer, even though the firm simplicity of con-struction allows a wide appeal. Damas's masterpiece 'Hoquet' has attracted many commentaries, but a less remarked feature is the scope it offers for an ironical play on Creole interferences in the mother's speech: the nasal vowels of *pain*, and [dž] of *banjo*, an expressive high note on the typical African reduplication of *français français*, etc.

Humour in Damas is an art of self-defence. He has the satirical imagination to reverse the stereotypes, and cast Hitler as cannibal, the European as trophy-hunting barbarian, the Christian God as an unfortunate who missed out on polygamy, and in 'Et caetera' turn round the European's nightmare image of the Tirailleur raping white women to send him to attack colonialism in Senegal itself. In *Pigments* whimsical fancies often turn out to be serious weapons, like the Blue Danube motif in 'Nuit blanche'. Disintegrating clichés and idioms, playing with satisfying sound patterns, and with a neat taste in puns, Damas seldom relaxes into verbosity, as if the underlying tension of his whole approach to things French kept his wit taut and short-winded.

Damas as poet dramatizing archetypal roles (the bogey man of 'Bouclez-la' or the stern mother of 'Hoquet') and calling on so many of the techniques by which the story-teller holds his audience: jokes, sung interludes, rhythms and repetitions, prepares us for the *conteur* of *Veillées noires*. Even if folklore did not figure extensively in his own

Cayenne childhood, Damas was doubtless keen to rediscover the oral sources which Dr. Price-Mars prized as the authentic voice of the Caribbean masses,[17] and to add his own contribution to making known African survivals in the New World. These are enriched in the Guyanas by the presence of the reconstituted tribal groups of early escaped slaves ('Bush Negroes'). Damas is still promising to publish an enlarged collection of Afro-Amerindian tales, *La Moisson des Trois Domaines.*

The bulk of the material retold in *Veillées noires* demonstrates the resilience of African folk-tales in their New World setting. We find the range of animal characters, irrepressible Rabbit, Deer and Monkey, fierce but stupid Tiger, gossiping Bird and devious Turtle, common to so many areas of the black diaspora. (Anansi the spider-man was apparently reserved for a later collection.) They often express the art of survival of the powerless, in trickery, flattery and a hard-won humorous wisdom. The plots too are familiar, blending with African story or creation myth, elements of European devil tale, or Amerindian legend. They mirror the cultural diversity of a plural society, but one which has coexisted for centuries in the same natural habitat. Damas builds up a portrait of the local life-style with its particular ways of cooking, fishing, cultivating, practising magic. This is a land of rivers (Turtle and Alligator figure more frequently than in the Islands), where the deep forest, the *Yan-Man*, is a constant point of reference. This rural milieu has changed little since M. de Préfontaine wrote his manual for settlers in 1763.

Thus Damas offers a critique of assimilation policies simply by showing the richness of the native local culture they threaten. He is also more specific. A few stories deal explicitly with an unjust social order based on race: 'Aux premiers âges', the old story of the magic fountain combining with a bitter parable of the talents in 'Les trois frères'. More often a sharp aside brings a story into focus: the wicked mother offers her prettiest daughter to a Devil who apart from a slight limp might be any plantation owner ('Grain de sel'). Such indications are sufficient to allow a second level of interpretation of all the stories satirizing the abuse of power. When Damas shows Little Pig learning class consciousness in the farmyard, or Monkey dressing up to pass for man, the parallels with *Pigments* are inescapable and direct us to decode in racial terms.

Naturally the extensive use of Creole songs and *dolos* (proverbs), stock jokes and riddles, underlines Damas's intention. Often the central figure of the tale is a musician, gifted like Ravet-Guitar with a subversive power to awaken the African vitality of the people in defiance of the landowner or ruler. The narrative incorporates these elements, usually without strain (though 'Echec et mât' almost gets out of hand). Damas relishes playing off the Creole elements and apparently naïve content against a literary level of formal French, gracefully archaic in flavour (e.g. 'Papa Mouton eut le vin fort gai', etc.). The result is a seductive little book, with all the wit of the best of *Pigments* at the service of a more richly human and *guyanais* version of the same project.

The third pre-war volume, *Retour de Guyane*, originated in a 1934 ethnographic mission to study the Bush Negroes which exploded with passionate indignation into a full-scale critique of French policy and mismanagement. Damas fills in the background by a brief history of exploration and settlement, then looks at the contemporary situation. The long history of failed projects, the 'gangrene' of the penal settlements, so much potential frustrated by obtuse direct rule from Paris and corrupt or lazy officials, such factors have created a specific local mentality despite the internal divisions of race and class. This book is essential reading both for Damas's own commitment to his homeland, and for a partisan view of French colonialism from a writer unusually well-placed to evaluate assimilation. Most often he allows a damning series of facts to speak for themselves, but we recognize his flair for the telling detail: 'un vrai budget colonial' which spends 7,000 Fr. on a uniform for the governor's chauffeur and 4,000 Fr. on the Public Library, or so much convict labour expended on road-building, to achieve communication with the interior by the dug-out canoes of the Boni tribesmen. Damas disentangles the various issues involved in assimilation: political status as a French department (in fact achieved in 1946), social equality with white Frenchmen (a mirage), cultural uniformity (neither desirable nor possible). With a firm 'no' he concludes that the colonial is and can be an equal but remains *other*. He rejects a change in political status as no more of a cure for the ills of French Guyana than suppressing the *bagne*, indeed such measures might serve to distract from vitally-needed economic development. An expert in the weight of words, he distrusts all the grandiose rhetoric, and warns against exchanging one set of labels for another on an equally empty package, or, to use his own image, 'pinning this *légion d'honneur* on a naked and starving breast'. Not surprisingly this book made Damas very unpopular both in official quarters and among some of his compatriots, though time has alas justified too many of his lucid commentaries on French policy in the Caribbean.[18] The factual approach and well-argued position of *Retour de Guyane* is a valuable companion to the emotional rejection expressed in *Pigments*, and usefully relates the folklore of *Veillées noires* to the territory as a whole. In the stimulating atmosphere of the pre-war black community Damas felt the pressure to contribute his message. Nothing he has published since shows quite the same urgent power. Indeed from 1947 on, a variety of enticing titles have been announced but not actually reached publication. Immediately after the war he worked on the first of the anthologies which collected the work of *Poètes d'expression française*[19] not to the greater glory of French civilization but to promote awareness of a shared colonial experience. Damas makes his position clear by featuring Léro in his preface and work by the militant younger generation, Georges Desportes, Lucien Attuly, Guy Tirolien, etc. together with his own *compagnons de route*, Césaire and Senghor. However in compiling a manual on historical lines, 1900-1945, he also included too much mediocre and imitative versifying, and the resultant volume has been inevitably overshadowed by Senghor's excellent *Anthologie de la nouvelle poésie nègre et malgache*, published the following year.

During this, the heroic period of *Présence Africaine*, Damas expressed solidarity by a little collection of African songs adapted from originals in indigenous languages. Though the themes are often close to his own songs of love, war or abuse, the tone is more confidently prosaic. Several tiny love-poems ('Idylle', 'Sérénade', 'Prière') charmingly suggest an underlying order of stable human relations. Poems like the satirical 'Cocu et content', 'Parti-pris' or 'La Maîtresse Servante' illuminate the links between Damas's own poetic technique and folk-song originals with their well-defined social functions.[20] However, the collection does not altogether avoid the quaintly stilted air of translation. In 1952 appeared Damas's own first collection of love-poems. These nine lyrics modulating the pangs of 'mon coeur malade' with often a hinted context of exile or hostility, reappear in slightly revised form in *Névralgies*.

However, 1948-51 saw Damas engaged in the purposeful parallel activity of representing French Guyana, now an overseas Department, in the Chambre des Députés. His record is a workmanlike though not outstanding one of sensible proposals to develop the territory: tax relief, agricultural credit, electoral and judicial reforms, setting up of various bodies to promote forestry, agriculture and an 'Institut Français d'Amérique tropicale'. Damas took an active part in attacking the delay in extending French Social Security benefits to the D. O. M., and finally displayed his intransigence over the official enquiry into the troubles in the Ivory Coast. He held to his views and did not seek re-election. Although brief, this career offsets the picture of Damas as hysterical racist composing 'hate-filled diatribes' (Coulthard). For a period at least he made an attempt to work the system, and cooperate both with the socialist group in parliament and other bodies concerned with French Guyana. The poetic image is of the victim of persecution and censorship, having the courage to say *merde* instead of keeping meekly silent. The full picture is more complex and shows unexpected patience with the compromises of concerted action and the prose of officialdom.

Since the immediate post-war phase Damas has worked towards the cultural liberation of the black man in a more international sphere. He has written tributes to Dr. Price-Mars and René Maran for *Présence Africaine*, and edited a second anthology, *La nouvelle somme de poésie du monde noir*, which charts the enormous vitality of the poetic resurgence and also the expansion of Damas's own horizons. Though based now in the United States at Howard University, he has been a regular participant in cultural missions and congresses round the globe, looking back in addresses and especially public readings on the Négritude experience.

Damas's poetry since *Pigments* lacks that initial verve, though offering much to reward the reader or listener. Extracts from *Black-Label* appeared in the 1947-48 anthologies, and this sustained poem in four movements elaborates without significantly advancing Damas's long debate with himself and the world. It has a confessional quality, as if under the influence of alcohol the exiled poet yields up 'le film du rêve recréé', a long fluid series of flashbacks into his past. The first section develops from tears of exile by the waters of the Seine, to a long apostrophizing of all those who challenge him, men of the Caribbean who betray their own dignity, men of Africa who betrayed their brothers, then blames with humorous blasphemy the Christian God and bitterly reiterates his stance *against* all the forces of repression. The second canto concentrates more on the sentimental memories of the lonely heart: a pastoral vision symbolizing the distant Caribbean, a fiasco with the blonde Ketty, voices calling long distance. The round of partners quickens into the consoling rhythms of the Cabane Cubaine, the blues singer, and then the Afro-Brazilian beat triumphantly bombards Paris with the black man's revenge. Damas next develops one encounter into a sustained conversation, a *dédoublement* which allows him to give another self-addressed account of his childhood, the experience of 'Hoquet' amplified and set in the real and ideal landscape of home. He ends in his favourite role as rebel, shouting 'Down with school' on behalf of all the underdogs and outcasts. In Section IV he pulls together many strands of experience to link his own poetic method to the *kamougué* folk-dance, trace his gift of language to the figure of Tètèche (the old woman storyteller presiding over *Veillées noires*) and invoke the heritage of the Maskililis, the little men, free spirits of the woods, Amerindian or African. He takes care to dispel the Christian overtones of this *testament;* to the last he defies the system, glass in hand.

The form of *Black-Label* is hauntingly obsessive, patterns sustained beyond the point of saturation, refrains used to structure an elusive flux of mental experience. Critics point to the essentially musical nature of the construction. The notorious war-chant 'Jamais le Blanc ne sera nègre' achieves a very exciting beat by its double accent on the Creole syllable *nèg*, and the ambiguity of *est/et* finds a triumphant climax in the absolute statements of the last four lines. The context shows Damas ruefully conscious that this explosion of black power and joy is sited in a tiny Parisian dance floor. However, without the support of a musical accompaniment this poem flags. The absorption with his childhood and with protest for its own sake needs a less self-indulgent expression at this stage in the poet's career, though this is Damas's own favourite work.

Some of the love poems in *Névralgies*, like *Black-Label*, set a personal relationship into the tormented context of black-white relations. The title itself implies a bashful confession of weakness nagging at the soul. Memorable lyrics here are often the brief fixing of a mood, for example 'Par la fenêtre ouverte à demi' with its unerring tense shift as the initial charm and consecrated attitudes of poet to the world and his muse give way to an avid urgency; 'Sur le sein' playing ironically on the poet 'in whiteface', uses the metre to give a woeful emphasis to 'flasque' and 'blême'. Among longer pieces, 'Toute à ce besoin d'évasion' constructs a lively pattern to ease the heartache: the woman totally absorbed in her holiday sunbathing, the poet just a key dangling in an empty piegeonhole. The verbal shrug of the final couplet is a typical play on an idiomatic nuance. Other pieces show in a more relaxed form the poet's sheer delight in language, whether punning on the European and Caribbean meaning of *marron*, composing nonsense proverbs and magic pass-words in the Surrealist manner ('Nul ne se rappelle avoir vu'), or building a collage on the sound waves ('Et maintenant'). Though a few poems stress race consciousness for lament or satire, overall this collection deals more playfully with the intimate

71

sense of loss and lack of fulfilment. The urgent passion of *Pigments* is not there to direct the games.

The verdict of the general public is thus right in giving a special place to *Pigments*, even if it is unrepresentative of Damas's range of interests and abilities. His original contribution to Négritude may not be extensive in terms of ideas, but his temperament and Guyanese background add a valuable and distinctive note. Above all he is an authentic artist with words, in that heightened popular vein of other *poètes-gueux* from Villon to Verlaine, like them gifted with a poetic ear of rare subtlety and a sure sense of form. We value his sense of humour, his wit and satire, his astringent refusal to be mystified. He transmits the pain and passion of blackness simply and clearly enough to reach his chosen people, and the audience for his work continues to grow.

NOTES

1. First published by G. L. M. (Paris, 1937) and in a definitive edition by Présence Africaine (Paris, 1962, reprinted 1972 with *Névralgies*).
2. Introduction to *Nouvelle somme de poèsie du monde noir* (*Présence Africaine*, No. 57, 1966). Translations are my own.
3. For a fuller biographical sketch see the valuable study by Merle Hodge (unpublished M. Phil. thesis 'The Writings of Léon Damas and their connection with the Négritude movement in literature', University of London, 1967).
4. *Névralgies* (Paris: Présence Africaine, 1966 and 1972), p. 122.
5. Paris, Stock, 1943. Republished with some slight amendments by Leméac (Ottawa, 1972).
6. Paris: J. Corti, 1938.
7. L. Kesteloot fills in some useful general background in the early chapters of her thesis, *Les écrivains noirs de langue française: naissance d'une littérature* (Bruxelles: Institut de Sociologie de l'Université libre, 1965).
8. Now available in Kraus reprint (Nendeln, 1970).
9. A point noted by W. Feuser, 'Négritude: The Third Phase', *The New African*, Vol. 5, No. 3 (April 1966), p. 63.
10. See 'Autour de René Maran' (*Présence Africaine*, No. 86, 2e trimestre 1973, pp. 165-171) and also 'René Maran, trait d'union entre deux négritudes' in *Négritude africaine Négritude caraibe* (Université de Paris XIII, 1973).
11. Conducted by Keith Warner (*Manna*, No. 3, Toronto 1973), p. 17.
12. Paris: Gallimard, 1956.
13. Introductory note to *Poèmes nègres sur des airs africains* (Paris: G. L. M., 1948).
14. Some general observations in Keith Warner, 'New Perspective on Léon Damas', *Black Images*, Vol. 2, No. 1 (Spring 1973), pp. 3-6.
15. See 1937 lecture collected in *Négritude et Humanisme* (Paris: Du Seuil, 1964), p. 20.
16. Work in *phonostylistique littéraire* under the direction of Pierre Léon suggests a useful approach, especially if developed on the balanced lines indicated by D.

Delas and J. Filliolet (cf. chapter on 'Matériaux pour le décodage sonore et prosodique' in *Linguistique et poétique*, Paris: Larousse, 1973). Research on the prosody of French-based Creoles is not as extensive as, for example, the work of Jack Berry, Richard Spears, *et al.* on problems of pitch, 'tone' and intonation in English-based Creoles. M. Saint-Jacques Fauquenoy, *Analyse Structurale du créole guyanais* (Paris: Klincksieck, 1972) devotes a scant page to 'Phonologie de la phrase' p. 52.

17. See his tributes to Price-Mars in *Présence Africaine*, Nos. 32-33 (juin-sept. 1960 and No. 71 (3e trimestre 1969).

18. Cf. articles in *Le Monde*, 'La Guyane en faillite', 19-21 juin 1974.

19. Paris: Du Seuil, 1947.

20. Some further parallels suggested in notes on Paramaribo Negro culture in M. J. and F. S. Herskovits, *Suriname Folklore* (New York: Columbia U. P., 1936), p. 23ff.

6

The Example of Aimé Césaire

by

J. MICHAEL DASH

It was a young Frantz Fanon who, full of admiration, wrote:

> For the first time a lycée teacher—a man therefore who was
> apparently worthy of respect—was seen to announce quite simply
> to West Indian society 'that it is fine and good to be a Negro'.
> To be sure this created a scandal. It was said at the time that he
> was a little mad and his colleagues went out of their way to give
> details as to his supposed ailment.[1]

This describes the impact made by Césaire on Martinican society
in the early 1940s. His ideas were disturbingly new to the conservative
and apathetic middle class. Yet Césaire's early radicalism eventually
became more acceptable. Martinique's first collective racist experience
occurred when nearly ten thousand French sailors were stationed on
the island for four years during the Second World War. This period in
Martinique represented a time of tremendous promise for Aimé
Césaire, armed with the ideology of Négritude and fresh from the
literary triumph of the *Cahier d'un retour au pays natal*. Indeed this
period can now be seen as the peak of Césaire's political career; he was
soon a popular and successful mayor of Fort de France and deputy
for Martinique.

From a political point of view, Césaire met with increasing reversals
during the next decades: the disappointments created by departmenta-
lization in 1946; his disillusion with the French Communist Party and
his subsequent resignation in 1956; the failure of the journal *Tropiques*
to create any general and permanent 'crise de conscience' among
Martinicans. In spite of his personal prestige, there was increasing
criticism of his politically moderate position and the contradictions and

compromises that seemed to exist between his actions as a politician and the rhetoric of his speeches.

Naturally, these problems coming after the optimism of the 1930s left their mark on Césaire. In 1939 he asked:

Being such as we are—can that rush of virility, the conquering knee of victory, the clodded fertility of that plain which is the future ever be ours?[2]

In 1960 the poet seemed haunted that this question remained unanswered:

... from the restive silence of this mouth of sand will there arise nothing but the rotting stumps of a dried-up forest?[3]

The desperate optimism of the 1930s spawned the ideology of 'Négritude'. Now confronted with the harsh, unyielding reality of post-colonial societies, this effervescence seems frustrated. The group which founded *L'Etudiant Noir* (1934)—Léon Damas, Aimé Césaire, Léopold Senghor—once bound together by what James Baldwin called 'that ache to come into the world as men', finds the political and cultural implications of Négritude under attack.[4] In their then justifiable attempts to create an authentic black 'prise de position' and correct the prejudices directed in the past against African culture, they created an ideology which made for brilliant poetry but, when followed to the letter, for pernicious political systems.

The spectrum of Négritude ranged from Damas's 'racisme anti-raciste' to Senghor's notion of a symbiosis of Africa's mystical cultural patrimony and the scientific materialism of the West. Césaire's definition of Négritude is the most tenable since from the outset it avoided abstractions and extremes. It is a simple personal attitude . . . 'la simple reconnaissance du fait d'être noir' (the simple recognition of the fact of being black). Césaire is only remotely connected to the bizarre Duvalierist experiment in Haiti or other attempts at a political order based on spurious biological or ethnic peculiarities. In a recent interview with Lilyan Kesteloot Césaire explained:

... négritude has brought with it some dangers, it has tended to become a school, a church, a theory, an ideology. I am for a négritude which is literary and somewhat like a personal ethic, but I am against an ideology founded on négritude. . . . I refuse to be considered, in the name of négritude, the brother of François

Duvalier (restricting myself to only the dead) and other sinister creatures who make my hair stand on end![5]

Neither the naïveté of an earlier optimism nor the painful ironies of history, however, can render invalid that surge of creativity in which Césaire's greatness lies. The ultimate validity of Césaire's 'engagement' resides not in the political consummation of his ideals but in the creation of a personal and authentic attitude towards the world and the articulation of a unique kind of experience in his writing. Thus Césaire's literary output is characterized not only by its sustained dialogue with history—which was its very 'raison d'être'—but by the desperate subjectivity and self-consciousness generated by a defiance of the past. History, in so far as Césaire and Martinique are concerned, is tainted by the harsh realities of slavery and the imposition of a colonial system which denied the very humanity of its victims. For the creative writer an ideological point of departure easily becomes an aesthetic 'prise de position'. The will to confront history—to be angered by the past—created in the poet a personal vision of the trauma of alienation and exile. This produced an acute insight into the way in which assimilation had subtly separated the educated from their people, from their beginnings and introduced them to a metropolitan culture into which they could not fit. Césaire's true creativity lies in his ability to fashion an aesthetic possibility for conveying the anguish and the ambivalence caused by the colonial experience.

Césaire is primarily a poet. The popularity of poetry among black writers stems from that genre's capacity for experimentation with language so as to allow for the rendering of a new and very special experience. It is Césaire who claims . . . 'In the beginning was the word . . . no one has believed this more fervently than the poet.' The power of the poetic 'word' becomes Césaire's miraculous weapon, the 'beating of the wave of the mind against the rock of the world.' Césaire's poetry represents a pioneering effort to impose a new subjectivity upon an inherited literary form.

It was Jean-Paul Sartre who, in one of the first anthologies of black poetry, pointed to the problem faced by the black writer and the emergence of a new 'voice' in creative writing:

For the white man has enjoyed for three thousand years the privilege of seeing without being seen . . . . The white man, white because he was man . . . lighted like a torch all creation; he unfolded the essence, secret and white, of existence. Today, these black men have fixed their gaze upon us and our gaze is thrown back in our eyes; black torches, in their turn, light the world.[6]

Inherited language and literary form came with its own associations, its own sensibility. Language for the non-metropolitan writer has indeed been described as a kind of prison. The black writer can easily find himself victim of stereotypes in his attempt to use a language which never before took into account his experience, his humanity. As George Lamming points out:

> A Negro writer is a writer who encounters himself in a category called Negro. He carries this definition like a limb. It travels with him as a necessary guide for the Other's regard .... He is a reluctant part of that conspiracy that identifies him with that condition that the Other has created for them both.[7]

A major preoccupation of all black writing is to define and illustrate the possibilities of a startlingly new vision of the world—the possibility for an authentic literary 'voice'. It is this attempt to impose a new 'will' on the world—to illustrate a new literary aesthetic—that makes Césaire's *Cahier d'un retour au pays natal* an original document. In his attempt to endow the French language with a new expressiveness— to write a 'Caribbean French'—he dramatically illustrates the disruptive and creative potential of the poetic 'word'.

Césaire's curious use of Surrealist technique is revealing. Surrealism was useful in removing French from its traditional cultural moorings and in generating freshness and originality, particularly in the dimension of figurative language. Surrealism had as its prime goal the creation of a liberating effect on language and form in poetry. In their attempt to give positive direction to the anarchistic 'refus' of Dadaism, André Breton and others had, through their search for 'l'insolite' and the systematic exploration of the unconscious, added a new dimension to literature. This 'pure' experimentation with language was in vogue during the 1930s and its attraction for Césaire is obvious. However, Césaire's relationship with Surrealism is peculiar in that there is a marked difference between his adaptation of this technique and the Surrealist experiments of metropolitan French poets and in particular the French West Indians who founded *Légitime Défense* (1932). One of the members of this group, Etienne Léro, is an example of a black writer whose work resembled that of 'orthodox' Surrealist

77

writers. He tended to reproduce the experimental exercises of Surrealism in his work, thus creating an imitative literature that preserves a preciosity and a stylized chaos from which personal torment is absent. In Césaire this experimentation with imagery and language does not appear to be a gratuitous game; it is the vehicle that eloquently articulates the tortured sensibility of the exile.

The random association of images, the radical juxtaposition of the incompatible is linked with that destructive fantasy of aggression which so poignantly expresses the poet's alienation and dispossession. One can feel the intensity and violence of Césaire's desperation in

We sing of poisonous flowers
exploding in meadows of fury;
skies of love destroyed by clots of blood;
epileptic mornings; the white burning of abysmal sands
the sinking of wrecks in nights blasted by savage odours.

We sense here more than experimentation with the unreal. The power of the poetic imagination seems bound to an inflexible obsessive resentment which unleashes a flood of destructive images. The attempt to represent the trauma of exile, to impose his defiance on the world is for Césaire not a purely literary exercise but intensely personal and moving literary improvisation. What we have is paradoxically a kind of 'directed automatic writing'—a literary technique harnessed in a paroxysm of hate:

words of flesh and blood, words which are tidal
waves and erysipelas, malarias and lava and bush
fires, and burning flesh and burning cities.

By imposing his vision on his medium, Césaire fulfils the major ambition of any artist—to contribute through his inspiration a new expressiveness to his genre.

The attempts made by Césaire's critics, in particular Lilyan Kesteloot, to create a 'lexique' of the poet's vocabulary and symbols suggest that in his verse language loses its traditional associations and acquires new values. Such a re-ordering is particularly noticeable as far as the connotations of black and white are concerned. The traditional hierarchy of black and white cultural values is inverted in Césaire's work. The example of Toussaint L'Ouverture's captivity and death in Europe is obvious:

This man belongs to me
a man alone imprisoned by white
a man alone defying the white cries of white death
... a man alone in the sterile sea of white sand
... death expires in a white pool of silence.

White, no longer the pigment of virtue, the essence of humanity, is changed under the scrutiny of someone who does not belong. He defines his Négritude as an attitude which is not a 'white speck of dead water' but a new elemental dynamism. In contrast to 'the disarmed day' we have 'the sun in bud at midnight'. What is evolved is a black subjectivity which sees the world in its own terms—the aesthetic achievement of a protest literature. In the *Cahier* and also later in *Ferrements* we see the formulation of an aesthetic which might be described as specifically Caribbean.

The prime requirement for a perception of the 'pays natal' would be a profound sense of identity with the Caribbean. African writers, inspired by a similar kind of sensitivity, have turned to the memories of childhood, thereby creating an African sensibility from this cultural nostalgia. Indeed the childhood universe of ancestral tradition constitutes a fundamental element in the inspiration of such writers as Léopold Sédar Senghor and Camara Laye. However, for the West Indian writer, the perception of his homeland from the distance of exile is not the marvellous world of a serene tribal past but a painful awareness of the devastation wrought by history. No longer is there the exotic Caribbean Eden of the early colonial writer—for exoticism demands an emotional distance, a sensibility based on surfaces and stereotypes. In the *Cahier* we have such a sense of intimacy with Martinique that the island's contours, its own sensuality, is brought vividly into focus:

this most essential country restored to my greed, not wanting any foggy tenderness, but the twisted sensual concentration of the fat nipple of the morne with the occasional palm tree as its hardened germ; the jerking spunk of rivers, and from Trinité to Grand Rivière, the hysterical licking of the sea.

The West Indies recollected cannot represent tranquility; all this has been disrupted by history:

How much blood there is in my memory. In my memory are lagoons. They are covered with death heads. They are not covered with water lilies.

Nostalgia cannot dim that pervasive meaninglessness and loss Césaire feels in Martinique. Nothing can gloss over that sense of tragedy as the very landscape seems to reveal the hurt of history—its every scar and deformation representing a figurative reference to the desolation of the past and the futility of the present:

At the end of the small hours, the contained fire of the morne like a sob gagged as it is about to break into blood . . . . At the end of the small hours, the morne squatting before hunger pains . . . alone with its bandages of shadows, its ditches of fear, its great hands of wind.

Defeat and docility are dramatically symbolized by a road:

a hump-backed road plunging into a hollow where it scatters a handful of huts; an untiring road charging at full speed towards a hill at the top of which it is brutally drowned in a stagnant pool of freakish houses.

Fort de France embodies the submissiveness of a people:

It crawls on its hands without the slightest wish to raise up and pierce the sky with its protest.

Césaire's 'pays natal' is not distant nor exotic; it is scarred and wounded by the colonial past. This terrified consciousness of belonging to a wasteland has created a literary aesthetic that reveals a historical awareness of the Caribbean and the painful sensation of 'knowing it for the first time'.

This quality in Aimé Césaire's writing is intensified in the poet's later work, *Ferrements* (1960), which marks the first real thematic departure from the *Cahier*. Produced in the period of the poet's maturity, *Ferrements* is a very personal and often bitter chronicle of Césaire's political disillusion. Césaire's various collections of poetry written in the 1940s—*Les Armes Miraculeuses, Soleil Cou Coupé, Corps perdu*— devote great attention to style, especially as far as Surrealist imagery is concerned, often to the point of being quite elusive and esoteric. The fact that the essential 'vision' of the *Cahier* is maintained in these

80

early works is not surprising, since it is really during the 1950s and after that the disappointments of leadership assail Césaire. By the time we come to the poetry of *Ferrements* we no longer witness the exuberance of the *Cahier* but now are swamped by an atmosphere of introspection and withdrawal. The poet's vision of himself is chillingly stated in 'Me centuplant Persée':

> Je parcours l'intime fosse alimentant
>   mes monstres.
> (I crawl through that personal ditch from
>   which my monsters grow.)

There are numerous references to himself as a snake crawling through a twilight of disappointment and compromise. Césaire in registering his despair reproduces an ironic and bitter vision of Martinique. Defeat and submission seem secreted into this wasted landscape—Martinique more trapped than ever is caught in a grim vision of failure:

> from the depths of a country of silence
> of bones burnt dry of stalks cast into fires
> of storms of cries unsounded and caught in
> their muzzles from a country of longings
> irritated by the branches of shipwrecks the
> black sand stuffed with that strange silence.

In some of his more hermetic and moving utterances Césaire explores the same landscape glimpsed earlier through the rhetoric of the *Cahier*. However, in 1939 devastated Martinique was presented on the verge of change; in 1960 complacent Martinique resists any real change.

This tortured sensibility cannot be advocated as the only possibility for West Indian literature; it certainly cannot preclude a more creolized aesthetic which would use the indigenous language and experience as the source of its vision. Indeed the imagination of the folk—the autochthonous and transplanted people who experienced colonial domination without being assimilated into the educated elite—will necessarily differ from the traumatized sensibility of the exile, transformed by the dubious privilege of assimilation. It is conceivable that the sensibility of the 'folk' will not contain the frenzied protest of the exiled, but will be involved in a more speculative view of history in which myths, legends, superstitions reach beyond the violations of slavery and indenture to present the reality of those who endured.

Yet Césaire's poetic achievement is obvious, a compelling and dramatic articulation of one kind of authentic West Indian experience.

No study of Césaire can be complete without some attempt to understand the relationship between his poetry and his more recent drama. Césaire published his first major play, *La Tragédie du roi Christophe* (1963), three years after some of his most hermetic verse, *Ferrements*. What we have here is an attempted separation of two features of Césaire's writing. The *Cahier* skilfully combined personal anguish and public rhetoric. It was at once the most accessible protest poetry and yet contained the poet's very private 'voice', which contributed to that quality of a 'lived experience' in the work. With his verse becoming increasingly personal and contemplative, we find that Césaire's public voice is attracted to a genre which offers the advantage of physically presenting his message. The need to fulfil his 'engagement' as a Third World writer makes the poet aware of the need to communicate with his public. Césaire sees the artist's role in terms of Rimbaud's concept of the 'poète voyant'. The poet's perception and awareness are more acute than those of ordinary men. Césaire emphasizes the need, however, to make things visible to his audience. He becomes a dramatist in this effort to communicate his vision and sensitivity to others.

Attention has often focused upon the ways in which Césaire's theatre approximates actual political and economic conditions. This is because his plays are largely concerned with the anguish of decolonization. In *La Tragédie du roi Christophe* we witness the attempts made by Christophe to build a strong Haiti after the wars of independence. This is symbolic of the efforts to achieve real autonomy in many emergent Third World states. In *Une Saison au Congo* (1965) Patrice Lumumba attempts to defy the forces of neo-colonialism in the Congo in 1960. Césaire's most recent work, *Une Tempête* (1969), is an adaptation of Shakespeare's play; through the relationship between Caliban and Prospero it dramatizes the problems of black American protest.

There is another quality that pervades Césaire's plays as well as his poetry. One always has the impression that his creative writing in some way complements his actual political situation, that a personal drama is associated with his creative imagination. As he said: 'J'écris pour m'aider á prendre possession de moi-même' (I write to help me to see more clearly into myself). This quality is particularly apparent in *La Tragédie du roi Christophe* and *Une Saison au Congo*.

The titles of these works indicate more than an attempt to document and offer solutions to the problems of independent, developing countries.

Césaire remains often ambivalent in so far as solutions are concerned. These works reveal Césaire's insight into the anguish of the failed political leader. 'Tragédie' and 'Saison'—the former is self-explanatory, the latter seems to derive from Rimbaud's 'une saison en enfer'—both are moving testimonies because they capture the dilemma of the Third World leader, disillusioned, betrayed, misunderstood.

Césaire's plays are shaped by a vision of tragedy as resulting from an almost inevitable collision of the subjective 'intention' of the hero and the implacability of the world—an almost Sisyphus-like confrontation of the human will and a reality oblivious to his presence and agony. To this extent Césaire's plays qualify not only as political commentaries but as psycho-dramas. The association between the political and the tragic is shown in Césaire's claim, 'la politique, c'est la forme moderne du destin' (politics are the modern equivalent of fate). His tragic heroes all epitomize that haunting condition which first appears in *Ferrements*—the image of Prometheus bound . . .

> et moi je le suis
> au bec du vent du doute de la suie

> (and here I am
> eaten away by wind by doubt by soot)

and again:

> sculpté au niveau du museau des vagues et de la fiente
> des oiseaux

> (fixed and moulded by the gnawing of the
> waves and excrement of birds).

These quotations offer an image of the poet-politician attempting to defy the inevitable; he is the lonely tragic figure inexorably being crushed by external forces. The prototype for such a protagonist can be found in the figure of 'Le Rebelle' whose solitary defiance is an integral part of the allegorical *Et les chiens se taisaient* (1956). He is related to Christophe, who, a victim of his hallucinations, brandishes his sword against the sky—a gesture at once heroic and futile.

La Tragédie du roi Christophe opens with a cockfight in which Christophe and Pétion are the two cocks in the arena. This image is the key to the whole play in that it neatly presents Christophe as a victim of external reality; Christophe is destined to be destroyed. Throughout the play we witness the sincerity and the grandeur of

Christophe's ambitions contrasted with his own fated inadequacy and the hostility of the times.

Curiously enough, for a tragic play, we have several scenes where laughter is produced from caricature. The comic element in the play has a special function. Christophe's attempts to be a king are the source of comedy. Travesty only works when the disproportion between the role played and the player is obvious and sustained, i.e. when the clown obviously can never be a king and as a result is nothing more than a caricature. This inability to quite fit the role of king is Christophe's weakness and makes him appear ludicrous. His grossness and his preposterous notions of respectability are obvious. But comedy disappears if the clown, for even a moment, has an insight into the real responsibility of a leader; even in the most farcical scenes, we see in Christophe a king in deadly earnest, obsessed by the need for dignity:

> Formerly they stole our names!
> Our pride!
> Our nobility, they, I say *They* stole them!
> Pierre, Paul, Jacques, Toussaint!
> Those are the humiliating labels with which *They* obliterated our true names.[8]

Thus, the farcical results from the character's frailty and is central to his most tragic feature, the fact that he is destined to failure in spite of his vision.

Failure comes even in spite of his lucidity. At times Christophe can clearly see the danger of servile imitation. This technique is almost Racinian; in spite of insights into his own weakness, Christophe cannot combat the forces that are creating an inevitably tragic dénouement. He is both conscious of the colonial legacy of doubt, insecurity and alienation, and also a victim of it:

> There is nothing I hate more than servile imitation....
> I think, Master of Ceremonies, that one must bring some civilization to these people (and I think I have done more than anyone in this direction), one must also allow free expression of the national genius.

In this character we are presented with an attempt to understand the blindness as well as the vision of Haiti's cook turned king. Through a figure whom History once considered as only a clown, Césaire attempts the indictment of a system that created the 'chosification' of men.

Christophe and Lumumba in *Une Saison au Congo* are both objects of Césaire's sympathy and symbols of hope. By their heroic efforts and self-sacrifice in dealing with the problems of independence and decolonization, both are even more powerful after their deaths. Lumumba claims:

> ... I incarnate an idea that cannot die! Invincible like the hope of a people, like the fire spreading from bush to bush, like the pollen from wind to wind, like the root in the blind earth.[9]

With Christophe we have the eulogies of his queen and Vastey and the telling remarks of those bearing the dead king: 'Not only is he heavy ... You notice that he gets heavier'. Césaire evidently sees History as an index of men born before their time. This is obviously a poet's conception of the political leader as a visionary; the leader is a herald of a new order and yet a victim of the uncomprehending present. Through his own experiences Césaire could understand and communicate the anguish of both these leaders and present the painful reality responsible for their failure. But he sees their ambitions, like his own, being fulfilled in more favourable times.

It was an over-enthusiastic Fanon who claimed 'Before Césaire, West Indian literature was a literature of Europeans.'.[10] There is evidence in Haiti,[11] Cuba and the British West Indies of an earlier awareness of the need for indigenous literatures. Nevertheless, Fanon's enthusiasm can be understood in that Césaire remains one of the most articulate and compelling spokesmen for the West Indian experience. Whether as a student in the 1930s or as a politician in his later years, every role Césaire has played has brought fresh insights into the torments and complexities of the West Indian experience. We are obviously distant from the exoticism that characterized nineteenth-century colonial literature but we sense in Césaire's violent protest over the disrupted past and in his fears and ambivalence over the precarious future that his aesthetic and ideological point of departure is always the cruel truth of 'nous vomissure de négrier'. Indeed very few writers have returned to the Caribbean in the way in which Césaire has 'returned', so much so that his works even defy being catalogued into that one monolithic bloc known as 'black writing'. Beyond rhetoric, beyond ideology, he displays in his poetry and his theatre a singular grasp of the ambiguities and tensions of the West Indian condition in particular and the black diaspora in general. What we have seen as an aesthetic based on that tragic familiarity with his world has created the literary possibility of conveying a region's historical and cultural experience. In this way has been realized the poet's vision that ... 'the Word becomes again a God and walks among us'.[12]

NOTES

1. Frantz Fanon, *Toward the African Revolution* (Harmondsworth: Penguin, 1970), p. 31.
2. *Le Cahier d'un retour au pays natal* (Paris: Présence Africaine, 1956), p. 65. The translations are mine.
3. 'Va-t-en chien des nuits', *Ferrements* (Paris: Seuil, 1960), p. 25.
4. The First Congress of Black Writers in 1956 brought to light criticism of the ideology of Négritude—James Baldwin, Jacques-Stéphen Alexis, George Lamming—all indicated a mistrust of this attempt at a universal, homogeneous black culture. Fanon's remarks in *The Wretched of the Earth* are also critical: 'Men of African cultures who are still fighting in the name of African-Negro culture and who have called many congresses in the name of the unity of that culture should today realize that all their efforts amount to is to make comparisons between coins and sarcophagi'. (Harmondsworth: Penguin, 1969), p. 188, originally published in 1961.
5. Lilyan Kesteloot, 'Entretien avec Césaire', *Aimé Césaire, l'homme et l'oeuvre*, (Paris: Présence Africaine, 1973), pp. 235-236.
6. J. P. Sartre, *Black Orpheus*, trans. S. W. Allen, (Paris: Présence Africaine, n.d.), pp. 7-8.
7. 'The Negro Writer and his World', *Caribbean Quarterly*, Vol. 5, No. 2, (February 1958.)
8. *La Tragédie du roi Christophe* (Paris: Présence Africaine, 1963), p. 39.
9. *Une Saison au Congo* (Paris: Seuil, 1967), p. 109.
10. *Toward the African Revolution*, p. 36.
11. As early as 1836 during Boyer's presidency, Emile Nau offered a blueprint for an indigenous literature in the pages of *L'Union*.
12. Edward Brathwaite, *Islands* (Oxford University Press, 1969), p. 109.

7

The Men Who Lived Underground: Richard Wright and Ralph Ellison

by

WILLFRIED F. FEUSER

When we follow the stream of Negro American fiction starting from its humble beginnings in 1853 with William Wells Brown's *Clotel, or the President's Daughter* and continuing through the rising foothills of the 'Negro Renaissance', we suddenly find ourselves transported among the mountain peaks, and the towering achievement of Richard Wright and Ralph Ellison comes into full view. They have given a new colour and a fresh impetus to American literature. And yet, before reaching those commanding heights, they had to cross the marshes, wade through the sewers, live underground—if not physically, then at least psychologically—in a society which attached a stigma to the pigmentation of their skin, and in a country which disputed their birthright as native sons.

Although their *oeuvre* taken together represents a major break-through in American writing, and they are often mentioned in the same breath to the extent of being jocularly placed in the same category of 'emotional hypochondriacs ... unhappy *when not unhappy,* and *when not expounding on their sadness*' by their friend and fellow writer Langston Hughes,[1] it would be futile merely to dwell on their similarities as black writers to the exclusion of the very real differences in their life, art, and outlook, or even to devise a spiritual father-son relationship between Wright, the elder of the two, and Ellison, six years his junior. For Ellison, Wright was a 'relative'; but his 'ancestors', he wrote in 1963, were Eliot, Faulkner, Hemingway, Malraux and Dostoyevsky.[2]

While Wright, who in his prime saw himself as 'a Western man of colour', claimed a similar literary ancestry, he had to undergo considerable hardship to develop his elective affinities with those writers. Born on a plantation near Natchez, Mississippi, in 1908, growing up in the streets of Memphis, where his father had deserted the family, a drunkard at the age of six, he first stumbled upon literature in the guise of the story of Bluebeard told to him by a young school-teacher who helped his mother in the household. The shock of recognition, related in Wright's searing account of his childhood and youth, *Black Boy* (1944), was total: 'My imagination blazed ... I vowed that as soon as I was old enough I would buy all the novels there were and read them to feed that thirst for violence that was in me, for intrigue, for plotting, for secrecy, for bloody murders.'[3]

When he grew older and had published at the age of sixteen his first short story, significantly titled 'The Voodoo of Hell's Half-Acre', in a Negro newspaper, he found it very difficult to obtain the books he wanted to read since Negroes were not allowed to patronize the public library. Finally a white fellow-worker lent him his library card, and Wright daringly scribbled a note to the librarian, counterfeiting the Irishman's signature: 'Dear Madam: will you please let this nigger boy have some books by H. L. Mencken?'. In Mencken's *Book of Prefaces* he first discovered the conscious use of words as a weapon, and the whole galaxy of writers from Anatole France to Nietzsche was suddenly thrust upon him.

Moving from Memphis to Chicago in the early thirties he arrived just in time to swell the ranks of the jobless in the Great Depression. Solely absorbed by the struggle for survival while in his native South-land, he had let the enthusiasm generated by the 'Negro Renaissance' pass unnoticed. But now, seeing the nation in the throes of an unprecedented economic upheaval and noticing that the old adage 'the last to be hired, the first to be fired' applied more than ever to people of his colour, his nascent political consciousness veered sharply to the left. He joined the Communist Party, after first having come into contact with radical intellectuals in the 'John Reed Club'. His first poems were published in the reviews *Left Front*, *The Anvil*, and *New Masses* in 1934, and were soon followed by short fiction culminating in *Uncle Tom's Children* (1938), three novellas (four in a later edition) about lynching, resistance and deliverance from the black man's burden through revolutionary action: 'Freedom belongs to the strong!' These stories made Richard Wright nationally known.

The position of Wright the artist and Wright the political activist is best epitomized in one of his early poems:

> I am black and I have seen black hands
> Raised in fists of revolt, side by side with the white
>   fists of white workers.

And some day—and it is only this which sustains me—
Some day there shall be millions of them,
On some red day in a burst of fists on a new horizon.[4]

Like Langston Hughes, who had visited the Soviet Union in the early thirties,[5] Wright was convinced that the black writer's place in the 'Red Decade' was with the most vocal spokesmen for the dispossessed masses. Here he found fellowship and a new sense of identity. On the other hand, the young Negro's unique experience enriched America's 'proletarian fiction', a vigorous current of literature which included James T. Farrell and John Steinbeck. Many Negro writers, encouraged by the Federal Writers' Project set up under the auspices of President Roosevelt's New Deal, followed in Wright's wake, the most gifted among them being William Attaway, Willard Motley and Chester Himes; the last, who continued the proletarian tradition well into the forties, may justifiably be called the greatest surviving American writer in the naturalistic tradition.

Wright's communism was never narrowly defined by party dogma; it was of the Popular Front variety. Two novellas from *Uncle Tom's Children* show Wright turning away from individual heroism to collective action. The outstanding character in 'Bright and Morning Star' is a church-going, hymn-singing Negro mother who avenges the murder of her son, a political activist. In 'Fire and Cloud', a story suffused with Old Testament images, it is the Christ-like figure of the Negro preacher, Reverend Taylor, complete with disciples (the vestry board), Judas (Deacon Smith), Pilate (the Mayor) and way of the cross (organized by the white vigilantes) who, contrary to the gentle Nazarene embracing the cross, launches into collective action: 'Sisters n Brothers, A *know* now! Ah done seen the *sign*! Wes gotta git together.'[6]

Communism for Wright was 'a key to the prison of colour', it was the 'Red Ladder' enabling him 'to climb out of his Black Belt'. Rejecting passive submission and gradualist thinking as he was later to reject Négritude, he felt at one with the oppressed of all countries, a passion which outlasted his episodic party affiliation: 'It seemed to me that here at last, in the realm of revolutionary expression, Negro experience could find a home, a functioning value and role'.[7] Since in his view racism was the American equivalent of Fascism, he was prepared to join those who seemed most determined to confront Fascism. Although he attempted, both ideologically and artistically, to subsume the race problem in Marxist categories, he soon realized that it was a phenomenon *sui generis:*

> The political Left often gyrates and squirms to make the Negro problem fit rigidly into a class-war frame of reference, when the roots of that problem lie in American culture as a whole; it tries to anchor the Negro problem to a patriotism of global time and space, which robs the problem of its reality and urgency, of its concreteness and tragedy.[8]

The most concrete expression of the American tragedy which goes under the designation of 'Negro problem' was Wright's novel, *Native Son* (1940). Bigger Thomas, the hero of *Native Son*, is an inarticulate youth who like many of Wright's characters has graduated from the frying pan of Southern racial injustice to the fire of impersonal Northern slum conditions. He lives in abject poverty with his mother, brother and sister in a rat-infested one-room apartment—the notorious 'kitchenette' described by Wright in all its degradation in his folk history of the American Negro, *Twelve Million Black Voices* (1941). Bigger detests his family and only finds a measure of togetherness in his street-corner gang that engages in petty crime. Offered a job as a chauffeur by a real-estate tycoon with humanitarian tendencies, who ploughs back some of the profits accruing to him from the black ghettoes in the guise of ping-pong tables for the black boys' clubs, Bigger kills the millionaire's daughter, incinerates her body in the furnace he has to attend, and writes a ransom note to the parents. When the crime is discovered, he hides in the abandoned slum houses of the Chicago South Side, and murders his Negro girl friend Bessie, who has turned out to be a hindrance during his flight. Caught in a giant man-hunt on the icy roof-tops and sentenced to death in a sensational trial, he ends in the electric chair.

The story of Bigger's crime and punishment is partly based on an actual murder case, that of the Chicago Negro Robert Nixon, executed in the electric chair in 1938 for having murdered a white girl. The author had studied the sociological findings about living conditions and delinquency on the Southside which went into the writing of that classic on Negro urbanization, *Black Metropolis:*

> It was from the scientific findings of men like the late Robert E. Park, Robert Redfield, and Louis Wirth that I drew the meanings for my documentary book, *Twelve Million Black Voices;* for my

novel *Native Son;* it was from their scientific facts that I absorbed some of that quota of inspiration necessary for me to write *Uncle Tom's Children* and *Black Boy. Black Metropolis,* Drake's and Cayton's scientific statement about the urban Negro, pictures the environment out of which the Bigger Thomases of our nation come; it is the environment of the Bosses of the Buildings; and it is the environment to which Negro boys and girls turn their eyes when they hear the word Freedom.[9]

Bigger whose actions evoke more terror than pity, whose stunted emotional responses to friends and foes look like the stigmata of degeneracy in an anthropological throw-back, shows the two traits Sigmund Freud has defined as essential in a criminal: 'boundless egoism and a strong destructive urge. Common to both of these, and a necessary condition for their expression, is absence of love, lack of an emotional appreciation of human objects.'[10] Wright had chosen the type of the 'bad nigger' from a deep sense of commitment to the 'underdog'.

The critic may ask whether this blend of sociology, criminal pathology, political philosophy and fiction has anything to do with art. If the proper aim of fiction, in W. S. Maugham's phrase, is 'not to *instruct,* but to *please',* an evocation of the seething hatred and dehumanization of the black *Lumpenproletariat* has no place in any literary discussion. But for Wright a third category—'to displease'—might be more appropriate. This third category is that of art as an agent of social awareness. There are in fact artistic flaws in *Native Son* since the author hammers away at his sociological theorem. In the words of Bigger's communist defence counsel, Boris A. Max, whose oratory is inspired by the great Clarence Darrow of Leopold and Loeb fame:

> Multiply Bigger Thomas twelve million times, allowing for environmental and temperamental variations . . . and you have the psychology of the Negro people. But once you see them as a whole, once your eyes leave the individual and encompass the mass, a new quality comes into the picture. Taken collectively, they are not simply twelve million people; in reality they constitute a separate nation, stunted, stripped, and held captive *within* this nation devoid of political, social, economic, and property rights . . . [11]

What casts a weird spell on the book, precluding any notable character development, is Wright's hard-line social determinism expressed by

Max: 'Men do what they must'. In another context the author sums up the unqualified conditioning of the individual by outside forces in an overtly mechanistic image:

> After studying the social processes . . . you cannot expect Negro life to be other than what it is. To expect the contrary would be like expecting to see Rolls-Royces coming off the assembly lines at Ford's River Rouge plant. The imposed conditions under which Negroes live detail the structure of their lives like an engineer outlining the blue-prints for the production of machines.[12]

The omnipotence of the social forces in *Native Son* is, however, tempered by fate. Events rush to their inexorable conclusion at the crack of an invisible whip: nine hours and thirty-five minutes elapse between Bigger's reporting to the Daltons as their new chauffeur and his full realization that he has murdered Mary—a scenario that would have caused any classical dramatist concerned about the unity of time and action to turn pale with envy. The ticking of the clock as a symbol of fate is one of the many metaphoric devices adding depth to Wright's professed factualism and his solicitude for environmental detail. Shortly before his capture Bigger realizes that his watch has stopped: fate has caught up with him.

Wright uses many other symbols masterfully. In the opening scene of *Native Son*, Bigger kills a rat, signifying both the hideous environment or the forces closing in on the doomed slum-dweller, and the trapped victim, baring its fangs and letting off a shrill note of defiance in the face of death. There is the symbolism of sounds and numbers in the tripartite structure of the novel: Fear—Fight—Fate; and the symbolism of names: Jan Erlone, Mary's communist boy friend (*erlone* being the Negro dialect version of *alone*), who offers the murderer his forgiveness, is a lone fighter in the struggle against racial prejudice, 'a particle of white rock . . . detached from that looming mountain of white hate'.

Wright's passionate involvement with those imprisoned in the lower depths of society is evident throughout the novel. Bigger,' being black and at the bottom of the world', confined to the street, the poolroom and the basement, day-dreams compulsively of rising: 'I wanted to be an aviator once'. He stares with equal awe and wonder at the plane flying over Chicago and the pigeon rising swiftly into the air. When riding in the car with Mary and Jan, shamed by the unwonted contact of black and white flesh, he craves to 'rise up and stand in naked space above the speeding car and with one final blow blot it out . . . '. Here the vertical escape mechanism in his consciousness is combined with another obsessive gesture, the blotting out—an act of total rejection countering the sense of rejection he has felt all his life—which recurs throughout the novel. In a further instance of wishful thinking he tries to catapult himself away from his family: 'He wished that he could rise up through the ceiling and float away from this room, forever.' Such symbolism is common in Wright's work, as in the foreword to *Twelve Million Black Voices:*

> This text assumes that those few Negroes who have lifted them-selves, through personal strength, talent, or luck, above the lives of their fellow-blacks— like single fishes that leap and flash for a split second above the surface of the sea—are but fleeting exceptions to that vast, tragic school that swims below in the depths, against the current, silently and heavily, struggling against the waves of vicissitudes that spell a common fate.[13]

When Bigger is trapped by the police on the roof top, he refuses to jump to his death among 'the sea of white faces . . . that ocean of boiling hate'.

This leads us to the most obvious symbolism, that of colour. To the grimness of the black-and-white confrontation, in the manner of a woodcut, other shades are added. Colour in *Native Son* is never purely descriptive but charged with visceral emotion at one end of the gamut ('black trouble', 'dead-black with hate'), whilst at the other it spells either coldness and distance or the vaguely supernatural terror of Nemesis and death. The twilight zone between life and death in Book One is steeped in a 'hazy blue', which after Mary Dalton's murder deepens into a 'blue darkness', then, after her incineration, into a 'red darkness' punctured by the hellish red glare of the fiery furnace symbolizing Bigger's guilt. Despite the subtly poetic interplay of those various colours the overriding impression left by *Native Son* is, never-theless, that of a bipartite world, a world that Fanon, in projecting it onto the scene of the anti-colonial struggle, full of Wrightian echoes, was to characterize as 'Manichean'. In *Native Son*, the black man's fractured identity emerges like a portrait by Picasso, if we put the pieces of the mosaic together:

> . . . twin eddies of blue smoke jutting from his *black nostrils*. . . And don't you ever set your *black feet* inside here again! . . . The man was gazing at him with an amused smile that made him con-

93

scious of every square inch of skin on his *black body* . . . He felt he had no physical existence at all; he was something he hated, the badge of shame which he knew was attached to a *black skin* . . . Bigger paused, swallowed, and looked anxiously at the dim reflection of his *black face* in the sweaty windowpane . . . He rested his *black fingers* on the edge of the white table . . . He was just a *black clown*.[14]

Is Richard Wright here laying the foundation for a black aesthetic? Hardly. To Wright, the acculturation of the American Negro, despite racial prejudice and oppression, has progressed to such an extent 'that the mode and pitch of Negro literary expression would alter as soon as the attitude of the nation toward the Negro changed'[15]. Negro expression, according to Wright, is therefore not a value in itself but a function of the prevalent attitudes in the majority culture. By the same token, Bigger's blackness is thrust upon him by the hostile white beholder. He sees himself as others see him and becomes the prisoner of the hateful image they have conceived of him. In analysing this psychological mechanism Wright anticipates Sartre, just as he does in Bigger's acceptance of an 'accidental' killing, born of dread and desire, as his own action, thus raising it from the subconscious level to the light of the conscious will. Bigger Thomas shoulders the responsibility for his crime and rejects his family's compassion:

> *They ought to be glad*! . . . Had he not taken fully upon himself the crime of being black? Had he not done the thing which they dreaded above all others? Then they ought not stand here and pity him, cry over him; but look at him and go home, contented, feeling that their shame was washed away.[16]

Murder as a 'supreme and meaningful act', an act of creation, an exorcism, is this not a glorification of violence for its own sake? For Wright it is rather a means to an end, a cold blast tearing through the web of hypocrisy and complacent lies, the explosion of the myth, as old as the plantation tradition, of the Negro's happiness in the best of all possible worlds, a thrust at America's democratic conscience. In Wright's wake, Jean-Paul Sartre, both in his *Critique de la raison dialectique* and his preface to Fanon's *Les Damnés de la terre*, and Fanon himself made violence—the blood-stained coin of history—the legal tender of the oppressed in their struggle for freedom from colonial domination.

Nobody had to tell Wright anything about what he had lived through as a black man in white America: about man's alienation in the modern world, the ordeal of extreme situations, and the isolation of the individual—concepts which were seminally present in *Native Son* and were further elaborated in Wright's second novel, *The Outsider* (1953). Although Wright's first treatment of the outsider theme in *Native Son* had preceded Camus's classic, *L'Etranger*, by two years, and Wright obviously did not need any letters of nobility from the French existentialists, American critics accused him of aping an alien tradition. Wright's grim existentialist fable of the Chicago Negro, Cross Damon, who in trying to escape from his old self emerges into a cold and ambiguous universe where God is dead, where, freed from the shackles of tradition, family, race and social morality he becomes an 'ethical criminal'—law, jury, and executioner at the same time—a man hovering between opposing totalitarian forces and in fighting them becoming like them, did not fit into any known pattern. The fact that Wright had left the United States to settle in Paris, that he had refused to remain forever chained to the Negro problem like a galley slave but reached out to the totality of the human condition, and, one suspects, that he had 'wasted' his time on such un-American activities as catching up on nineteenth-century philosophy and writing a novel replete with *Weltanschauung*, was hardly conducive to arousing sympathy for his book. Towards the end of the novel Richard Wright pours his scorn on the yellow press which puts a false construction on the double murder his hero committed:

> Hardened Metropolitan police circles were stunned late yesterday by the freakish Greenwich Village double murder of a Communist by a Fascist and of a Fascist by Communist. The Medical Examiner has technically dubbed the crime double manslaughter. It was learned through unusually reliable sources that these men's brains had been poisoned by the dangerous doctrines of communal property advocated in the writings of the notorious German author Karl Marx, and the Superman ideas sponsored by the syphilis-infected German philosopher Friedrich Nietzsche. . . . [17]

Few of Wright's critics rise above such pettiness and incomprehension. *The Outsider* is the work of a man grappling honestly and painfully with the main currents of modern thought.

'The Negro is America's metaphor'. Nowhere is this statement by Wright more fittingly illustrated than in his parable, 'The Man Who

Lived Underground', where an innocent Negro, presumed guilty by the representatives of the white order, probes for life's hidden truth in the bowels of the earth, peering full of compassion through the chinks and crevices of his dark abode at a society of dancing shadows in 'a wild forest filled with death'. When he emerges with the newly acquired knowledge of man's boundless liberty and innate existential guilt, he is rejected as a raving fool by the community and liquidated by the police as a potential threat to the existing order.

It is out of the same cave of sibylline wisdom that Ralph Ellison's fictional hero, living 'rent-free in a building rented strictly to whites, in a section of the basement that was shut off and forgotten during the nineteenth century', speaks to us: 'I am an *invisible* man. Thus I have come a long way and returned and boomeranged a long way from the point in society towards which I originally aspired'.[18] Like Wright, the author dramatizes the basic ironies of Negro existence, which becomes a metaphor of human existence, because it is hearing without being heard, feeling without being felt, and seeing without being seen: 'I am invisible, understand, simply because people refuse to see me'. Whereas in Wright's story the name of the antagonist is disclosed as 'freddaniels' halfway through the action, Ellison's hero squirms out of any situation which might allow us to identify him and remains the 'Invisible Man' whose name is possibility.

The critic confronting Ralph Ellison's novel is like the character in the fairy-tale nibbling at a mountain of cake made up of many tempting layers; he finds it well-nigh impossible to tunnel his way through. On one level, the novel represents in a bold sweep the historical migration of the Negro Americans through space, along the South-North axis, and their often frustrated advance through time. On another, it is the secularized quest of the individual not for Logos or the Light that shineth in the darkness but for self-knowledge through experience. It is thus both an outward and an inward journey. On the linguistic level, it resembles a vast musical score with its ritardandos and crescendos, moving with magic verbal virtuosity from canto to canto, from the pastoral to the orgiastic. On yet another level, it tries to come to grips with reality—material, social, and spiritual—a reality defying definition in the same way as the identity of the novel's picaresque hero who is in the constant process of becoming, sustained by the ancient knowledge that one can't swim in the same river twice: 'Time was as I was, but neither that time nor that "I" are any more'. He is a cousin germain of Perceval, the pure at heart ('no hero . . . short and dark and with a bottomless capacity for being a fool to mark me from the rest'), but also related to Dostoyevsky's 'paradoxalist', the analyst of self and others, though lacking his venom and causing neither loathing nor pity. He is the artist as a young man inspired by Dante and Uncle Remus, a tragi-comedian enraptured alike by Beethoven's Fifth and Louis Armstrong's 'What did I do to be so black and blue?'. All through his life the cryptic words of his dying grandfather resound in his mind:

> Son, after I'm gone I want you to keep up the good fight. I never told you, but our life is a war and I have been a traitor all my born days, a spy in the enemy's country ever since I give up my gun back in the Reconstruction. Live with your head in the lion's mouth. I want you to overcome 'em with yeses, undermine 'em with grins, agree 'em to death and destruction, let 'em swoller you till they vomit or bust wide open.[19]

From a potential Booker T. Washington playing the role reserved for him by the Southern whites, first in his home-town where he engages in a fierce Battle Royal against other black boys staged for the benefit of a drunken mob, then in the famous Negro college where he overplays his hand at yessing and gets expelled for having revealed the guilty secrets of the black community to a visiting white philanthropist, he becomes a candidate for the industrialization process. Despite his college president's confidential letter of recommendation reproducing the injunction revealed to him in a bad dream, which becomes a leitmotif of his life, TO WHOM IT MAY CONCERN: KEEP THIS NIGGER BOY RUNNING, he obtains a job in a paint factory, LIBERTY PAINTS. The Negro operator in the basement illustrates the whitening effect of their prime product to him: 'Our white is so white you can paint a chunka coal and you'd have to crack it open with a sledge hammer to prove it wasn't white clear through'.

But a shattering explosion touched off by industrial strife between the black and white producers of white paint sends the hero to the company hospital more dead than alive. The hospital in its antiseptic whiteness is a modernized version of Dr. Caligari's horror cabinet and the patient's bed a mechanical womb on which 'a pair of eyes peered down through lenses as thick as the bottom of a Coca-Cola bottle, eyes protruding, luminous and veined, like an old biology specimen preserved in alcohol'. Rising from the machine in a ritual second birth the man whose case 'has been developing some three hundred years' walks out with a new personality only to be told that he is not yet prepared for work under industrial conditions. He now delves into the warm atmosphere of Harlem, where in the motherly care of Mary, a stout Southern black woman, his bruised ego finds new hope, and identifies with the folk culture through culinary communion: 'I yam what I am'.

His talent as a valedictorian and debater which he developed 'down home' stands him in good stead when he chances upon an eviction scene, quickly turned into a riot through his spontaneous oratory. This feat brings him into contact with the 'Brotherhood', a world-wide radical organization searching for support among the black masses. The leader of the group, Brother Jack, enlists him as a propagandist. He tells him, '*History* has been born in your brain'. The young proselyte, thus stumbling into the class struggle like a drunk slipping on a banana peel, soon runs into stiff competition from 'Ras the Exhorter', the West Indian Negro leader reminiscent of Marcus Garvey. In his campaign to stir up the souls of black folk Ras tries hard to win the lost sheep of the Brotherhood back into his fold: 'It took a billion gallons of black blood to make you. . . . You black and beautiful— don't let 'em tell you different!'.

The protagonist's popularity increases when by the graveside of his friend and comrade Tod Clifton, murdered by the police, he makes a speech worthy of a Mark Antony. But since Tod was a renegade the Brotherhood disapproves of this. It sees the waxing of the young man's influence with a jaundiced eye, calling him a 'petty individualist'. In this period of increasing disillusionment with the party he has to hide one day behind a pair of dark glasses to escape from Ras and in this disguise is taken for Rinehart the trickster, the lover, the numbers runner, and finally the Rev. B. P. Rinehart, spiritual technologist. The existence of this con man who defies all scientific definitions of reality, who is appearance and essence, 'rind and heart' at the same time, opens the protagonist's eyes and shows him the congenital blindness of his fellow-men:

> His world was possibility and he knew it. The world in which we lived was without boundaries. A vast seething, hot world of fluidity, and Rine the rascal was at home, perhaps *only* Rine the rascal was at home in it. It was unbelievable, but perhaps only the unbelievable could be believed. Perhaps the truth was always a lie.[20]

This realization of possibility as a basic mode of human existence, which is at the same time an option for the freedom of the individual in a world ruled by statistics, is one of Ralph Ellison's main points of divergence from Richard Wright's universe of cast-iron necessity, although later in his life Wright also discovered 'the rich infinities of possibility looming before the eyes of men'.[21] Ellison's happy childhood in Oklahoma City, where he was born the son of a construction foreman and a church janitress,[22] and his youthful dreams of being a 'Renaissance man' seem to have fashioned his more flexible outlook on life. But later on, during the Depression, when he used to ride freight trains like a hobo to attend Tuskegee Institute—where he trained to be a musician and composer—or when he faced unemployment, he underwent the same kind of grim experiences as his friend Richard Wright. Common to both is the throbbing pain, the descent into chaos, and the dream of rising above conditions imposed from the outside, as in Ellison's magnificent short story 'Flying Home', where in the fate of a black pilot crash-landing in the Alabama backwoods the Negro's South-North migration is symbolically reversed. Common to them is their passionate ECCE HOMO: behold the image of man destroyed, or reduced to invisibility.

But their divergences are even greater. They differ in their view of the literary craft, which to Wright is primarily an instrument for social action, while to Ellison, who was attracted to writing not because he considered words as weapons but because he was curious about 'the aesthetic nature of literary power', it is its own justification. Often accused by black critics of being ensconced in the cocoon of his craftsmanship, he considers craft 'an aspect of morality'. While Wright is a tone-deaf giant, his feet immunized against dance and rhythm, Ellison is all music. Wright is the embittered pessimist whose final stance would seem to coincide with that of his hero, Fishbelly Tucker in *The Long Dream*, the last novel he published in his life-time. The closing scene of the book shows Fishbelly during his symbolic flight from his homeland on the plane to Paris, surrounded by white passengers, ominously staring at his black hands: a double rejection. Ralph Ellison is deeply convinced that pleading the Negro's humanity by underscoring his malformation through environmental forces is a false issue. He feels that the current of Negro American literature and culture is not confined to a separate gutter but forms the deepest and most powerful channel of the American mainstream. Acceptance to the point of joyous affirmation is therefore his prevailing mode of thought. Acceptance of self and acceptance of life as a whole.

In his famous politico-literary feud with Irving Howe, reprinted in *Shadow and Act* (1964), Ellison expounds 'Negroness' as a cultural phenomenon not conditioned by the genes and adds: 'More important, perhaps, being a Negro American involves a *willed* (who wills to be a Negro? *I* do) affirmation of self as against all outside pressures . . . .'[23] And in the epilogue of *Invisible Man* the hero, having achieved true self-knowledge, sets forth:

> So it is that now I denounce and defend, or feel prepared to defend. I condemn and affirm, say no and say yes, say yes and say no. I denounce because though implicated and partially responsible, I have been hurt to the point of abysmal pain, hurt to the point of invisibility. And I defend because in spite of all I find that I love . . . I sell you no phony forgiveness, I'm a desperate man—but too much of your life will be lost, its meaning lost, unless you approach it as much through love as through hate . . . . [24]

NOTES

1. Langston Hughes, *I Wonder as I Wander: An Autobiographical Journey* (New York—Toronto: Rinehart, 1956), p. 120.
2. Ralph Ellison, *Shadow and Act* (New York: Random House, 1964), p. 140.
3. Richard Wright, *Black Boy* (Cleveland—New York: The World Publishing Company, 1947), pp. 34-35.
4. Quoted in Richard Wright, 'Negro Literature in the United States', published in his book *White Man, Listen* (Garden City, N. Y.: Doubleday, 1957), reprinted in Addison Gayle, Jr., ed., *Black Expression* (New York: Weybright and Talley, 1969), p. 225.
5. At least one of Hughes's short stories in *The Ways of White Folks* (1934) was written in Moscow.
6. Richard Wright, *Uncle Tom's Children* (New York: Signet, 1954), p. 152.
7. Richard Wright, 'I Tried to Be a Communist', in Richard Crossman, ed., *The God That Failed* (New York: Bantam, 1965), p. 106.
8. Richard Wright, Introduction to St. Clair Drake and H. R. Cayton, *Black Metropolis* (New York: Harcourt, Brace, 1945), p. xxix.
9. *Ibid.*, p. xviii.
10. S. Freud, 'Dostoevsky and Parricide', in René Wellek, ed., *Dostoevsky. A Collection of Critical Essays* (Englewood Cliffs, N.J.: Prentice Hall, Inc., 1962), p. 99.
11. Richard Wright, *Native Son* (New York: The Modern Library, 1940), p. 365.
12. Richard Wright in Drake and Cayton, *op. cit.*, p. xx.
13. Richard Wright, *Twelve Million Black Voices*: A Folk History of the Negro in the United States of America (1941), (London: Lindsay Drummond, 1947), p. 5.
14. *Native Son*, pp. 33, 38, 43, 63, 67, 105, 173, 192. Italics mine.
15. Richard Wright, 'Negro Literature . . . ' in Gayle, *op. cit.*, p. 228.

16. *Native Son*, p. 275.
17. Richard Wright, *The Outsider* (New York: Signet, 1954), p. 283.
18. Ralph Ellison, *Invisible Man* (New York: Signet, 1952), pp. 9, 496.
19. *Invisible Man*, pp. 19-20.
20. *Invisible Man*, p. 430.
21. Richard Wright, *Pagan Spain* (London: The Bodley Head, 1957), p. 191.
22. John Hersey ed.: *Ralph Ellison. A Collection of Critical Essays* (Englewood Cliffs, N.J.: Prentice Hall, Inc., 1974), p. 4. Its introduction contains a lengthy discussion of Ellison's second novel, still unpublished, on which he has been working for the last nineteen years.
23. Ralph Ellison, *Shadow and Act*, p. 132.
24. *Invisible Man*, p. 501.

8

Léopold Sédar Senghor's Poetry

by
JOHN REED

Towards the end of a long essay which is still the best introduction to Senghor's poetry, Armand Guibert reflects that Senghor, who had recently become the President of his country, was perhaps already at the end of his career as a poet.

> As this problem of the coexistence of political leader with poet has been posed it is worth noting that circumstances have already slowed down the career of the poetry which has been the subject of this essay. In the last five years, only five elegies have been added. Will the demands of public life in the end have the better of the inward man? Strictly every poet carries the rank of prince, whether he is a cut-purse like Villon or a ploughman like Burns. But if the Prince also holds real temporal power, he will envy cut-purse and ploughman the obscurity that guarantees their freedom.[1]

Guibert was writing in 1961. Senghor's last new volume of poetry was *Ethiopiques*, published in 1956. The recent *Nocturnes* (1961) was really a revised version of *Chants pour Naëtt* (1949) with the addition of the five elegies. In the years that followed, the slowing down became very nearly a standstill. There was one more elegy published in *Présence Africaine*. Then nothing. The Editions du Seuil hard-back collected *Poèmes* of 1961 included a small additional section, *Poèmes Divers*, but these are evidently juvenalia or at least poems earlier than *Chants d'Ombre*. Thus it had all the appearance of finality.

As the years passed, the incompatibility of poetry and political power seemed demonstrated. Then the tide of intellectual opinion in Africa began to turn against the cultural theory of Négritude which Senghor had assiduously elaborated in speeches and essays. Through the sixties as the political spectrum formed by the new states in Africa

102

grew clear, Senghor appeared rather to the right. His interest and influence hardly seemed to reach English-speaking Africa, and the poet of *Chaka* had little to say about the south. At the Second International Conference of Africanists in Dakar in the late 60s he spoke of the political problems of Africa as having been solved, leaving only social and cultural problems to be tackled. Later in 1972 he was advocating dialogue with South Africa, long before this became politically respectable. Senghor's poetry was, in some parts of Africa at least, as suspect as his politics: but not therefore neglected, for the meteoric rise of African literature as an academic subject and the expansion of French studies in English-speaking Africa were bound to make much of an *oeuvre* which had the advantages of being substantial and evidently complete.

Then in 1973 appeared, simultaneously under the imprint of Seuil in Paris and Nouvelles Editions Africaines in Dakar, Senghor's first volume of new poems since *Ethiopiques,* seventeen years before. The title, *Lettres d'Hivernage* (Letters of the Rainy Season).[2] It has now been incorporated into, and is most easily accessible in a second, paper-back edition of the complete *Poèmes.*

Asked in an interview the same year how he was able to reconcile his two roles, Senghor replied:

> One complements the other. I've always liked to have several projects on the go at once, and everything interpenetrating. It's a matter of organizing one's time practically.
>
> I work on poems during my holidays—that's about six weeks a year—especially in the summer when I take off a whole month. During the rest of the year I draft out poems, make notes, write *versets*—and, more important, I live my poems. At the moment I'm living an *Elegy for the Queen of Sheba.* Then when I have a bit of time to myself, I get down to it. Living my poems, that means imagining them. Then the poem inside me grows richer and richer in images. It feeds on my ideas and feelings.[3]

The practical man of affairs can make arrangements to accommodate the composer of *versets.* But has the poet survived the long reign of the secular prince? I think on the evidence of *Lettres d'Hivernage* that he has. The years have not transformed Senghor's poetry. There is no radical difference in technique, in subject matter or mood. But these new poems are not vapid self-imitations—even if they seem full of specific reference to the earlier poems, as though for Senghor himself these now have a kind of classical status. These poems add to and enrich although they do not transform or compel a complete reassessment of Senghor's poetic achievement.

Lettres d'Hivernage is a sequence of thirty poems. In length, and in the relation of the separate poems to the sequence, it resembles the *Chants pour Naëtt*, poems which Senghor wrote to his first wife. But in theme and also in imagery, especially in the contrasted images of Africa and Northern—or at least non-Mediterranean—Europe, they are much closer to the set of six poems in *Ethiopiques* entitled *Epîtres à la Princesse*. In these poems the poet addresses a European princess from whom he is separated by his responsibilities in Africa. These *Epîtres* have usually been interpreted as a celebration in poetry of Senghor's love for the woman who was to become his second wife. Yet the circumstances are not directly presented. Senghor gives himself the persona of a traditional, tribal, almost patriarchal ruler, owing more probably to Saint-John Perse's *Anabase*, than to his own earliest memories of Africa and a far cry from the incisive leader of a mass party which at the time he was; and his lady is some snow princess from a Nordic fairy-tale. The sequence ends with a poem entitled *The Death of the Princess.* These longer, mythologically elaborate *Epîtres* or epistles have become simple letters, much concerned in content with waiting for, receiving, and sending letters. They are thus tender poems of an aging man to his wife, written during periods of separation. The background, though other resounding landscapes also occur, is often simply Dakar itself with its view of the Ile de Gorée lying just off shore and the poet seems to see his scenery not from camelback as once but through the windows of descending aircraft or helicopters.

An example of one of the briefest of these poems will give the quality.

Ta Lettre sur le Drap

Ta lettre sur le drap, sous la lampe odorante
Bleue comme la chemise neuve que lisse le jeune homme
En chantonnant, comme le ciel et la mer et mon rêve
Ta lettre. Et la mer a son sel, et l'air le lait le pain le riz, je dis son sel
La vie contient sa sève, et la terre son sens
Le sens de Dieu et son mouvement.
Ta lettre sans quoi la vie ne serait pas vie
Tes lèvres mon sel mon soleil, mon air frais et ma neige.

(Your letter on the sheet, beneath the sweet-smelling lamp,
Blue as a new shirt a young man smooths,
Humming to himself; as the sky and the sea and my dream
Your letter. And the sea has its salt, and the air milk, bread, rice, I
    say its salt
Life holds its sap and earth its meaning
The meaning of God and his movement.
Your letter life would not be life without
Your lips my salt my sun, my fresh air and my snow.)

There is much in the *Lettres d'Hivernage* that is pitched more
eloquently and elaborately than this, and passages which could be
taken as coming from the earlier volumes. Yet the comparative simpli-
fication of manner found in *Ta Lettre sur le Drap* is characteristic of
Lettres d'Hivernage as a whole. The difference does not amount to a
change of poetic manner. Senghor is writing in a less dense and over-
grown area of his familiar wood, but he has certainly not gone seeking
fresh woods. From the immediate experience in sensation—in this
poem not an emotion but something seen, a still life, the blue notepaper
lying on the white sheet under the lamp—the poet moves with a directness that might seem self-assured or merely facile, to the stark lists of
nouns which are like a basic inventory of the cosmos. The poet, to
affirm his love, affirms succinctly because urgently the whole human
and natural universe in which he lives and breathes and is. Some of
the words he uses—for example, sun and snow—have a special, as
well as the more general, significance from the theme of the whole
poetic sequence. But still, the elements are named, invoked, or as it
were implicated (as when a person is named in a legal enquiry), not
merely referred to. Here the process is so abrupt that it is unmistakable
but it is the same process—the transition from the immediate and
personal to the cosmic by way of a naming and implication, which
on a larger scale and to the accompaniment of a more decorative
rhetoric is found throughout Senghor's work.

It is not difficult to relate this structure in Senghor's poetry to the
French poetry of his time. French critics see Senghor's poetry as deeply
influenced by Paul Claudel whose most important single poetic collection, the *Cinq Grandes Odes* appeared in 1910. Senghor has never
denied this debt. Signs of his familiarity not only with Claudel's poetry
but his thought about the nature of poetry are evident everywhere
in Senghor's work. The other major influence is Saint-John Perse.
Here Senghor insists that he had read no work of this poet until 1945

when all the poems that were to appear in *Chants d'Ombre* and *Hosties Noires* were already written, but that on his reading of Saint–John Perse's poem *Exil* in that year, he was 'struck blind like Paul on the road to Damascus'.[4]

Senghor himself stresses the variety of his sources. 'I have read a great deal from the troubadors to Paul Claudel—and imitated a great deal.'[5] Senghor reads English and knew the work of the black American poets of the 1920s and 30s. In 1948 he edited the important *Anthologie de la nouvelle poésie nègre et malgache*. This anthology of work by black poets writing in French was mainly Caribbean. Most of Senghor's critical writing is an attempt to characterize this black poetry rather than to examine the nature of his own poetic inspiration. There are throughout Senghor's poems allusions to and imitations of other black poets. In one of the poems in *Lettres d'Hivernage* there is the following scrap of dialogue:

--Fais que toujours tu me sois joie, mon Prince
    mon Athlète et mon ébène.
—Point n'ai pris habitude des promesses; je sais
    oui mon amour de toi

—(See that forever you may be joy to me, my
    Prince, my Athlete, my Ebony.
—Never have I caught the habit of promises: I
    know Yes my love of thee.)[6]

This catches the flavour of the *Vieilles Chansons* of the Madagascan poet Rabéarivelo, themselves adaptations into French of the Madagascan folk poetry of the Hain-teny. Senghor had already made a similar imitation in his *Elégie des Saudades* in *Nocturnes*.

Yet these are hommages to other poets. They do not affect the texture of Senghor's own poetry. It is natural to be led, in the critical examination of Senghor's poetry, by what he says in his own criticism about the nature of 'black poetry'. Yet Senghor's thought about his poetry, as distinct from his practice as a poet, has found its literary associations not in the tradition of Claudel, but, in what in the 1920s and 30s when Senghor lived in Paris was the most *avant garde* and revolutionary movement of poetry, with surrealism. In Senghor's exposition of black poetry it is Aimé Césaire's and not Senghor's own poetry which is the central model. Even when he is writing about traditional poetry in African languages Senghor seems to interpret its qualities through the critical vocabulary of surrealism. These qualities which he finds in traditional African poetry and in the new black poets (who, he asserts, have only been enabled to express Négritude in the French language because of the surrealist revolution[7]), the violent image, the disintegration of the phrase, the destruction of syntax, elimination of tool-words or connectives, are none of them characteristic of Senghor's own verse. Here and there in Senghor there may occur a passage of pastiche surrealism but Senghor's violence to language characteristically goes no further than

> sous les cris blancs des mouettes
> (beneath the white cries of the gulls).[8]

And in Senghor the omission of tool-words amounts to no more than a fondness for omitting *and* between nouns. Sometimes there are syntactical ambiguities in Senghor, as in all poetry and indeed all speech. In *Ta Lettre sur le Drap* the fourth line might seem to be devoid of all syntax, permitting us to arrange the words together, to allow them to interact with each other as we wish. But a closer look reveals that there is nothing more extreme here than the omission of commas between the items of a list and having the verb *have* understood and not repeated in the second clause. This is as natural in French as it would be in English.

Significantly it is in an article on Saint-John Perse that Senghor seems to clarify the distinctness of his own kind of poetry from that of surrealism. The article appeared in *La Table Ronde* in 1962—after the publication of Senghor's main volumes. In this article he notes that Saint-John Perse's poetry is a tissue of images or symbols. Symbols, uttered by speech, are an elucidation, an order. Through them, the poet, who is 'Ordinateur et Ordonnateur'—one who both sets in order and ordains—maintains or restores the order of the world, the ordered world without which man cannot have full existence, since he is, as Teilhard de Chardin says, 'a cosmic being'. But if it can create order, the symbol can also by perversion of its true function sow confusion. The contrast between the images of Saint-John Perse and the surrealists is made:

> The images of Saint-John Perse are as new as those of the surrealists. They are more beautiful. Why? Because they are clothed in the grace of language. Because they are more taking, gripping you at the very root of *being*. Because they are not gratuitous. They share in the truth of the *archetypal images* laid down in the depths of Man's Collective Soul.[9]

The surrealists were without the grace of language because language was one of the objects of their destructive rage, a social institution to be swept away with the rest of an oppressive social order for the total liberation of the individual. The link between surrealism and black poetry is a common interest in revolution—but a revolution which swept away civilization and technology would be as self-contradictory as a poetry which succeeded in destroying language. Those who do not find with Teilhard de Chardin that man is a cosmic being but for whom 'this is not our place', will not in any case be blessed by 'the grace of language'.

In the same article Senghor identifies poets like Saint-John Perse with the Priests and Magicians of African and traditional civilizations, and the world of his poetry with the articulated symbolic worlds of Africa. This seems to me a mistake, the mistake of using the myth of the poem as the guide to the critical understanding of its true nature. The urge to create a poetry in which the poet himself appears centrally as the Mage, Demiurge or Logos of the poetically summoned cosmos can only arise when the poet has in the social reality of his day no magic powers and there are no more Priest-Kings or Mages whose powers of ordering and maintaining the universe are accepted. The need to make the evocation of the world and the acceptance of it central to poetry only arises when the sense of cosmos has been lost and when rejection instead of acceptance is conceivable.

During the nineteenth century it became possible—and so necessary— for poetry to move beyond the expression of personal experience and personal vision through a shared literary tradition which reflected and ultimately implied a whole, diverse, developing but still shared civilization. Poetry itself would have to assert its own cultural cosmos— the alternatives were to keep traditional poetry going as a kind of folklore, or to be resigned to côterie verse and hermeticism. Of course this cosmos was not a clean creation of the poet's. Just as socially shared cultures depend on the inescapable realities of the natural world and shape the raw material of human psychology, so the poet has to draw and select and shape from the conflicting and incoherent diversity around him. Hence the main poets of this tradition are men like Senghor whose life has been shaped by diversity of cultural experience. Claudel's *Cinq Grandes Odes* were written mostly in China where he had a diplomatic posting. Saint-John Perse was born and spent his earliest years in Guadeloupe. His mature poetry was written in exile in the United States where he was driven after the fall of France in 1940. The cosmos of the poem depends on the assertion of the poet. He is at its centre and he has to create for himself a persona of a kind that does not appear in earlier poetry. The cosmos of the poem is also the world of the poet's own experience, is indeed the medium through which his own experience can find coherence, meaning and hence expression. Thus he cannot abandon his real self in the poem and adopt a purely formal or mythic role. At the same time he has to assume inside the cosmos of the poem the central, princely, demiurgic role.

The kind of poetry we have been describing was first created by Walt Whitman, working in the cultural diversity and unrooted quality of American life, and with only a trivial poetic tradition to break free of. The strange quality of the 'I' figure in Whitman's poetry, firmly identified by name and experience with the real man, yet also functioning in the poems as a kind of Son of Man, has engaged much attention from the critics. The poems, out of widely varied sources in Whitman's reading and experience, by listing, naming, evocation, assert a universe. The poetry created great interest in Europe, especially in France where the American experience was more likely to be understood than in England with its traditional continuities unbroken by recent revolutionary change. Whitman's breakthrough made a new, more powerful poetry available but only where individual genius and a certain set of conditions occurred. What is common to all is that the poet asserts his own universe. We should not expect the universes to look alike. Whitman's is democratic, libertarian, ordered by opportunity not hierarchy; both Claudel's and Saint-John Perse's are aristocratic and exclusive. Senghor's cosmos shows great similarities to the two French poets who are not only direct influences but created their poetic worlds out of material that overlaps directly with his own. Senghor observes that Saint-John Perse like Senghor himself spent his childhood in the black world. Yet in some ways Senghor comes closer to Whitman's inclusiveness than either of his French predecessors. I think we should see his poetry as much in its place within this modern supranational tradition belonging to the times of the melting pot, of interacting and conflicting cultures, as belonging to French poetry or to African poetry.

Senghor's poetry asserts a universe on the poet's authority, a universe which is an ordering and an ordination of African, Mediterranean, Gallic, Catholic, Islamic elements. At the centre of these is the 'I' of Senghor himself, a figure both mythic and actual. Senghor has never confused the princely role he plays in his own poetry with his own political position and nor should his readers. Yet his own personal experience is central to the cosmos of his poems. The two guiding experiences of Senghor's poetry are imprisonment—the poems in

Camp 1940 and in a sense the whole of the collection *Hosties Noires* of which this forms a part—and love. In the *Lettres d'Hivernage* we can see how personal poetry of a direct kind can rest within the cosmos of the poet's creation and yet through each new occasional poem succeed in articulating it further and in maintaining the rhythm of its connections and correspondences.

Auden said that time would pardon Paul Claudel and his views— 'for writing well'. It would certainly be sad if we rejected all the poetry which did not reflect our own views. It would after all cut us off from almost all the poetry of earlier generations. But the point I think is not to go to this kind of poetry looking for views to overlook. Certainly there are in Senghor's work poems which are direct reactions on a public level to political events, poems of protest. *Tyaroye* in *Hosties Noires* is one of these, though no one I think is likely to raise objections to the views it expresses. But my suggestion is that poetry like Whitman's, Claudel's, Senghor's does not, except incidentally, express views. It asserts not opinions or doctrines but a cosmos. Among the elements of that cosmos there may be doctrines and opinions. With the advent of Whitman the poet surrenders the role of teacher—or becomes as Whitman says, the teacher of 'no lesson'. We can only teach within the settled conventions of a stable and accepted culture.

I have tried to suggest a description of the kind of poetry to which I think Senghor's belongs. I have no theory of the way this poetry works on the reader, of the nature of the delight that comes from reading Whitman or Claudel or Senghor except that taking them together, the soothing of our political opinions cannot be any part of it. Some lines from Whitman do not provide that missing theory but may perhaps illustrate the delight.

> The words of the true poems give you more than poems,
> They give you to form for yourself poems, religions, politics, war, peace, behavior, histories, essays, daily life and everything else,
> They balance ranks, colors, races, creeds, and the sexes
>   . . . .
>
> Whom they take they take into space to behold the birth of stars, to learn one of the meanings,
> To launch off with absolute faith, to sweep through the ceaseless rings and never be quiet again.[10]

1. Armand Guibert. *Léopold Sédar Senghor* (Poètes d'aujourd'hui, Paris: Pierre Seghers, 1961), p. 96.
2. *Lettres d'Hivernage* (illustrations originales de Marc Chagall, Paris: Seuil, 1973 and Dakar: Nouvelles Editions Africaines, 1973).
3. Interview with René Minguet, published in *Les Nouvelles Littéraires*, 17-23 December 1973.
4. *Comme les lamantins vont boire à la source*, Postface to *Ethiopiques* (Paris: Seuil, 1956), p. 106.
5. *Ibid*, p. 106.
6. *Ta Lettre Trémulation*.
7. 'L'Apport de la Poésie Nègre au Demi-Siècle', in *Liberté* 1: *Négritude et Humanisme* (Paris: Seuil, 1964), p. 143.
8. *Je Repasse, Lettres d'Hivernage*.
9. 'Saint-John Perse ou Poésie du Royaume d' Enfance', in *Liberté* 1: *Négritude et Humanisme*, p. 343.
10. From 'Song of the Answerer' in *Calamus*.

9

Camara Laye

by

ADELE KING

Camara Laye is one of the founders of modern African writing. His first book, *L'Enfant Noir* (1953), is perhaps the best known work of francophonic African literature, and it is likely to remain one of the classic portrayals of traditional tribal life. Its subtle affirmation of the dignity and worth of African culture appeared at a time when colonialism was still justified by the white man's 'mission civilisatrice'. *L'Enfant Noir* and Laye's second novel, *Le Regard du Roi* (1954), were among the first African novels to reflect the mood of the Négritude movement of the 1940s and 50s. By evoking a rich, warm African community, in contrast to cold, rational European individualism, they showed that African civilization had its own contribution to make to the world. The affirmation of traditional African values was an important arm of the movement for political independence. The criticism of recent African politics in Laye's third novel, *Dramouss* (1966), needs to be seen in the perspective of his previous work and the hopes of other well-known writers of his generation.

Camara Laye was born in 1928 in Kouroussa in Upper Guinea.[1] He grew up during the period of colonialism when traditional African village culture was subject to fewer outside influences than it is at present; but it was a time when European schooling was becoming necessary for a career in modern Africa. One had to leave home and often go abroad for schooling and further training. The effect of travel was to make the African student conscious of his heritage and the difference between his culture and that of the European. *L'Enfant Noir* tells the story of an African child, whose early years are spent in the security of the family compound and within a traditional Malinké community in Kouroussa. His father is a respected blacksmith and goldsmith; his mother is a woman of great dignity and authority to whom he is deeply attached. The child is sent to a French school, and feels torn between traditional village life and the modern world. Later, he goes to a technical school in Conakry, and, at the end of the novel, he is given a scholarship to France.

The novel seeks initially to describe the best of village life, so as to create a permanent record of the values of traditional culture before they are lost. The people of the village live harmoniously; each has a role to play, each shows a natural warmth and sympathy for his fellow men. There is no poverty in Kouroussa. Standards of behaviour are strict; children are both loved and well disciplined. Life follows a series of rituals: harvesting, initiation; even the work of the goldsmith is accompanied by ritual ceremonies. The world is full of divine presences, such as the little black snake which guides Laye's father in his work. When Laye must leave the village he is still protected by the extended family; he lives with an uncle who works in Conakry and who encourages his desire for a modern education. Laye is unsure, however, what his role should be. His father tells him to continue his studies in France, in order to become a leader in the changing world. He must follow God's will; as he can never fully understand the pattern of life, he must accept his destiny.

As African writing of the 1950s was still addressed to European readers, Laye explains the seasons in his country, describes the family compound, and avoids African expressions. He often points out how his family, school days and friends are similar to those in other cultures. Little African school boys, for example, pull the school girls' hair. Laye's aim is both to make the reader appreciate the orderliness and harmony of this African childhood, and to make him understand what this society shares with other societies.

The story is told by a mature narrator looking back from Paris with nostalgia on his childhood experiences. He tells his story in a style which shows the changing perspective of the boy as he grows up. He responds to the recurring rituals of village life in a direct, sensuous manner. Later, in Conakry, he sees life more intellectually and abstractly, as a sequence of separate events. The novel conveys the gradual widening of the child's world and his accompanying loss of security.

L'Enfant Noir is written in a classical manner, aiming at clarity of expression, at a concise recounting of major events, with a great control over personal feelings. Laye places a distance between himself and his memories of childhood, purposely creating a narrator who seems much further removed in time from his experiences than was Laye himself when he wrote the book six years after he had left Guinea. He presents

113

the major events of his childhood in a carefully arranged pattern of parallels and contrasts. The father's pride in his work as a goldsmith is contrasted with the uncle's refusal to work faster than his neighbours during the communal rice harvest at Tindican. The initiation ceremonies are juxtaposed with Laye's departure for Conakry; a contrast is implied between a formal social ritual for attaining manhood and the more frightening individual experience of going off to a modern city to study. Laye continually recounts events so that the happiness of the past is set against the feeling of loss and the nostalgic mood of the moment of narration. After describing the powers of his mother's totem, he comments: 'Oui, le monde bouge, le monde change; il bouge et change à telle enseigne que mon propre totem—j'ai mon totem aussi—m'est inconnu.' The characters in the novel are, with few exceptions, admirable men and women. They are often types, standing for general cultural characteristics. Laye's mother represents Mother Africa, traditional life close to the forces of nature. The conflict between the mother and father concerning the son's desire to go to France is portrayed as a noble one, in which both parents express their views with great dignity.

If *L'Enfant Noir* is essentially autobiographical, it is a stylized autobiography in which, as in for example James Joyce's *Portrait of the Artist as a Young Man,* the author's reminiscences have been given an artistic form and become representative of widely shared forms of experience. The book records a typical pattern of Laye's generation, as it tries to meet the demands of the modern world; it also shows a universal pattern of growing up and moving beyond the warmth of the family.

The portrait of traditional African society in *L'Enfant Noir* is similar to the views which other African writers were expressing during the 1940s and 50s. Many of the themes of Laye's novels can be found in Placide Tempels's *Philosophie bantoue,* or in articles in *Présence Africaine* during this period. Senghor, and other Négritude spokesmen, said that if there is something known as European civilization, despite the variety of national characteristics, then it is necessary to speak of an African civilization, the essentials of which are shared throughout the continent. Laye's novels assume such a culture. Even the title, *L'Enfant Noir,* is significant. Laye wishes to show what is common to African life: the extended family, the close ties to the natural world, the social role of the artist, the rituals which define the place of each individual within his age-group and within the community. He seldom mentions any detail which would seem particular to the Malinké. One may even feel that he underplays the importance of the Islamic influence in Kouroussa, in order to give a universalized picture of an African childhood in which an imported religion exists alongside animist beliefs and ancient rituals: it is a picture which would be valid for Christian as well as Moslem parts of West Africa.

Without attempting here to disentangle the various, often contradictory, strands of the Négritude movement, it is useful to recall some of Senghor's ideas about African culture. While Laye might be described as holding a position similar to Senghor's, there are interesting differences. Senghor holds that the black man has a distinctive way of understanding the world: he feels a unity of being with the universe, which he approaches more often through his senses and his emotions than through logic. (The change in kind of perception in *L'Enfant Noir* perhaps is meant to illustrate the difference between an African response to the world and European analytical logic.) This mentality, 'l'esprit négro-africain', is equal to the western mode of knowledge. The African has as much to teach Europe as to learn from it. European civilization, however, is not to be rejected; once the dignity and value of African culture have been recognized, black and white values are to be combined. Indeed Senghor spoke of himself as a 'cultural mulatto' and said that most great civilizations in the past were the result of cultural cross-breeding.

As can be seen both from the uncle's advice in *L'Enfant Noir* and from the narrator's hope for a modern, industrialized Africa in *Dramouss*, Laye, who was by training an engineer, was particularly concerned that the restoration of African culture be accompanied by the acquisition of European scientific knowledge. While he writes persuasively of the harmonious society of his childhood, he accepts that the world is changing. The traditional tribal life of the village co-exists alongside the urban life of Conakry. Even in Kouroussa, the railway and a modern hospital had been built. One should record the past before it is forgotten, but it is impossible to prevent the future which, in any case, is in God's hands. Laye sees his own role—following in a new way in his father's footsteps as craftsman and community leader— as necessitating the study of modern technology. Perhaps more directly than Senghor he accepts his place as between the old and the new, as combining the best of two cultures.

If Laye's writings are influenced by various Négritude ideals, including the restoration of African dignity and the struggle against assimilation into French culture, the novels reveal strongly held personal opinions. Laye's writing, while using African subject matter

115

and concerns, tends towards the universal. As we will see in *Le Regard du Roi*, race is less important than man's relationship to God. Indeed it could be argued that Laye's novels are shaped by a religious vision in which all temporal events are part of God's plan.

Le Regard du Roi, Laye's second novel, is a strange, dream-like story of Clarence, a white man who struggled against a reef to get to Africa. Once he arrives, he loses all his money through gambling and tries to find the black king of the country in the hope he will be accepted into his service. Clarence begins his journey in the city of Adramé, in the North of an unnamed West African country. When he cannot pay his bill, his hotel keeper demands his jacket. The jacket is later stolen. Clarence is called into a law court where he cannot explain himself and undergoes a travesty of justice. Escaping the law, he is taken to the South by an old beggar, who sells him into slavery to the local ruler, the *naba*. Aziana, the *naba's* village of the South, is filled with heavy, sensuous odours; Clarence experiences strange, magical visions. In this community he finds a role, although he performs it unknowingly; drugged at night by strange odours, he becomes the stud to the *naba's* harem, producing many half-caste children. Humiliated by his own behaviour, Clarence has given up hope when the young king comes to Aziana and, in a powerful scene, accepts Clarence into his arms.

Le Regard du Roi appears to be an illustration of African values. Clarence, the rational white man, is overwhelmed by his sensations of the colours and odours of Africa. He must undergo a series of adventures in which his strong ego and his belief in his 'rights' are changed by the apparent irrationality of an alien society, and by the humiliation of his economic disaster and of the role he is given in Aziana. He gradually rejects the cold, analytical world of western technology, and accepts that he is part of the natural African world. He learns that he cannot save himself by his merits; the king, whose coming is unpredictable and whom he can never hope to please, offers salvation through grace.

Le Regard du Roi reverses the usual autobiographical pattern of the African studying abroad. Instead of the black student in Europe who feels alienated by a strange, urban, economically dominated culture, and who has to adapt to its ways, the white man is an incompetent stranger in Africa and he must become part of a black society. Clarence undergoes experiences similar to those of Laye himself in Paris, as he will later describe them in *Dramouss:* the problems of adjusting to a different type of clothing, the greedy hotel keeper who

116

takes clothing when the bill is not paid. Clarence's long, arduous journey to the South is a parallel to Laye's long and seemingly endless walks through Paris in search of work. Laye in Paris often felt the nightmare quality of life in a modern bureaucratic state, governed by a soulless technology and by a mad search for money. Clarence also feels that his experiences are initially a nightmare, although of a different kind; he does not understand the beggar's seemingly irresponsible way of life; he is lost in a jungle of thick foliage and overpowering odours; he is unable to comprehend his role in Aziana, but realizes that people are laughing at him.

Clarence's experiences are an ironic reversal of the black man's relationship to Europe. As an outsider, he does not understand the legal system; he cannot defend himself when he is unjustly accused of stealing. He is laughed at as helpless, and sold into slavery. His one recognized accomplishment is his sexual prowess, an obvious ironic reversal of western attitudes towards black men. He learns to accept a black God-King, whereas colonialism brought Africans the white God of Christianity.

Le Regard du Roi is more than a protest novel in which the white man must undergo assimilation into black culture. It goes beyond a racial theme to a religious one. Laye said in an interview: 'Clarence, mon héros est un Blanc en quête de Dieu. Je ne devrais même pas dire un Blanc, mais un homme à la recherche de Dieu'.[2] Clarence's nightmarish experiences are not just a result of living in the culture of another race; they result from the material world in which we all live, ruled by an unknowable God. Clarence's journey shows how the soul must gradually lose its feeling of individual importance, if it is to find God. The novel may even be an allegory of the birth of the soul into this world, its experiences, and its return to God. Laye is a practising Moslem, but the religious vision in his works is not tied to any specific dogma. We are aware from *L'Enfant Noir* that older animistic beliefs were combined with the Islamic faith in the Kouroussa of his childhood. In *Le Regard du Roi*, the young, loving king whose coming cannot be foreseen, may remind us of Christ, but he is also described with many characteristics which recall the Benin statues. *Le Regard du Roi* might be seen as an often humorous allegory of what mystics, both Sufi and Christian, call the 'negative way', the approach to grace through the denial of the self. Although the God-like king is black, Laye has tried to make the description of Clarence's union with him universal.

Le Regard du Roi often suggests that the African way—the acceptance of one's role as part of a community, the superiority of feeling over

117

reason—is more natural and more attuned to the divine purpose of life than is the European way. There is an emphasis on physical sensations as a means of overcoming the pride of the individual ego, which seems in tune with Senghor's claim that Africa must teach the white man to feel as well as to reason. Clarence is not saved, however, because he gives way to sensual pleasure, or because he has become a stud for the *naba's* harem. He is saved because, humiliated by his experiences, he feels unworthy of salvation; at this moment he receives divine grace. Laye himself spoke of Clarence's need to feel shame: 'lorsqu'il a honte de regarder le Roi, en raison des fautes qu'il a commises, alors toutes les conditions sont remplies, en réalité, pour que Dieu lui ouvre ses bras'.[3] Neither white nor black culture is an adequate way towards salvation; salvation is an unmerited gift of God which comes only to the humble soul. Senghor felt that the quest for God in *Le Regard du Roi* was not a black quest. For the black man, Senghor insisted, the flesh is a support not an obstacle.[4] The conclusion of the novel may to some extent parody Senghorian ideas. Perhaps even the half-caste children Clarence produces for the *naba* are a humorous parody of Senghor's ideal of the cross-breeding of great civilizations. Laye's vision is ultimately religious.

Because the story is told indirectly through the point of view of Clarence, the confused white man, *Le Regard du Roi* contains a wealth of contradictory, irrational events, impressions of a world which seems to have no coherence or permanence. Clarence sees the African world around him as sometimes a mirage (did he really hear the screams of sacrificial victims?), sometimes a maze (is the beggar leading him in circles through the dense rain forest on the journey to the South?). Events may take place or may be dreams. Sometimes we never know what happened. Did Clarence make love to Dioki, the old sorceress, or not? In the combination of naturalistic detail and confused, shifting perspectives, *Le Regard du Roi* captures a dream-like atmosphere. It is also, however, rich in comic incidents and ironic misunderstandings. Adramé and Aziana, the North and the South, seem like caricature African settings. Samba Baloum, the easy-going eunuch who guards the *naba's* harem, and Nagoa and Noaga, the identical twins whose nonchalant, amoral pranks seem the reverse of Clarence's continual moral questioning, are richly comic figures.

Le Regard du Roi was influenced by the Czechoslovakian writer, Franz Kafka.[5] During the 1940s and 50s Kafka was almost a cult among literary intellectuals, who saw in his comic, ironical works a spectrum of meanings ranging from protest against the modern

118

bureaucratic state to a record of man's search for salvation in an absurd world. Laye learned from Kafka, especially from *The Castle*, how to make comic irony suggest a metaphysical dimension. *Le Regard du Roi*, like *The Castle*, turns the comic mode into the symbolic; the illogicality of life shows our incomprehension of the divine. The story also uses the quest motif which, as can be seen from the works of D. O. Fagunwa and Amos Tutuola, is usually an allegory of man's search for salvation, or an attempt to bring harmony between God and man. *Le Regard du Roi*, like Senghor's poetry, evokes an Africa of symbols, mysteries and past empires. There are fish-women, magical snakes and antelopes; the king himself, encircled with bracelets, resembles a Benin statue. In the novel, as in many folk–tales, strange metamorphoses occur; dreams and visions are often an important source of truth.

The spiritual quest in *Le Regard du Roi* is similar to that of 'Les Yeux de la Statue', a short story Laye published in *Présence Africaine* in 1957. Here the protagonist is an African woman rather than a white man, but she too searches for some kind of salvation. Like Clarence, she travels through heavy bush; she feels she is losing her way and that objects are indistinct as in a dream. She arrives at the ruins of an abandoned city, where she believes that the fallen statue of the former ruler is calling out to her in despair, but that she is unworthy to respond. Eventually she is overcome by a sea of weeds that engulfs the ruins. The story is not overtly African; it is, rather, a modern parable of the soul's longing for a god to give life meaning.

'Les Yeux de la Statue' is more pessimistic than *Le Regard du Roi*. It suggests that a culture capable of supporting the woman's spiritual quest has fallen into ruins. Perhaps it reflects Laye's own feeling of the disintegration of the Africa of his childhood. The woman feels that she cannot understand the statue she sees; the artistic tradition of the past has been lost. In *L'Enfant Noir* Laye's father, in his role as goldsmith, is to some extent still a traditional artist. Although as an individual he is proud of his accomplishments, he is an instrument through which communal religious forces are at work and he is given divine guidance by the black snake. The individual artist is not merely expressing his own thoughts; the work of art he produces, by capturing the spiritual forces of the community, is more than merely an object. In *Le Regard du Roi*, Diallo the blacksmith produces a series of axes, striving to come as close as possible to perfection, although that goal can never be attained. The finest axe he can produce will be offered by the *naba* to the king. Later, in *Dramouss*, the father speaks of the artist's role in the traditional world: 'c'était un temps où la biche qui surgissait sous l'herminette servait au culte, à la magie. Un temps où le forgeron-sculpteur était sorcier, était prêtre, et où il exerçait plus qu'une pure activité artisinale'. In 'Les Yeux de la Statue', since the community has been destroyed, the art left behind no longer expresses its spiritual impulses; it is merely a sterile relic.

The communal nature of African art throws light on Laye's aims in his novels. While each novel is partly based on personal experiences, it also has a representative quality. The personal is given a fictional form which makes it universal in the sense that it can be said to represent Africa or mankind collectively. This representative aesthetic is shown clearly in the dedication of *Dramouss*, where the author addresses other Africans who have studied or are studying abroad 'à la recherche de moyens de lutte plus efficaces'. *Dramouss* is meant to be understood as more than a mixture of autobiography, criticism of Guinean politics, and personal mystical vision. It is representative of those who, during the colonial period, like Laye, felt that their quest for education and their writings were preparatory for the achievement of an ideal Africa, and who, like Laye, were disappointed by the actual results of independence in many parts of the continent.

Dramouss takes up the autobiographical story of *L'Enfant Noir*, although the main character is now called Fatoman. The story is told in somewhat disjointed, stylized fashion. The past, present and a vision of the future are narrated without a clear chronological order. The novel begins with Fatoman's return to Conakry during the period of self-rule ('la loi-cadre') which preceded independence. He marries Mimie, who has been waiting for him for six years and is presumably the girl named Marie in *L'Enfant Noir*. Her jealous comments about his French girlfriend, his impressions of the changes in Guinea, and his visit to a bauxite plant where he sees the contributions French technology has made to the Guinean economy, make him think of the relationship between Guinea and France. He spends a restless night recalling his life in Paris. His memories recapitulate many of the themes of earlier West African writing: the feeling of alienation, the joys and difficulties of life in Paris, the organizations of African intellectuals working with sympathetic Frenchmen to justify African culture. Fatoman has favourable memories of many Frenchmen. Stanislas, a typical French worker, is pro-African and holds similar socialist ideals to Laye's own. While Stanislas tells Fatoman to kick the colonialists out of Africa, Fatoman is in favour of continuing cooperation between France and Africa. Colonialism, we are told, was on the whole beneficial in bringing modern industry to Africa. Fatoman like Laye, seems to desire a mixture of western technology and traditional African values. Europe is criticized less for colonialism and more for its money economy, in which men exploit others rather than work together towards communal goals.

Fatoman and his wife travel from Conakry to his family home in Kouroussa, where a 'griot' tells a story about a jealous husband; the tale recalls an older way of life, a time when men believed in God's mysterious powers. This glimpse of a dying culture is followed by episodes which show how Guinea has changed. Since Guinea has been inundated with cheap trinkets, art has become part of the market economy rather than an expression of spiritual values. At a rally Fatoman learns that party politics have divided the people; opponents of the ruling party are being treated brutally. After returning home, he has a strange dream of Guinea's future; there will be a cruel period of dictatorship, when all men will be imprisoned, followed by the coming of a redeemer who will save the country and Africa. Later, after several more years abroad, Fatoman returns to a now independent Guinea. The worst aspects of his dream are becoming true. Fatoman's father complains of the lack of meat and rice in Kouroussa. Social harmony and the natural tendency of the African to help his fellow men have broken down under the party system. Pan-African ideals have been lost. Fatoman finds that several of his friends have been accused as political plotters against the regime and executed.

Dramouss is in part a picture of what Laye feels has happened to destroy the traditional cultural and social values of Africa, and the hope that independence would contribute towards a new humanism blending the best of Europe and Africa. Fatoman learns that the Guinean R.D.A. (*Rassemblement Démocratique Africain*) has gone its separate way from the main body of the party. This is of particular historical significance since the R.D.A. was a leading force in the independence movement and included many of the Négritude writers such as Bernard Dadié. If *Dramouss* gives voice to the hopes and subsequent disillusionment of Laye's generation, it also contains a vision of the future. In his dream of Dramouss, Fatoman is shown how the Black Lion will eventually save the nation and all of Africa from tyranny. The dream has obvious political significance; it suggests that although the nation is at present a police state in which the rule of law has been replaced by sheer force, salvation will come through God, who will provide a leader.

In a Conference at Fourah Bay College, Freetown, in 1963, at which he told the dream of the Black Lion, Laye said that beyond the political allegory lay a deeper reality, the relation between man and God. This he felt was in keeping with the traditional folk tale: 'telle est la manière des conteurs d'Afrique, dont les fables s'éclaircissent seulement à la lumière des rapports *entre Dieu et ses créatures*'. Dramouss, he said, is a figure of justice, and her eyes, which resemble 'phares' (locomotive headlights), foretell the Last Judgement. (The description is an interesting example of combining African with western technological images.) The Black Lion is thus a saviour. The novel moves beyond the political problems of modern Africa to include a mythic presentation of the soul's search for salvation. The dream sequence captures a feeling of the terror of modern life and combines it with an allegory of God's power to save man. It is closely related to the theme of *Le Regard du Roi,* where, just when he feels most humiliated, Clarence is taken into the king's arms.

Laye's relationship to his readers in *Dramouss* differs from that in his earlier novels. There he addressed Europeans; here he is writing for Africans. Traditional African symbols are used with the expectation that the reader will feel something of their significance. Magical incidents are related without any explanation. Laye uses expressions in Malinké (translated in footnotes) and refers to contemporary events which would puzzle a foreign reader.

Dramouss is a strange and not wholly satisfactory mixture of autobiography, folk-tale, political discussion, and allegory. While it aims at expressing important communal problems, its form is not well adapted to its themes. If the pressure of public events sometimes makes Laye speak out more as a commentator than as an artist, there are moments when we wish *Dramouss* had more political detail and was less stylized into a work of art. The novel is too disjunctive. The characters do not seem real, the political discussions are hardly dramatized. The most successful parts are the recounting of the folk-tale and the powerful dream sequence of Dramouss and the Black Lion.

In *Dramouss* Laye attacks those whose racial or ideological views prevented cooperation between Guinea and France. He recalls that the ruling powers were initially voted into office on a programme of cooperation. All Laye's work is infused with a spirit of assimilating the best of past and present, of Africa and Europe, in order to make human life better. It is also shaped by a religious vision, in which it is essential to submit oneself to God's will and to seek salvation in the life to come. Laye can often take a longer, calmer view of political and social problems because he believes that a divine plan, overriding racial, economic and cultural concerns, directs human life. This resignation to God's will is undoubtedly part of his Islamic upbringing.

Beyond the Négritude themes and the Islamic religious sensibility present in the novels, Laye is also writing about mankind in general. His work is set in an African context, but it shows that African culture shares the fundamental preoccupations of all men. He creates scenes and characters true to a moment of African history and also memorable as general types. Laye uses in his work a stylized form to express, as he feels traditional African sculpture expresses, 'un type universel'.[6] As a modern novelist, writing in French, however, he cannot produce traditional art. Just as he wants an assimilation of African spiritual values and European technology, Laye also seeks an assimilation of artistic forms. His work combines elements of the traditional folktale with modern European modes and styles.

At his best, Laye is a poetic novelist, combining strong images of the natural world with a delicate portrayal of human emotions. Before Laye, there was very little African fiction, in either English or French, which deserved critical attention. Laye's achievement in his first two novels may be said to have set standards of craftsmanship, style and artistic purpose for such later writers as Oyono, Béti and Achebe. As it is less successful artistically, *Dramouss* will perhaps be read primarily for insight into a difficult moment of contemporary history and for a fuller understanding of Laye's thought. *L' Enfant Noir* and *Le Regard du Roi*, however, are fully achieved works of art, of lasting value beyond their historical and cultural circumstances.

NOTES

1. Camara is the family name. Following European usage, we should refer to him as Laye Camara. He has, however, preferred to publish as Camara Laye.
2. 'Entretien avec Camara Laye' in *Afrique*, 26 (July 1963), p. 56.
3. Ibid., p. 56.
4. Léopold Sédar Senghor, 'Laye Camara et Lamine Niang ou l'Art doit être incarné', in *Condition humaine* (22 April 1955). Reprinted in *Négritude et Humanisme* (Paris: Seuil, 1964), pp. 173-174.
5. For a detailed study of Laye's use of Kafka, see Patricia Anne Deduck's unpublished thesis, 'Franz Kafka's Influence on Camara Laye's '*Le regard du roi*' (University of Indiana, 1970).
6. 'L'Ame de l'Afrique dans Sa Partie Guinéenne', an address given at the Colloque sur la littérature africaine d'expression française, Faculté des Lettres de Dakar, March 1963. Also published in *African Literature and the Universities*, ed. Gerald Moore (Ibadan University Press, 1965).

10

Tchicaya U Tam'si

by
CLIVE WAKE

Tchicaya U Tam'si is a major African poet, the most outstanding French-speaking African poet of the younger, or what one might perhaps call the post-Négritude, generation. His work has not, however, made the same impact on the black world as Senghor's, for reasons which are more closely related to the political evolution of Africa than to literary merit.

Tchicaya's poetry, like Senghor's, is deeply rooted in an African consciousness torn by colonialism (although unlike Senghor, Tchicaya is also profoundly affected by the memory of slavery). Their attitude of mind is, however, very different. Whereas Senghor knows who he is and where he is going—it was part of the essential confidence and optimism of Négritude—Tchicaya is frustrated by the apparently insuperable difficulty of finding his identity, in relation both to the past and to the present, and has no certainty at all about his future either as a black man or quite simply as a man. It is precisely because he is unsure about the ability of man in general to overcome his weaknesses that he can feel so little confidence in his future as a black man. Senghor, starting from an absolute confidence in his own race, is able to face the rest of humanity with an equal confidence. The tone of their writing is therefore very different. Senghor's poetic diction embodies the calm dignity of the poet's self-assurance, with which the almost biblical rhythms of his verse are very much in keeping. Tchicaya's sense of frustration, anger and loss produces a more aggressive diction which expresses the ups and downs of an unsatisfied self-exploration. Sure of his links with the African past, Senghor constantly refers by name to the heroes of African history and to the particularities of the traditional culture. Such references are almost totally absent from Tchicaya's poetry. For him, there are the general images of a suffering past—slavery and colonialism—and the particular images of twentieth-century misery—the lynched black American

Emmet Till, the murdered political leader Patrice Lumumba and the Congo: the Congo, a river as well as a place, above all. This is the region where he was born in 1931 and the scene of one of Africa's most traumatic experiences of the twentieth century. Although he was born on the Brazzaville side of the Congo, he identifies in his poetry with the nightmare of the other Congo's history between 1959 and 1961, both because of the significance of the events themselves and because they reflected with symbolic intensity his own sense of violation and loss. The specific events of the period find their place almost naturally in a poetic universe which was by then ready to receive them. This was a poetic universe made up of two primary elements, the suffering human body in all its parts and the Congolese landscape of savannahs, forests, rivers (and chiefly one river), birds, animals, sun and sky. These are the realities of his world, and the necessary sources of his imagery and his symbolism.

Tchicaya writes a difficult poetry. Much of it remains impenetrable to even the most assiduous and sensitive of readers, although there is little doubt about the main lines of his thought. Tchicaya has, however, with justification, denied the charge of hermeticism: '... personally I do not think myself hermetic. I admit I have a big nose, I admit I have a club foot, but I do not admit being hermetic. It is quite easy to read my poetry if one takes time, if one is careful to pause in the right places; there is no trick about it'.[1] There is no evidence that the poet is deliberately trying to make his work inaccessible to the reader. The poetry is constructed around a very vivid, startling use of imagery and symbolism of a chiefly visual kind. One is tempted to define it as Surrealist, but this would be a mistake. The use of enigmatic visual imagery, largely without referents, along with ellipsis, non-linear argument, ambiguity, lack of punctuation and a refusal generally to make allowances for the reader are common to much modern French poetry which is not Surrealist. Surrealist poetry is concerned with subconscious experience and ought, if it is genuine, to be based on spontaneous (called 'automatic') writing. The structure and imagery of all of Tchicaya's poetry are very carefully controlled, and throughout his work there is broadly the same recurring pattern of images, phrases and themes. Moreover, Tchicaya seems to be much more concerned with conscious experience than with the subconscious; he is anxious for the self-knowledge which will tell him where he stands in relation to other men. This would certainly be in keeping with Tchicaya's rejection of the description of his poetry as hermetic. He goes on to say: 'It is as when I say: I lend a pack of cards to a passer-by. I lend. I give. One must visualise the pack of cards and one must visualise the hands of the passer-by, and the passer-by himself. And if the passer-by is a Fortune-teller one must wait for the prognostication. . .nothing could be more direct.'[2] He is stressing here the conscious quality of his poetic experience. The purpose of this essay will be to try to suggest some of the ways in which one might gradually penetrate the mysteries of this complex, highly-charged but very immediate poetry.

Tchicaya has so far published six volumes of poetry: *Le Mauvais Sang* (1955), *Feu de Brousse* (1957), *A Triche-coeur* (1960), *Epitomé* (1962), *Le Ventre* (1964), and *Arc Musical* (1970). The first three volumes were re-issued (with a number of significant alterations to *Le Mauvais Sang*) in a single volume, in 1970. *Epitomé*, which also incorporated a number of significant textual amendments, as well as additions, was re-issued in the same volume as *Arc Musical*.[3]

In his first volume, *Le Mauvais Sang* ('Bad Blood'), the young poet evokes the emotional impact made on him by the realization that the human condition, and in particular that of the black man, condemns him to the role of victim, not hero. Although the black man's situation in the world is central to his theme (it is mentioned in the very first poem and the notion of 'bad blood' refers to the black man's supposed congenital inferiority), it is not again directly referred to until the end of the volume, and in the final poem it literally explodes into prominence. This approach has the effect of strengthening Tchicaya's point by bringing us to the poet's awareness of himself as a black man via his awareness of himself as a human being first and foremost. But Tchicaya is not so much concerned with his lot as a black man as with that initial realization of his human condition. Like his admired predecessor Rimbaud, Tchicaya expresses it very aptly through the image of the child, and occasionally through the image of the bird, when he wants to stress more the idea of the poet as a singer and a lonely figure. The child's imagination is particularly sensitive to the experience of alienation and hostility. Family ties are important to him, so Tchicaya's child has no family, 'neither father, nor mother, nor brothers', he is 'a bird without feathers, a bird without a nest'. He has an instinctive longing for joy, purity and love ('sun', 'gold', 'love', 'heart' are all words carrying these ideas which recur frequently), but he seems to be held by a 'destin' ('destiny') which is corrupted at source; he is led to believe that his very life blood, his very blackness are impure. In his quest for an answer to the riddle of this paradoxical conflict between aspiration and hopelessness, he is torn alternately

126

by hope and despair, by apparent success and a profound sense of defeat. He meets a fortune-teller who describes his life as 'a long journey at the end of which you will be hanged'. His frustration provokes intense resentment, emotions which come very forcefully through the imagery and the rhythms. Passive sadness, in verses perhaps deliberately reminiscent of the nineteenth century French poet Verlaine, alternates with outbursts of aggressive revolt which are in turn reminiscent of Verlaine's companion Rimbaud. The intensity of the emotion is maintained by its being held tautly in check, its only outlet an irony which makes no allowances for the unwary.

The volume is not, however, merely a random collection of mood poems. There is a unity of imagery and theme, but also an evolution in the poet's attitude to his predicament. A poem of hope seems to be cancelled out by a poem of despair and so on, like a pendulum. But as the volume nears its close, the feeling of hope comes to dominate more and more. In the poem 'Espérance, o savanes', while the penultimate stanza ends with the exclamation 'Défaite!', the last stanza ends with a resounding 'Espérance!'. The first and last poems of the collection themselves indicate the distance covered by portraying exactly opposite states of mind through the same image of 'le mauvais sang'. The first poem asks a question without any hope of an answer:

> Heave your song—Bad Blood!—how then to survive
> the soul bloomed with shit. . . .

In the last poem, 'The Sign of Bad Blood', rather like Césaire in the *Cahier,* the poet ironically accepts the squalor and ugliness of his physical and moral condition as it has been presented to him. He rejects the temptation of self-pity and fatalism. 'A toad's destiny is pure enough', he exclaims. Another of the last poems is entitled 'Le Gros Sang', where 'bad' (or 'impure') is replaced by 'big' as the qualification for 'blood'. This poem contains an important line which expresses the mood of the final poem: 'I am the tempered steel, the fire of the new races'. The poet acknowledges the virtue of pride: 'In the memory of man pride has been a vice I make it a God . . . I am a man I am black'.[5] Along with the transition from defeatism to a more aggressive self-assertion comes the realization that what he has so far seen as a private predicament is one he shares with all the 'new races'. The poet's sense of isolation disappears and he is able to declare: 'I create Brotherhood'. Where he had once taken seriously the idea of the inherent impurity of his blood, he now uses the phrase 'le mauvais sang' with an irony which indicates his new state of mind:

That's it they are of course tractors grumbling across my savannah.
No it is my blood in my veins!
A bad blood it is![6]

Tchicaya's concern with colonialism is more explicit in *Feu de Brousse* ('Bush Fire'). Although he tells us his 'love is sad', this volume has none of the passive sadness, with its hint of self-pity, to be found in *Le Mauvais Sang*. Instead there is a much greater firmness of purpose, already evoked in 'The Sign of Bad Blood'. The central theme of *Feu de Brousse* is the idea that the black man has been deprived of the spiritual continuity of his African tradition, and without it it seems he cannot find his identity. Colonialism, coming in the wake of slavery, and bringing with it the cultural arrogance of Christianity, has undermined his tradition and created in him a sense of rootlessness; in terms of the book's symbolism, the fishermen have abandoned the river. In the poem 'Long Live the Bride', he illustrates his argument by taking what was at the time one of the great events of Africanized Christianity. The *Messe des Piroguiers* ('The Fishermen's Mass') had recently been performed in the Cathedral of Saint Anne in Brazzaville. Less well-known than the *Missa Luba*, it was nevertheless one of the fashionable 'African' masses of the day:

> uncle nathanael writes to me of his astonishment
> at hearing the drums
> over radio-brazzaville.

Tchicaya was not to be taken in by the novelty of drums in a Christian church. In allowing their use, the missionaries had been careful to exclude any of the 'lewdness' they associated with traditional African dance and music. Tchicaya regards this emasculation as a travesty:

> my catafalque is ready
> and I lie dead murdered on the altar of christ.

Tchicaya returns constantly in his work to the way European education and religion have alienated him and Africans in general from themselves, and at the same time destroyed the links that once bound Africans of different tribes together. The poems of this volume evoke the poet's attempts to rediscover his own lost spiritual continuity with his people. There are false solutions: he pretends to accept the white man's ways, but this leads to a hypocrisy which can only give him 'the life that kills'. He seeks the answer in the vision of an ideal, represented here by the love of a woman, especially Sammy; the

128

theme and Sammy recur throughout his work. But idealism is no solution either. He comes finally to realize that he has to stand on his own two feet and walk, as the titles of the last two poems in this volume indicate: 'Debout' ('On your feet') and 'Marche' ('Walk').

This summary is a gross oversimplification, inevitably, of a complex and subtle exposition in poetic terms of the poet's conception of his predicament. Imagery drawn from the human body, especially the various associations with blood, is significant, but he expresses his theme mainly through the medium of imagery suggested by the Congo landscape. The river itself is the central symbol, standing for the continuity of life and the spirituality it ensures. Often the poet identifies himself directly with the river:

> His river was the gentlest dish
> the firmest
> it was his most living flesh.[7]

Some of the images, such as the dish in this quotation, seem odd at first. The dish can be associated with the later image of the matrix, equated with the poet's eyes, the symbol of the true self.

The river must be bridged, the two banks linked again, and the spiritual continuity of his soul in space and time restored. It seems to him that only the rainbow—perhaps an image of the ideal—can achieve this. The last poem, 'Marche', draws the imagery and themes of the volume together in the form of a fable which seems to suggest ultimate success for the poet. The river Congo is created from the eyelash of a waking child, and the banks of the river are joined by time; the poet crosses and is restored to his origins, able to undergo the purification by fire which will clean away his shame.

> the bell tolls it is time
> across time and river
> time fords the tolling of the bell
> on its mounts of silence
>   and crosses
> my soul is ready
> peace on my soul
> light the fire that washes away shame.

A Triche-coeur ('By Cheating the Heart') stresses the theme of the poet's quest for purpose. In the opening fable-poem, 'Agonie', the poet ('the black boatman') crosses the river to a bird on the other bank who represents his soul. Filled with his ambition to 'heal with the mud of his sad eyes/the lepers of their leprosy', he learns that he must instead set his sights much lower. The bird tells him:

I am your soul farewell
my body is only a shadow farewell
your arms will be untied
I am not a leper
do not die waiting for me
with your arms stretched out in a cross.

A later poem, 'L'Etrange Agonie', develops the theme of the poet's quest more fully and in a more intensely personal way. The outcome is, however, the same: his future will not be that of a conqueror but a club-foot.

The poet's concern with the purpose of his own life is always inextricably tied up with his awareness of 'the orphan' Africa's three centuries of suffering through slavery and colonialism. In a very vivid and moving fable-poem, 'Equinoxiale', Africa is portrayed as a mother who has lost her child and during her centuries of mourning ploughs and sows her body in readiness for the birth of a new child. In several poems, Christianity's role is developed more fully, in readiness almost for the next volume, *Epitomé*. It enables the poet to exploit the image of the cheating heart. The Christianization of Africa by men who use methods that betray Christ also leads to duplicity on the part of the poet who hides his real preoccupations from them and even from his own people:

Devoted to my illusions
I never laughed
I never showed my teeth to anyone . . .
I pretended they were bad.

In turn he betrays the betrayed Christ (who is later to be presented as the betrayer himself) and turns back to the pagan Sammy, whose pure song rises from among the devastated trees of Africa like a clear river flowing through green fields. In the title poem of the volume, Tchicaya contrasts the apparent sterility of his own suffering and his sense of having betrayed Africa by his cheating and hypocrisy with the falseness of Christ's sacrifice (Christ is symbolized as a wild boar),

130

for did he not instruct the 'corner-stone' Peter to bring into being
a religion of violence?

> with the sword break bread
> stretch forth your hand make love.

The unifying idea of this volume is the moment of death (agony)
and death itself, for death sums up a man's life and, as the Gospels say,
inaugurates a new life. Christ dies so that a religion based on violence
and violation might emerge; the mother mourns for her child while
she prepares her body for a new birth; the death of the orphan Africa
is evoked in yet another fable-poem, 'Le Corbillard' ('The Hearse');
and so too is the mystery of the poet's own agony as he strives to free
himself from a destiny that prevents him from realizing the real purpose
of his existence.

A Triche-coeur reads like a prologue to Epitomé, although all three
volumes so far discussed reach their climax in this last one. Epitomé/Les
Mots de Tête pour le Sommaire d'une Passion ('Epitome/Epigraphs for the
Summary of a Passion'), published in 1962, is perhaps Tchicaya's most
important work to date, the two subsequent volumes notwithstanding,
not only in terms of the poet's artistic development, but also, as it is
clear from the title, in terms of his awareness of the stage reached by his
intellectual and emotional development. 'Epitome' indicates a
quintessential bringing together, or summary, of the elements that
constitute his 'passion' (in the religious sense), and the word 'summary'
in the sub-title on the one hand reinforces this intention and on the
other it includes the now less common meanings of summa, the 'sum
or substance of a matter', to quote the OED, and the notion of the
highest point or climax of an experience. This is clear from Tchicaya's
use of the preposition in the title of the poem's first section: 'Au
Sommaire d'une Passion' ('At the Summary of a Passion'). These
intentions are made very relevant when we consider the events which
provided an essential element in the inspiration of the poem. These
were the events that followed on the outbreak of violence in Leopoldville (which Tchicaya refers to throughout his work as Kin) in 1959
(the date is mentioned in the text), a year before the country's independence. Something like two hundred African civilians lost their
lives in clashes with the Belgian forces of order. These events, in all
their brutal reality, force the poet to come face to face with himself,
to confront the introspection of a perhaps too theoretical poetry with
the facts of life.

131

In 'Préface', Tchicaya acknowledges the ambiguities of his attitude to the world around him. During the course of the poem, he refers to himself as the man with a limp, anxious to do what is right, but imperfect and aware of his own treachery. People, he says, demand purity, but he is not pure in the accepted sense. There are sides to his personality and his behaviour which deserve criticism. He has seemingly identified with the white world, spent time on that 'society beach' which crops up from time to time in his poems. But real purity, he argues, comes from the experience of all aspects of life, with its many pressures and temptations. They are the cause of the 'headaches' that constitute the matter of his poems. 'Nothing is pure which excludes a mixture of everything; I shall say that real purity doesn't care a damn for purity . . . . The darkest night has greater brightness than the flash of lightning that shatters it.'

The poet is faced with two main problems. Firstly, there is the urgent need to know who and what he is, the nature of his destiny. This is the continuing anxiety. He wants to find the roots of his 'genealogical tree', which is his tree of life. This quest remains an apparently hopeless one. He is reluctant to opt for the artificial answers provided by movements like Négritude—

> The cross the banner négritude in overalls
> who wants to get involved?

Secondly, he senses a conflict between his quest for his racial and cultural roots and the intense anger he feels about the events taking place in Leopoldville. There is, in fact, a shift of emphasis from the hitherto essentially egocentric nature of his quest to the poet's relationship with the here and now of the African situation and the problem of the poet's commitment to it. The long first section of the poem, 'At the Summary of a Passion', poses the problems and indicates the poet's hesitations. In the last section, he seems to reach a conclusion. He rejects the attitude of mind that is represented by van Gogh and Matisse who withdraw from 'the noises of the city' in order to create an art which has nothing to do with everyday realities. They work in isolation—perhaps to some extent he has also done so up until now—while

> on the pavements the passers-by
> have a deluge in their hearts.

His own passion—the word already indicates this—is paralleled with Christ's, and he too assumes the suffering of his fellow men. But, whereas he has so far tended to reflect mostly on the pain caused to himself by the wearing of the poet's crown of thorns, he will instead now concentrate on the pain felt by others, and thus in a true sense assume their suffering:

> by the salt of a wine
> explain the weather as it is
> turn away from all the sores that condition
> the growth of thorns on my crown.

The poet's commitment is to an awareness of the suffering of others, not his own, and to its poetic expression:

> From what love
> at what cost
> I die with each song of love.

The poet becomes a Christ whose passion and death are the poem, the verbal realization of the people's suffering. This brings him back, as so often is the case with this poetry of exploration, to the first poem, 'Préface': 'Nothing is closer to the Word than the word when it is made to resound'.

Much of the imagery and many of the key phrases of the earlier volumes are present in *Epitomé*, which is a bringing-together in a special way of all that has gone before. More stress is laid in this volume, however, on the image of the sea, the symbol of 'the human adventure', than on that of the river, the symbol of an individual culture, ultimately only part of the whole into which it flows. The shift is in line with Tchicaya's anxiety to decide whether his duty is to all men or to those who make up his own people. He is fascinated by the figure of the salt-gatherer, working on the sea-shore, gathering the essence of all things. In the end he decides, 'I shall no longer go down to the sea'. This is, too, the volume in which Tchicaya's Christological imagery plays its most important role, for, not only does he deliberately parallel 'the analysis of his suffering' with Christ's, using the imagery and terminology of Christology throughout the poem, but he also makes a bitter attack on Christ (especially in the section entitled 'The Scorner'), who is contaminated by association 'with the bourgeois', and Christianity, which is epitomized in the Cathedral of Saint Anne at Brazzaville. He plays on the ambiguities of Christ's betrayal of Africa and his own, but finally shifts the true dignity of the Cross from the white man's God to the black poet.

Le Ventre ('The Belly') is Tchicaya's most difficult poem; the concentration of the poem's language makes the text often intractable. Although it is based on the by now familiar imagery of the human body, the belly of course in particular, and although many other key images and phrases return, if with less insistence, there is an air of unfamiliarity which must strike the reader who has followed Tchicaya's poetry this far. He is clearly still preoccupied with the development of the situation in the now independent Congo-Kinshasa (Zaïre), between the date of independence on 30 June 1960 (once again, the date is given in the text) and Lumumba's assassination in February 1961: violence continues, the African leadership is compromised with international big business and the former colonial power has sent in troops to protect its interests (there is specific reference to the landing of Belgian troops at Kamina and Kitona). The name Kin recurs almost obsessively,

> the town
> where the river has its hand
> on my heart.

Nor is Katanga forgotten. The opening section recalls the imagery of the closing section of *Epitomé:* the rain continues to fall, and there is 'nothing to take away from that crown (of thorns)'.

Lumumba is not mentioned by name in the text, although he is given as the author of an epigraph: 'I am the Congo'. He is, however, the poet's central preoccupation, the basis of his angry reflection on the political and human situation and on leadership and sacrifice. Continuing the imagery of *Epitomé,* he presents Lumumba as a Christ figure, betrayed by his own people for money:

> Ah the jews know too well
> that this messiah was for sale.

(Tchicaya often refers to himself and black people metaphorically as Jews.) Money dominates:

> at Kin where blood
> has its exchange rate I don't know what it is:
> Is it measured by the dollar?

The poet even foresees the time when his own poetry will be quoted on the stock-exchange.

Gerald Moore suggests that 'in *Le Ventre* there is less reference to external events or to the past. The poet is here involved in a long interrogation of himself.'[8] The past certainly does have little place in the poem, and the quest for the genealogical tree has disappeared (although the river symbol remains). However, it is because the pressure of the present is even more overwhelming than it was in *Epitomé*, and it determines the nature of the self-interrogation; this becomes a reflection on the life and death of another person with whom the poet identifies. The dominating image of the belly (closely linked with blood, which is perhaps the second most powerful image in the poem) suggests concern with the most basic of everyday human experiences, with the elemental human realities of sexuality and birth, greed and generosity, the physical satisfaction of hunger and thirst. As an image the belly is a kind of visible presence in a way that the more traditional symbols of the heart and the head cannot be. The latter remain curiously abstract because they are dominated by what they stand for, whereas the belly, unusual, almost grotesque as a poetic image, seems to have a physical reality which imposes itself on the imagination. The poet's reflections range from:

> the belly. For sale everywhere with that pestilential
> heat of old charnel houses,

to Lumumba's death:

> He died with his back to the wind:
> turn over his belly:
> if his belly is hard
> it shows he died on his feet!
> Do not weep.
> Walk erect!

In the opening section of the poem we are presented with the vivid, startling picture of upturned bellies floating among the water hyacinths in Stanley Pool. The upturned belly is likened to the visible part of a seamark, for which he uses the word *voyant*, normally associated with the idea of prophecy. But prophecy does not seem to be his preoccupation here. He is using the more down-to-earth meaning of the word to stress a very down-to-earth meaning of martyrdom: the inspiration that the martyr gives through his example. Tchicaya uses the image to bring the poem to an end, associating the marker with the dead martyr:

But love for life
the love one gives from the belly
the earth takes care of that
Thank God markers fall
mostly on their back
mostly with their arms outspread
mostly with their belly facing the sky!

During the course of the interview quoted earlier in this essay, Tchicaya mentioned his feeling of sadness at the failure of men of different races to form community: 'An overflow of misery, undisguised and physical, a moral misery I would like to call it, and there was this odd impression of forlornness, of utter solitude, a barred horizon. Certainly there is in my writing this universe, this loneliness, sadness of man—man everywhere, whether he be black, white, yellow etc.'[9] He had spoken of his 'sad love' before in his poetry, especially in *Epitomé*, but it is with *Arc Musical* ('Bow Harp') that the feeling itself comes through. In earlier volumes, the sadness was spoken of but not evoked; it was kept in the background by the more imperious nature of the poet's anger and frustration. The tone of *Arc Musical* is strikingly different from its predecessors. We are made to share his sadness that

a cry cannot pass
unless it is covered in blood,
unless it promises its blood . . .
but this cry is
there has been enough bloodshed!

His whole work is haunted by the spilling of human blood, so the need for love is what becomes most urgent for the poet now, 'love, love at last satisfied'. With it goes an equally urgent longing for peace:

The treasure . . .
is in the voice of the man
where no storm rages
over the corn in the plains at dawn.

In the first of two poems entitled 'Communion', Tchicaya evokes his own discovery of communion with men, a discovery which, to his surprise, was not painful, which did not dismember him, and for

136

which he would now be prepared to suffer anything. The second poem of this title opens with one of those striking lines which one constantly meets with in Tchicaya's poetry:

Quand l'homme sera plus féal à l'homme
(When man will be more loyal to man).

When this happens, 'life will rediscover my body'.

There is a lyrical quality about most of these poems which is sometimes reminiscent of *Le Mauvais Sang*, but it is a parallel which only serves to show how far Tchicaya has come both as an artist and as a man since that first volume. His style is now very much his own. There is no trace of Verlaine or of Rimbaud, and there is, above all, a depth of feeling and a depth of sincerity which could only have come after the experience of suffering recorded in the previous volumes. The confrontation between the egocentric poet and external reality at the heart of *Epitomé* seems to have come to complete fruition. Similarly, Tchicaya is able to transcend the specifically racial concerns of his earlier poetry to write poetry which is unambiguously universal in its representation and understanding of the human condition. He is not afraid to go down to the sea. He does not, however, fall victim to sentimentality, as could so easily happen. He is very much aware of the human realities, and it is his recognition of the fact that love and peace are not often enough preferred to hate and bloodshed that forms the basis of his sadness and prevents sentimentality. He constantly reminds himself of the need to return to reality from the world of music in which he would prefer to live. These poems are about the interplay in the poet's life of his dream and reality. In the final poem of the collection, entitled 'Sinaï, bis', he offers to inscribe a new decalogue on the cheeks of the men of peace, the poem he cannot set down on the printed page:

the poem I have seen
the poem this page suppresses
which would have saved the blood
so that a hand might dash
both sphinxes and wanderers
so that birds might trust
in the innocence of man.[10]

137

1. 'Tchikaya U Tam'si interviewed by Edris Makward during the African Studies Association Conference held at Montreal, October 1969', published as a Supplement to *Cultural Events in Africa* (London: The Transcription Centre), no. 60 (1969), p. III.
2. *Ibid.*
3. Much of Tchicaya's work has been translated into English. A translation of *Feu de Brousse* (Paris: Caractères, 1957) entitled *Brush Fire*, by Sangodare Akanji, was published by Mbari of Ibadan in 1964. *Selected Poems*, translated by Gerald Moore, was published in 1970 in Heinemann's African Writers Series. This selection included the whole of *A Triche-coeur* (Paris: P.J. Oswald, 1960) and the first version of *Epitomé* (Tunis: S.N.E.D., 1962), as well as extracts from *Le Ventre* (Paris: Présence Africaine, 1964) and *Arc Musical* (P. J. Oswald, 1970). Translations from the whole range of Tchicaya's work, including *Le Mauvais Sang* (Caractères, 1955) are to be found in *French African Verse*, edited by John Reed and Clive Wake and published by Heinemann in the African Writers Series in 1972. Unless otherwise indicated, translations from Tchicaya's work quoted in this essay are by the present author.
4. Reed and Wake, *op. cit.*, p. 47.
5. *Ibid.*, p. 49.
6. *Ibid.*, p. 53.
7. *Ibid.*, p. 93.
8. Tchicaya U Tam'si, *Selected Poems*, p. xiii.
9. *Cultural Events in Africa.* no. 60 (1969), Supplement, p. III.
10. Reed & Wake, *op. cit.*, p. 199.

11

Sembène Ousmane: social commitment and the search for an African identity

by
MARTIN T. BESTMAN

Sembène Ousmane was born in January 1923 in Casamance, the southern region of Senegal. Unlike most Senegalese writers, he does not have a university education. He was expelled from school before obtaining his 'certificat d'études', and had to earn a living. Before trying his hand at writing novels, he was a fisherman, a plumber, a bricklayer, an apprentice mechanic and a soldier. He joined the French army at the outbreak of the Second World War and travelled extensively across Africa and Europe. Demobilized in 1946, he left for France clandestinely in 1948 and worked as a docker at the port of Marseilles for ten years. It was there he learned to write. His first novel, *Le Docker Noir* (published in 1956), reflects his personal experiences. He was still a docker when he published *O pays mon beau peuple!* (1957) and his masterpiece, *Les Bouts de Bois de Dieu* (1960), translated as *God's Bits of Wood*. As a trade-union leader, Sembène Ousmane took an active part in several workers' demonstrations and was influenced by socialist and communist thought. His leanings towards socialism are reflected in his writings.

It is astonishing how determination, courage, hard work, travel and experience have enabled this self-taught individual to become a man of culture and one of the most remarkable of all African writers. In addition he is a film director and producer who has created nine films which have won several international prizes. His social background and his direct contact with the masses enable him to express the spontaneity of the language, and the ideas and attitudes of the characters he delineates in both his films and his prose. Devoted to the cause of the people and interpreting their legitimate aspirations, he is suspicious of the bourgeois African intellectuals who cut themselves off from the masses.

As a revolutionary writer, Ousmane occupies a special place in African literature. His work shows a passionate social commitment and an ardent desire to reconstruct a sound and dynamic society. While condemning racial oppression, discrimination and injustices attendant on colonial rule, he is not blind to the social ills that plagues modern African society. He paints the image of an Africa that is convulsive, a world that questions its norms and values. He plunges us into an atmosphere of social tensions and explosive situations. He wages a relentless crusade against out-of-date customs or traditions. He diagnoses the evils that weigh down on society, such as the impact of imported religions, the lack of effective dialogue between parents and children, polygamy, the bourgeois tastes of an elite, and corruption that has become a way of life.

The words which Ousmane puts in the mouth of a character in *Le Docker Noir* throw light on his commitment: 'You are aspiring to be a writer? You will never be a good one so long as you don't defend a cause. You see, the writer must go to the fore-front, see things in their reality, not fear his ideas.'[1] A character in *L'Harmattan* adds: 'Who sees better the harvest of tomorrow, if not a writer? he alone can search consciences, that of the agronomist, of the physician, of the blacksmith, of the shoemaker, of our present leaders. The writer is not a unique person. He is a multitude of people.'[2] Faithful to his conviction that African writers should engage in revolutionary action, Ousmane rejects the notion of 'Négritude'; he feels it is used to mystify the masses, to mask real and pressing problems. The Africa that he depicts is at a cross-roads, rife with internal contradictions; it is a theatre of violent clashes between two apparently antagonistic worlds. It is pertinent to analyse some of the different social, political and psychological attitudes with which he invests characters who face the conflict between traditional and modern ways of life and who seek an African identity.

The rupture between tradition and modernism is deeply felt in the family system; the antinomy between the values of the past and those of the present finds poignant expression in the revolt of children against parental authority. This problem is not peculiar to African societies, but it is made more acute by the pressure of external forces and the opposition of traditional African and modern European values. The conflict is symptomatic of the disintegration of the traditional family structure, which seriously undermines the foundations of the society. In Ousmane's novels the revolt against parents is triggered by differences of opinion on marriage, religion and political ideology. This is particularly acute in areas where traditionally old age was synonymous with intelligence and wisdom.

According to tradition, parents have the prerogative to marry off their children, but Oumar Faye, the hero of *O pays, mon beau peuple!*, breaks this tradition by marrying a French woman. The disapproval and mounting hostility of his parents become so unbearable that Oumar leaves his father's house. Oumar also rejects custom and convention by abandoning the occupation of his family. The confrontation between Tioumbé, a teacher and local leader of the Marxist Party, in *L'Harmattan*, and her catechumen father, Koéboghi, is even more violent, more dramatic. But Tioumbé's revolt, unlike Oumar's, stems from religious and political inclinations. While she regards the 1958 Referendum on the political future of the country as an occasion to exercise her right to vote according to her convictions, her father, following the traditional way of life, insists on voting for all the members of his family. He sets upon his daughter, beats her savagely, binds her hand and foot and locks her up, with the help of other catechumens, swearing that she will only be released if she recognizes Jesus Christ as her saviour. Tioumbé turns a deaf ear to the threats of her father and stands up to him. Gradually the scales fall from Koéboghi's eyes and he realizes, to his great discomfiture, that the sacred rights of the father are collapsing; he comes to grips with the bitter fact that separates the present from the past. The crisis reaches its climax in the dramatic episode where the recalcitrant daughter pushes her father during a quarrel over her voter's card. In the ensuing struggle she butts into him, thus violating ancient precepts and condemning herself irrevocably. Even her mother, who has been sympathetic, is stupefied: she is so aghast at this turn of events that she wishes to die. In the end, Tioumbé, like Oumar Faye, leaves home after her father has disowned and cursed her. From *O Pays, mon beau peuple!* to *White Genesis* the development of the father-child conflict is perceptible: from simple friction it becomes more and more exacerbated, degenerating progressively into parricide when Tanor, a mentally deranged veteran, disowns and kills his incestuous father.

In Ousmane's novels the head of family is presented as narrow-minded, fanatical and dogmatic. His intransigence inevitably causes his children to burst the fetters of ancestral customs. This conflict is more than a family matter; it symbolizes the radical discord between the present and the past, the collision of two hostile, incommunicable worlds. It is the expression of a profound social malaise. The revolt has both positive and negative significances: it is positive because it affords the children liberty and the opportunity to develop their capacities, thus paving the way for social progress; it is negative when the family structure—the soul of Africa and the foundation of social order—becomes dismembered.

If it is true that harmony in the family system promotes stability and progress in society, it is also evident that no society can develop its national consciousness in a healthy manner without the active and full participation of women in its cultural, political and intellectual life. Ousmane's writings show that in some traditional African societies, particularly in those where Muslim culture has left its mark, women are relegated to the background. He criticizes traditional education which is shown to encourage a blind submissiveness and passive docility in women:

> Like all the women of these parts, Ngoné War Thiandum had her place in society, a society sustained by maxims, wise sayings and recommendations of passive docility; woman this, woman that, fidelity, unlimited devotion and total submission of body and soul to the husband who was her master after Yallah, so that he might intercede in her favour for a place in paradise. The woman found herself a listener. Outside her domestic tasks she was never given the opportunity to express her point of view, to state her opinion. She had to listen and carry out what her husband said.[3]

Some women like Ngoné War Thiandum, living in an atmosphere saturated with outdated ideas, cannot see things objectively. Years of physical and moral submission have blurred their reasoning faculty. When illumination comes the reaction is volcanic. In *L'Harmattan* there is the unparalleled outburst of Ouhigoué against the brutality of her tyrannical husband. The crucial scene in which her smouldering revolt blazes out constitutes an expression of her self-awakening, of her will to resist alienation. We find an echo of this unleashing of bitter indignation and open rebellion in 'Ses Trois Jours' in *Voltaïque*. Exasperated by protracted hours of weary vigil and expectation, humiliated and hurt, Noumbé gives vent to her repressed anger. In the dramatic final scene she gives a cold welcome to her callous, stone-hearted husband. This short story, which recalls the satirical vein of Montesquieu's *Lettres persanes*, exposes the moral tortures of some Muslim wives subjugated to the implacable laws of polygamy.

Changes in social structures and in attitudes are necessary if the African woman is to free herself and realize her potential. Agnès,

142

in *O pays*, suggests that better economic conditions, the elimination of ignorance and of mass illiteracy will inevitably improve the status of the African woman. Ousmane, perhaps more than any other African novelist, gives a privileged and dynamic role to women. The most striking example in this respect is provided by *God's Bits of Wood* in which women constitute a catalytic element and take an active part in the demonstrations of the railworkers during the strike. Full of buoyancy and in an unbending determination to ensure the success of the strike, they trek from Thiès to Dakar. Their relentless efforts and unflinching moral support eventually force the men to change their traditional attitude towards women.

Ousmane, as a keen observer and critic of society, stresses the need to break with those African customs which retard progress. He crusades against social parasitism. In *The Money-Order* he focuses attention on the degenerate state of African social customs and throws more light on the perennial conflict between traditional and modern ways of life. Witness the bitter remark of a character who measures the divorce between the past and the present: 'I am afraid times are hard. Life isn't what it used to be. You can't count on your neighbours any more. Nowadays, everyone looks after himself.'[4] Communal living has become debased by new economic structures, the introduction of the monetary system and rapid urbanization, which have given birth to parasitism. *The Money-Order* draws an intimate but disenchanted picture of Dakar: it shows how individuals motivated by need and self-interest can reduce a man to a state of destitution by playing upon the laws of the extended family system, fraternity and mutual assistance.

In the milieu depicted by this short story, everyone is aware of the slightest movement of others; consequently, social life easily engenders suspicion and distrust. This is one of the reasons why Dieng, whose generosity is proverbial, says it is imprudent to talk about money on the street. He adds: 'Now the whole quarter will know that I've had a money-order.'[5] Indeed, the jobless father of nine children gains a higher status because he has received a money-order on which the whole quarter builds its hopes. The news spreads far and wide, facts are distorted, the whole community becomes excited and pours into the household, assailing Dieng with interminable solicitations. This makes Mety say with an acid note, 'Parasites! As soon as they hear someone has money, there they are like vultures'.[6] It is deplorable that after Dieng's untold suffering at the photographer's everyone apparently rejoices complacently about his vicissitudes: 'For several days, the Dieng family had been observed: everyone, deep down,

143

wished them ill without admitting it to themselves'.[7] Bewildered, shattered, crushed by obscure forces, Dieng resigns himself to fate; he distributes desperately the sack of rice given to him by the unscrupulous Mbaye as a compensation for his stolen money. The behaviour of the common people can be explained by the fact that they live in a prosaic world, in a *cul-de-sac*. Poverty reduces them to a state of total abjection.

Ousmane acutely and sincerely examines both traditional and modern African society and insists on the necessity of adapting traditional customs or structures to the needs of a fast-changing world. While waging war against what Fanon termed 'sterilizing traditions', Ousmane is highly critical of the new breed of political leaders who are indifferent to the endemic poverty of the masses; he denounces their corruption, their incompetence, their lack of devotion to the people, their complicity with foreign powers. In *The Money-Order* he satirizes the complicated administrative system which defies the illiterate masses. Dieng has to go through intricate procedures to cash his money-order; he inevitably becomes a victim of incongruous incidents, of unpredictable short circuits. His misfortunes are due to the inefficiencies of an administrative mechanism inherited from the colonial system. Some disillusioned characters realize that independence, paradoxically, has not changed the old situation. They have been fed on slogans, on unfulfilled electoral promises. Indeed, independence has seen the birth of a privileged caste, which has become an instrument of oppression and of shameless exploitation of the proletariat.

Political leaders who place personal above national interest are criticized for wallowing in opulence instead of alleviating the sufferings of the masses. They make no positive efforts to bridge the gap between the rich and the poor. In this respect *Le Docker Noir* constitutes a pitiless indictment of the profiteering leaders who enrich themselves fraudulently and live in an artificial paradise. Lèye, the journalist and poet in *L'Harmattan*, stigmatizes in a biting article the ministers who squander public funds in order to satisfy their taste for luxury and ostentation. We find the same satirical mode and caustic virulence in *God's Bits of Wood*, where Bakayoko castigates the unscrupulous parliamentarians. The short story 'Prise de Conscience' illustrates vividly the cynicism and *embourgeoisement* of the 'parvenus'. Ibra, regarded as 'the hope of the working class', fights for equal pay for black and for white workers, but as soon as he is elected deputy he amasses wealth and private property in dubious ways. His secret aspirations fulfilled, he breaks his links with the proletariat and becomes deaf to their grievances. His nonchalant attitude makes one of his former companions remark with acrimony: 'People like this don't have anything in common with us! They are black on the surface . . . . Inside they are like colonialism.'[8]

The ruling class is also criticized for being a tool of imperialism. *L'Harmattan* offers concrete examples. During the Referendum of 1958, Tamban Youssido, the President/Prime-Minister, under the pretext that Africans are incapable of controlling their political destiny, encourages the population to vote in favour of the continuation of colonial rule. He rejects independence and dignity, thus perpetuating the state of bondage, and attempts to discredit the young militant nationalists as being extremists 'intoxicated by communism'. To justify his compromise with the colonial regime, he stresses the country's apparent economic weakness. In the same novel, Lèye makes a sharp criticism of certain black parliamentarians for dancing to the imperialists' tune during the debate on the Algerian question and the participation of young Africans in the Indo-China War. He attacks Tamban Youssido, the black deputy in the French National Assembly, for compromising his position.

Undoubtedly, as he intimates in the preface to *L'Harmattan*, Ousmane sees himself as an awakener of the people's conscience, performing the same role as the *griot* in pre-colonial Africa. Not only does he concentrate on the negative aspects of the African scene, he also wages war against economic, political and cultural alienation. His protagonists undertake a search for an African identity. They realize that 'in countries placed under foreign domination, individuals gradually lose their creative force and from generation to generation their energy diminishes'.[9] They propound salvation through revolutionary action; their prime objective is to liberate the people from exploitation and alienation, and to fight for collective dignity.

In their quest for identity, the chief characters struggle for economic, political and cultural emancipation. It is in this perspective that *O pays, mon beau peuple*! seeks an economic revolution with the ultimate objective of rehabilitating the alienated village community. The novel relates the singular experience of a young, resourceful, Marxist-oriented Casamancian who, motivated primarily by the pursuit of an African identity, by an overflowing love for his people, conceives and puts into practice a bold plan for an agrarian revolution. The fusion between Oumar and the soil is striking: enchanted by the secret forces of the land, he establishes physical, mystical and spiritual ties with nature. In a moment of exhilaration he tastes a piece of earth, a gesture which could be interpreted as total identification and communion with the motherland. It is worth noting that the hero's deep-rooted, inviolable attachment to the land is the expression of an ideological commitment: it translates his ardent search for identity, for a protective mother, symbolized by his country. He embodies '*l'inconscient collectif*'.

In order to realize his dreams of economic emancipation Oumar introduces modern techniques of farming and plans the creation of agricultural co-operatives. He is disenchanted with the foreign commercial companies who, thanks to the colonial structure, buy agricultural products at absurdly low prices and resell them eventually at exorbitant prices. It is to put an end to such economic exploitation that Oumar wishes to live for a hundred years. But his promethean enterprise of rehabilitating the community is ill-fated, for he has to fight against conservatism and indifference on the one hand, and foreign domination on the other. As the big companies dread competition and are highly apprehensive of Oumar's projects, they make him a victim of their infernal machinations. The protagonist's fate is a collective tragedy; it could be interpreted as the inability of the colonized to win their freedom and assume their destiny in a country where all the initiatives are left to foreigners who control the people's social evolution; or again, it could be interpreted as a sacrifice to achieve national consciousness. He becomes a collective *persona* and lives beyond the grave. The village community worships this man of initiation like an illustrious ancestor or a legendary hero.

Thus, *O pays* expresses the lyricism and violence of the secret aspirations of the colonized. It is an important stage in the African Odyssey, for it is illusory to believe that there can be real independence without economic emancipation. The search for identity reaches new dimensions in Ousmane's fourth novel. *L'Harmattan* is a continuation of the 'Quest for the Grail' undertaken by Oumar Faye; it answers the question of lack of political consciousness raised by Dr. Joseph in *O pays*. Just as Oumar fought against overwhelming odds to show the peasant farmers that agricultural development is a means of ameliorating their social and economic condition, the militants in *L'Harmattan* deploy their efforts to arouse a spirit of national consciousness.

Ousmane draws his inspiration from an historical event. The novel evokes the *ambiance* of the Gaullist constitutional referendum of 28 September 1958 which offered the Africans under French rule the opportunity to decide their future political status. The population is thrown into a dilemma over the choice between freedom with all its consequences and the perpetuation of colonial status by association with the 'Métropole'. It is revealing that the author does not limit the struggle to a particular country: to give coherence and a continental breadth to the epic struggle for political identity, he harmonizes and amalgamates the characteristic features of the various geographical areas and creates a unity of place by situating the action in an imaginary, anonymous country. This technique abolishes the arbitrary and artificial boundaries which divide the different countries. It is significant that the young radicals who incarnate the forces of unification and resistance to foreign domination are drawn from different regions. Thus the novel can be considered as the literary expression of continental patriotism. Ousmane has attempted to realize, on the literary plane, the ideal of Pan-Africanism.

L'Harmattan, which is interesting as an historical and social document, paints a relatively objective picture of the political manoeuvres mounted against the nationalists: it depicts the atmosphere of insecurity and the tense psychological climate characterized by ruthless repression and intimidation of the masses. The local government, with the complicity of the colonial authorities, has recourse to diverse tactics: it mobilizes the customary chiefs to persuade the people to vote in favour of continued French domination and reverts to corrupting the people. The entire procedure is a mockery of democracy. Freedom of movement, of speech, of assembly is abolished. Consequently, the revolutionary group is isolated from the masses and suffers set-backs; its defeat becomes imminent. Discouraged by the overwhelming victory of their adversaries, the members of the Liberation Front realize the urgent need to educate the masses, who know nothing about politics and are ignorant both of the implications of the Referendum and of the meaning of independence. After their defeat, some of the militants leave for Guinea, 'the Promised Land', which had voted in favour of independence; others, in their unflagging devotion to the common cause, stay, convinced that only unswerving struggle will restore the people's dignity and rehabilitate the past.

Ousmane's imaginative world revolves around the search for an African identity. His main characters fight not only for political and economic independence but also for cultural and linguistic identity. They deplore the up-rooting of African culture by centuries of colonial domination. As Bouki suggests in *Le Docker Noir*, to rehabilitate the cultural patrimony it is essential to preserve the positive values which are fast crumbling and to eliminate those aspects of the culture which inhibit progress. But the preservation of a culture demands the promotion of a national language.

A language identifies a homogeneous social group and constitutes a corner-stone of a people's culture. Literature—a crystallization of the emotions, experiences, joys, sufferings, hopes and aspirations of a people—forms an integral part of a national culture. A genuine African rebirth requires the development of indigenous, national languages—for it is paradoxical that Africans who advocate a cultural revival should write in the languages of their erstwhile dominators. Even old Niakoro, in *God's Bits of Wood*, is conscious of this problem. That is why she deplores the neglect of African languages, adding that the enthusiasm the young show in learning the white man's language generates their inferiority complex and contributes to their cultural alienation. In *L'Harmattan* Ousmane condemns the colonial educational system which expressly forbade Africans to use their mother-tongue, even outside the walls of the school or at home. In the same novel, Lèye, a fervent nationalist, artist and renowned poet who suffers from 'linguistic orphanage', revolts against the use of French as a medium of literary expression. His frustration and psychological conflict culminate in his decision to renounce writing in French: writing in French enriches 'a foreign language. A language which is not that of the people!'[10] He prefers painting and drawing, by virtue of their universality, and he translates his poems into several African languages.

Although Lèye's situation may seem dramatic, it exemplifies the cruel dilemma that confronts many African writers. A striking parallel could be drawn between Lèye and his creator: like him, Ousmane deplores writing in a foreign language inaccessible to the great majority of the people. He confessed in an interview that he does not have a mastery of his mother-tongue and that he also feels frustrated when he writes in French. Just as Lèye resorts to graphic art, Ousmane turns to cinema and is making a laudable effort by using African languages in his films. Thus, the incessant war he wages in his novels against social ills, against political, economic and cultural alienation, is prolonged on the screen and his 'message' is communicated to the people.

Social commitment animates Ousmane's imaginative world. His films and fiction do not offer an idealized image of the African scene. He depicts African society with its explosions of revolt and sufferings, with its great expectations and joy of life.

148

1. Sembène Ousmane, *Le Docker Noir* (Paris: Nouvelles Editions Debresse, 1956) p. 152.
2. *L'Harmattan, Livre I: Référendum* (Paris: Présence Africaine, 1964), p. 137.
3. *Vehi-Ciosane ou Blanche de la Genèse* with *Le Mandat* (Paris: Présence Africaine, 1965). Translated by Clive Wake as *The Money-Order* with *White Genesis* (London: Heinemann, 1972), pp. 14-15.
4. *The Money Order*, p. 108.
5. *Ibid.*, p. 81.
6. *Ibid.*, p. 92.
7. *Ibid.*, p. 119.
8. *Voltaique* (Paris: Présence Africaine, 1962), p. 34.
9. *O pays, mon beau peuple!* (Paris: Le livre contemporain, Amiot-Dumont, 1957), p. 94.
10. *L'Harmattan*, p. 135.

12

Chinua Achebe

by
M. J. C. ECHERUO

The Title Poem of Chinua Achebe's only book of verse, *Beware, Soul Brother*[1], acknowledges that 'we are the men of soul'.

> . . .we measure out
> our joys and agonies
> too, our long, long passion week
> in paces of the dance.

But Achebe recognizes the danger in that characterization, especially if as a result we become forgetful of what he calls 'the lures of ascension day',

> the day of soporific levitation
> on high winds of skysong.

Achebe compares his generation of dancers and poets with their ancestors who never forgot this:

> . . .they understood
> so well these hard-headed
> men of departed dance where a man's
> foot must return whatever beauties
> it may weave in air
> where it must return for safety
> and renewal of strength.

It is to this Earth—which our fathers called Ala, patroness of the arts—that Achebe asks all fellow African artists (his 'soul brothers') to dedicate themselves, for it is to this 'patrimony' that they and their children have to return

. . .when the song
is finished and the dancers disperse
. . .

for they [your children] in their time will want
a place for their feet when
they come of age and the dance
of the future is born
for them.

Here then is a direct statement of the ultimate concern of Achebe's work. Behind his novels, short stories and poems there is this immense presence of a patrimony, a land, a people, a way of life. But while characterizing that land, detailing the history of its many crises, Achebe sees it as the one unchanging feature of the artistic and moral landscape, as the one permanent Being to which all the efforts of the children of the land must be devoted. If we recognize this, we can then appreciate why Achebe is not the urban African, why his art is not the art of the metropolis. Rather Achebe is the artist in the traditional communal sense of the term, the man of great wisdom, working within the limits and through the norms of his society. His 'truth', therefore, depends as much on the immediacy and the integrity of his society as on the universality of his own personal vision. That is to say, without that inner communal conscience—the ultimate veracity of his understanding of Igbo society and of the traumas and conflicts it has experienced—Achebe would have had no worthwhile truth to relate, no essential theme to express.

Achebe's is both an absolute achievement and an achievement in context. It is absolute in the sense that his novels demonstrate that it is possible for a writer with his roots firmly planted in the local African soil and writing in a foreign language to produce work that is authentic as regards local colour and universal in terms of the humanity and the empathy that informs it. It is an achievement in context in the sense that this fiction is both a rejection of some traditions of fiction which preceded it and a fulfilment of others. For example, Achebe's novels constitute a firm rejection of the tradition of the white man's novel of Africa, the kind of fiction—no doubt, powerful in its own way—that responds to Africa from the superior and condescending distance of the Government Hill or the Mission Station, or the kind that regards Africa as the fitting locale for the dramatization of spiritual and metaphysical conflicts of relevance only to the foreign conscience contemplating Africa.

Achebe's novels are part of a tradition whose roots are to be found in every African nation that has had to seek its own fulfilment in cultural nationalism, or else in the rejection of the supposedly redemptory significance of white colonial contact. This tradition of fiction was essentially one of self-recognition and understanding. It included both those novels based on folk-tales and folk manners and the Onitsha-market kind of fiction of social realism which served as a record of the changing contemporary world.

Achebe fulfilled this tradition of fiction in two ways. First, he chose to use a form of English which, without embarrassment or hesitation, reflected the rhetorical genius of his people, the ultimately untranslatable expression of their native Igbo civilization. Indeed, Achebe's rhetorical strength lies in the ease of his performance, the total absence of a straining after an effect or a manner. It is as if, because he is completely aware of his hearers and understands them thoroughly, he can afford to devote his energies fully to his art, that is to the modulation of his effects and to the establishment of his meaning. Achebe can do this, too, because he has the necessary scope, the range of English registers to allow him to adapt the language to several uses. Achebe thus makes the best of his two worlds, and it is refreshing when one sees it in this way, to recall that casual remark of his about the language of his fiction: 'I have been given this language [English] and I intend to use it'.[2] It is in this use—the range, and subtlety, the variation of word, phrase and structure—in this creative use of both *cliché* and idiom that Achebe shows how to triumph over the problem of language.

Achebe fulfilled this tradition of fiction in a second, and perhaps more important, way: he provides a cosmos, a world with physical, moral and human dimensions into which the specific tale or event can be placed and understood. He thus succeeds in making true 'villagers' of his readers and thereby reminds them that, surrounding the otherwise simple story of Okonkwo's suicide, Obi's disgrace or Ezeulu's agony, is a coherent and full, even if changing, civilization.

Things Fall Apart (1958), his first novel, was the first full-fledged indication of this talent, though the earlier short stories did occasionally point to a sense of irony, an awareness of the complexity of the human and moral problems underlying the specific examples of parental solicitude and communal tyranny. The title of the novel seemed, of course, to place it squarely in the tradition of the novels of culture conflict, which explains why it appeared to its first readers as a study primarily in the effects of European culture on Igbo society. In fact, as is becoming apparent from closer study, Achebe was doing more than that. He was anxious to demonstrate that our very troubled present and anxious future could best be understood by looking at the experiences through which the African has passed in the last century. Those experiences included contact with Europe, and Achebe clearly sees this contact as crucial; but he is equally concerned with recording the world-view—the mores, codes, attitudes—which shaped men's response not only to colonialism but to life itself.

Historically, therefore, the action of *Things Fall Apart* (and *Arrow of God*) belongs to the first phases of colonial contact with Igboland. Philosophically, the two novels point to the eternal constant that is part of Igbo life before and since the colonial experience. The hero of the novel, Okonkwo, is a man 'well-known through the nine villages and even beyond'. But he is a fated man, in a sense, because he had, they said, a 'bad *chi*' inherited from his father Unoka. He too, 'had a bad *chi* or personal god, and evil fortune followed him to the grave, or rather to his death, for he had no grave. He died of the swelling which was an abomination to the earth goddess.' Such was Unoka's fate, and such the coherent world which his son Okonkwo was to inherit. Okonkwo's fate might have been the same—fatal, final and unambiguous. In fact, it is not. What *Things Fall Apart* reveals, in the process, is the uncertainty of values in the ensuing world; the beginning of the disintegration of the original coherence.

To the extent that the novels, as Achebe himself has said, seek to argue that the African past—'with all its imperfections —was not one long night of savagery from which the first Europeans acting on God's behalf delivered them',[3] they, of course, imply a celebration of that past, or more exactly, they affirm the existence of a past, the same past that most of the other Igbo novelists also record. The difference is in 'Achebe's philosophical stance, his insistence that this past is part and parcel of our present and already a predeterminant of our future. It is a tragic view of life which is deliberately meant to deny us a catharsis. Okonkwo, the hero of *Things Fall Apart*, is fit subject for tragedy because he looked life in the face and did what he thought was right. But he is destroyed in the process, and Achebe deliberately lets the District Commissioner decide to allot to him an untidy and insignificant place in the official history of the times: 'not a whole chapter' he says, 'but a reasonable paragraph'.

No Longer at Ease (1960) has basically the same kind of tragic denouement, only in a context of changed external circumstances. In the earlier novel, Achebe made the final conflicts violent and even bloody, beginning with the death of Ikemefuna and ending with the murder of the messengers and Okonkwo's eventual suicide. In *No Longer At Ease*, violence is totally excluded and the conflict is now shown through spiritual agony within the hero—or rather the non-hero, the 'beast of no nation', as he is called by one of the out-patients outside the Lagos General Hospital. Obi's tragedy is that of a man caught between an ideal in which he believes and a reality which impels him to compromise that ideal; between an independence of mind and purse which only can secure his identity and a sense of tradition and of communal responsibility which constantly rebukes him. In *Things Fall Apart*, the fact of Okonkwo's bad *chi* is faced directly by both novelist and the world of the novel. In *No Longer At Ease*, because *chi* is, in a sense, only part of the new world of Lagos, fate is behind all the action but is never fully faced. Only close to the end of the novel, following the death of Obi's mother, does Achebe remind us of this fact. 'You see this thing called blood. There is nothing like it. That is why when you plant a yam it produces another yam, and if you plant an orange it bears oranges. . . . A man may go to England, become a lawyer or a doctor, but it does not change his blood.'

It is this argument that is hinted at so beautifully in the scene in *No Longer At Ease* where the people of Umuofia resident in Lagos pay Obi a formal visit of condolence. According to the tale being told by one of them, the tortoise, in order to escape the burden of his mother's funeral, went on a journey and left word that he should not be recalled 'unless something new under the sun happened'. His mother died—which is nothing new under the sun—but to bring him home, word was sent that his 'father's palm tree had borne a fruit at the end of its leaf'. The sense of guilt which Obi felt after overhearing this story marked the turning point in his career. As the guilt about his neglect of his mother wore away, however, Obi felt a new sense of self. He, too, the idealist in him, 'had died'. There is no place for idealists to stand in order to move the earth. 'We all have to stand on the earth itself and go with her pace. The most horrible sight in the world cannot put out the eye. The death of a mother is not like a palm tree fruit at the end of its leaf, no matter how much we want to make it so'.

Ironically this new peace was his doom, for immediately after this passage, Achebe shows Obi accepting his first bribe and seducing his first candidate for a scholarship. The only evidence left of his former idealism is a muttered admission when he woke up with a start in the middle of the night: 'Terrible. . .This is terrible'. No one else knew

154

that these changes had taken place in Obi. As the novel says at its close: 'Everybody wondered why'. To the extent that *No Longer at Ease* assumes the existence of *Things Fall Apart*, its conception of tragedy includes an unavoidable continuity of family (or communal) and individual life. Hence the functional significance of the non-violent nature of *No Longer at Ease*. As Obi explains to the interviewing panel, the experience of tragedy is like that of 'an old man in my village, a Christian convert, who suffered one calamity after another. He said life was like a bowl of wormwood which one sips a little at a time world without end. He understood the nature of tragedy.'

Achebe once said that his aims in fiction and the 'deepest aspirations' of his society 'meet'. 'For no thinking African can escape the pain of the wound in our soul.' It would seem that his insistence on the conflicts and paradoxes of his world is to delineate its pride and integrity. Achebe makes this point with passion and conviction in his third novel, *Arrow of God* (1964), a novel about the death-throes of an age. It is a novel of great fear and great tenderness. Achebe achieves this through a carefully worked out demonstration of the disparity between Ezeulu's sense of the values of his world and the facetious and uncomprehending view of them held by the District Commissioner, Captain Winterbottom. As far as the District Commissioner can tell, the events of which the novel is a record, relate to some petty 'feud' over a piece of land, a feud 'made worse by the fact that Okperi welcomed missionaries and government while Umuaro on the other hand, has remained backward'.

In fact, we know that we are watching the turning-point in the history of a people, the moment when their chief priest, Eze-Ulu, and the god he serves and which protects the town, yield to the disruptive force of Christianity and British colonial administration. The novel describes this moment through an account of the career of Ezeulu, spokesman of the god, guardian of his people; a man shaped by the requirements of his sacred calling and by the same self-pride and worship of strength which brought disaster and shame to Okonkwo in *Things Fall Apart*. This disparity between his and Winterbottom's interpretation of history is not Achebe's theme; but Achebe uses it to establish the immensity of Ezeulu's responsibilities in the community, to establish the dimensions of his tragedy and that of his people. What the novel asserts at the end is the sanctity and the precariousness of his office—hence the title of the novel. In the tragic humiliation of the last scenes of the novel, Ezeulu is allowed to live out his last days, as the novel says, 'in the haughty splendour of a demented highpriest', since his god had, as it were, chosen 'to strike him down and cover him with mud' and then taken sides with his enemies against the chief priest. 'What could it point to but the collapse of all things?'

It is a heavily ironic yet sympathetic conclusion. By it, we are made all the more aware of Achebe's purpose: to portray a past that is only a moment, though a revealing moment, in the continuing history of a people; a full past that is still very much part of their being now and from which they should expect guidance in coming to terms with the future. Achebe offers no simple explanation for Ezeulu's fate. He leaves us with the terrible truth of his hero and his ambiguous fate, allows this priest that heart-rending final soliloquy on his disaster, and concludes in his authorial voice with a rather ominous reservation: 'In destroying his priest he had also brought disaster on himself, like the lizard in the fable who ruined his mother's funeral by his own hand.'

This might be thought an inconclusive ending to a story which seemed to demand a final and vigorous termination. In fact, it is typical of Achebe to end his novels on just that note of doubt and hesitation, leaving us with the very strong sense of life, including national life, continuing in spite of the preceding events. These conclusions are, moreover, phrased in that allusive language of Igbo proverbs and so retain some of that prophetic stature which alone could redeem their assertions. In *No Longer At Ease*, it is the final and cynical truth that the death of one's mother is not quite the same kind of thing as finding one's father's palm tree bearing fruit at the end of its leaves. In *Arrow of God*, it is the vast claim that is, in its own way, true: 'that no man however great was greater than his people; that no man ever won judgment against his clan'.

The complexity of an Achebe novel derives from the various layers of association and cross-reference, from a tradition of story-telling which prides itself on economy, allusion and indirection. In retrospect, one can see how unique this style is. In Cyprian Ekwensi, for example, we do find traces of the traditional story-telling techniques which he adapted early to his use in *Ikolo, the Wrestler, and other Igbo Tales*. We can also see his interest in the narrative traditions of the nineteenth century European novel, in writers like Stendhal, Zola and the French Naturalists, including de Maupassant.[4] But Ekwensi was unable to impose enough discipline on himself as artist to become master of either tradition of story-telling.[5] It was Achebe, in fact, who first mastered both traditions. His short stories[6] showed how plot can be made to serve the purposes of both the traditional tale and the modern short story. The substance of his stories is practically the same as in Ekwensi's novels and his versions of the folk-tales. But Achebe's control of the pace of his story, his awareness of the reader as a collaborating but discriminating intelligence, and his shrewd sense of a literary style which could be both listened to and read, made him perhaps the simplest and still the most technically competent of Nigerian novelists. Commentators on Achebe's work have often recalled the self-admitted influence of Conrad and Joyce Cary but they have not as frequently also drawn attention to Achebe's interest in Chekhov — an interest which is revealing, in this connection, because it brings us back to the folk tradition of understatement and simplicity now acknowledged to be the hallmark of Achebe's art. Conrad and Cary provided a view of Africa which Achebe had ultimately to refute; Chekhov offered the example of kindred style in which sophistication was differentiated from mere technical experimentation.

Achebe uses the form of his novels to support his artistic vision. The plot of *Things Fall Apart* is linear and its conclusion almost melodramatic, as is appropriate to a story which the British District Commissioner believes is about 'this man who had killed a messenger and hanged himself'. But Achebe knows more than the officer; he preserves this simple plot and melodramatic conclusion, but so tells the actual story that we believe Obierika when he says to the District Commissioner: 'That man was one of the greatest men in Umuofia. You drove him to kill himself; and now he will be buried like a dog.' Quite as appropriately, too, *No Longer At Ease* has a circular and inclusive framework which begins in the court-room on the day of Obi's trial and ends in the same court with 'everybody wondering' at the causes of the hero's fall. 'The learned judge, as we have seen, could not comprehend how an educated man and so on and so forth. The British Council man, even the men of Umuofia, did not know.' *Arrow of God*, a much denser and more technically sophisticated novel than the two earlier novels, tells three stories in one integrated stride: the trials of Ezeulu, the disintegration of the indigenous political and religious order in Umuofia, and the establishment of British rule and the Christian religion.

Achebe's kind of technical sophistication, with its use of an omniscient, or rather anonymous, narrator, its use of long speeches (both direct and in paraphrase), of 'detailed and leisurely description of proceedings, even commonplace proceedings', its 'high mimetic' language — these may be said to belong to the tradition of the oral folk narrative, and especially to the heroic style so suited to the great

157

human events of which they tell.[7] It is equally important to add that though there are other Nigerian novelists who adopt an apparently identical style, they do not achieve a comparable sophistication because they do not also have our novelist's philosophic vision, his austere sense of the tragic irony of history and character.

This is especially evident in *Arrow of God* where Achebe chose for a hero a man who is the strongest exponent of tradition and at the same time the major instrument for the disintegration of that tradition. Ezeulu is that complex combination of pride, dignity and commitment which, given the times—'these are not the times we used to know'— could not but provoke confrontation and crisis. The novel is right, therefore, in drawing attention to Ezeulu's egotism and to the price he pays for it. But character and history are inseparable. Hence the novel is also careful to add that a 'deity who chose a time such as this' to abandon his chief priest was taking liberties. The crucial phrase is, of course, 'a time such as this'. It is a phrase echoed in one form or another throughout this novel and in the two earlier ones. The meaning of Achebe's novels depends as much on this sense of the 'times' as on the quality of his heroes.

Chinua Achebe was born in 1930 and grew up at a very crucial period in the definition of the intellectual and moral character of the modern Igboman. It was with his generation that the average Igbo boy of scant means was able to have university education and at home, too. That generation brought into the life of the Igbo intellectual a kind of exhilarating and refreshing humour formed from a combination of past and present. It was this generation that chose or learnt to face life with both innocence and shrewdness, with a jovial but serious attitude which enabled it to face modernity without anger and without equivocation. Achebe's first roots have to be sought in that milieu.

Achebe's work was also part of the Ibadan movement of the 1950s and 60s; though one should remember that Ibadan, then, was in fact, even if not in name, a colonial university. A popular joke among some of the expatriate lecturers in the Department of English following the enthusiasm generated by *Things Fall Apart* was about the imminence of a 'Chaucer to Chinua' English syllabus! But writing in the *Horn* in 1958 about the new poets publishing at Ibadan, one of the students, the poet J. P. Clark, pointed out that 'side by side with Black Nationalism, Black Culture is striving for a hearing. Great currents like Leopold Senghor and Diop, rivers like Achebe and Laye and others— oh, others — are flowing towards the great ocean of Négritude.' We do not now associate Achebe with Négritude; yet it is true that he and his generation felt a kinship with the leaders of that movement and considered themselves independent enough of Europe to feel able both to understand and to reject it.[8] At heart, then, these young men felt themselves to be a new people.

University College, Ibadan, inevitably became a venue where the brightest of the generation gathered for a four-year term of meditation; it also became the medium through which the idiom of the generation became that of the nation itself — a native idiom. Achebe belonged to a movement which University College, as an institution, did not initiate. If anything, it was by a technical accident that the University of Ibadan became the most important concentration of the best minds of the time reacting strongly and fervently against colonialism and finding fulfilment at that phase in the unity of African culture. It was in Achebe and his generation that the political agitations, the philosophical speculations, of the 1940s bore their first fruit, long before actual political independence in 1960.

There was, of course, very little correspondence of views between this new generation and the older politicians and leaders. Indeed, the estrangement between the politicians and the new generation was not a post-independence phenomenon. As Achebe's *A Man of the People* (1966) shows, it represented more than the reaction of the younger generation to the failure of the politicians to meet the promises and obligations of nationhood. It included the despair, which had set in as early as Mokwugo Okoye's *Vistas of Life,*[9] of the leadership maintaining the high goals of national politics prefigured in the nationalist movements of the 1940s.

One source of discontent was the struggle for power and wealth. In *Arrow of God* Ekemezie prophesies:

> Everything was good in its season, dancing in the season of dancing . . . leave dancing and join the race for the white-man's money . . . the race for the white-man's money would not wait till tomorrow or till we were ready to join . . . other people from every clan, some people we used to despise, they were now in high favour when our people did not even know that day had broken.

One consequence of this attitude towards power and wealth was estrangement between these leaders and that aware and articulate part of the population which was in a unique position to reject Ekemezie's contention. In actual political life, this led to that bitterness of the young Nigerian radicals like Mokwugo Okoye and Osita Agwuna,

159

to mention some names, who spoke scornfully of those 'prophets of yesterday'. This conflict between the two groups, which is central to the argument of *A Man of the People*, might have resolved itself differently, if the 'hybrid class of western educated and snobbish intellectuals', the Odili's, was itself as dedicated to its own goals as the politicians were to theirs, or as certain of its ideals.

A Man of the People is a story, then, of corruption in both the older and the younger generation as told by one of the second group who, unlike both Christopher and Obi of *No Longer At Ease*, has come to terms with his disenchantment and now uses it to some personal advantage. Like Chief Nanga, Odili is committed to both financial and political power; like Christopher, he believes in making the best of the situation of amorality which he has inherited. Like Obi, there is something of the idealist in him, or rather vestiges of the remembered idealism of his generation, though its ideological foundations are uncertain, as we discover in his arguments with Max. But unlike Obi, Odili has learnt to smother his conscience with his rhetoric and hide his own corruption and ambition behind the moralizing and highmindedness of the so-called new class.

By having the novel told in the first person, Achebe obviously succeeds in creating the necessary authenticity of narration which would give a further illusion of intimacy to the events being related. But this first-person narrative device also enables Achebe to avoid that interpretation of events in an authorial voice which could have been regarded as intrusive since it would have amounted to a condemnation of both Odili and Chief Nanga, and would, thus, have left him without a moral centre for his novel. The result of Achebe's choice of point-of-view — an important one because it is also a departure from that of his earlier novels — is, predictably, doubly ironic. As in Ford Madox Ford's *The Good Soldier* and in James Gould Cozzens's *By Love Possessed*, Achebe's narrator, without meaning to, implicates himself in the corruption which it was his primary purpose to expose in other people. Odili's comments on the military coup — that 'the Army obliged us by staging a coup at that point and locking up every member of the Government' — which has been regarded as simply 'prophetic',[10] is in fact deliberately cynical in the context of Odili's telling of the story. The catch is in the phrase 'obliged us'.

A Man of the People is not Achebe's best novel; it is certainly neither as strong as *Things Fall Apart*, as supple in its development as *No Longer at Ease*, nor as dense as *Arrow of God*. However, the explanation is not to be found, as one critic has suggested, in Achebe's supposedly explicit intention to 'teach' or to write 'applied art'[11] but in the moral character of the world of that novel, in the absence of a system of accepted values by which the character of Odili or of Chief Nanga can be evaluated independently of history. And Achebe allowed himself a cynicism which did not permit him to invent such values. Odili himself remarks in the novel that when 'in the affairs of the nation there was no owner, the laws of the village became powerless.' This is the very antithesis of the situation in Achebe's other novels.

In *Things Fall Apart*, we had the voice of the community, even if it is that of Obierika, still supreme as law or at least as 'conscience'. In *No Longer at Ease*, even when that traditional community is only represented by the Umuofia Union in Lagos — whose wisest member admits that 'when I return to Umuofia I cannot claim to be an old man. But here in Lagos, I am an old man to the rest of you' — yet the Union does act as though it constituted a link with a still existent past. In *Arrow of God*, we have the two strong but different voices of Akuebue and Nwaka and the neutral but triumphant voice of Ofoka. In *A Man of the People*, however, no such community exists; only what is now called a country, a geographical or administrative construct. Cynicism and opportunism, therefore, have no corrective force to check them, and the nation is now no more than several million Ekemezie's on Government Hill. The proverbs that appear in the novel, in fact, emphasize this change of circumstances. As Nanga puts it in one beautiful misapplication of a common proverb which he uses to show why the country's intellectuals should tolerate his corrupt style of leadership: 'If you respect today's kings, others will respect you when your turn comes'. Achebe's failure in *A Man of the People* was in allowing this cynicism to involve him, too.

Achebe's kind of disgust in *A Man of the People* and in his more recent short story, 'The Vengeful Creditor',[12] suggests that his kind of natural restraint has its limitations and is, in fact, alien to his real role as the communal artist. This cynicism may have been the price paid by Achebe and his generation. However, as he pointed out in 1967: '*A Man of the People* wasn't a flash in the pan. This is the beginning of a phase for me in which I intend to take a hard look at what we in Africa are making of independence .... Right now my interest is in politics or rather my interest in the novel is politics.'[13]

Since the end of the Nigerian Civil War, this interest in politics has become central to Achebe's thinking and has been reflected in all his critical statements. It is not, of course, a new interest; but the war sharpened his awareness of the centrality of politics, in the widest sense of that term, in human life and in the artist's consciousness: 'an African creative writer who tries to avoid the big social and political issues of contemporary Africa will end up being completely irrelevant— like that absurd man in the proverb who leaves his burning house to pursue a rat fleeing from the flames.'[14]

Given the pattern of Chinua Achebe's development as an artist and as conscience for his people, it would indeed be surprising— it would be doubly disappointing — if his next major work did not deal with that truly traumatic experience: The War. Reflecting on his earlier novels, Achebe once described his generation as 'a very fortunate' one in the sense that the past was 'still there', even if not 'in the same force'.[15] He *was* there when the Nigerian Civil War was fought; he saw it coming, left his post in Lagos as the Director of the External Service of the Nigerian Broadcasting Corporation to throw in his lot with others who felt like him. In circumstances, in fact, other than those now prevailing, he would have been known simply as an 'Igbo' novelist, or else as a 'Biafran' writer, as the man who in only four novels showed his people what their past was like, what stock the future held for them and with what kinds of wisdom to deal with that future. Today he is Nigeria's (and Africa's) foremost novelist, the man who created the heroes and the failures from whose experience the conscience of his adopted fatherland and his continent will, for a long time to come, mould their communal consciousness.

NOTES

1. *Beware, Soul Brother* (Enugu, Nigeria: Nwankwo-Ifejika, 1971).
2. See Gerald Moore, *The Chosen Tongue: English Writing in the Tropical World* (London: Longman, 1969), p. xxiii.
3. 'The Novelist as Teacher', quoted in John Press, ed., *Commonwealth Literature* (London: Heinemann, 1965), p. 204.
4. See Cyprian Ekwensi's contribution to *The Novel and Reality in Africa and America* (Lagos: United States Information Service, 1973), pp. 8-10.
5. E. Emenyonu, *Cyprian Ekwensi* (London: Evans, 1974), pp. 70-72 gives a brief discussion of the influence of Ekwensi's father on his short stories: 'a famed story-teller in his times . . . and still one of the most captivating oral performers of all times'. Emenyonu writes: 'Any one who sees him [Ekwensi's father] will agree with Cyprian Ekwensi that he has been striving for but "has never quite captured the humour of his father, nor the vigour of his stories" (p. 70).
6. First published in the University [of Ibadan] *Herald* (1958, 1959), collected with additions and an introduction by M. J. C. Echeruo in *The Sacrificial Egg*

and other short Stories (Onitsha, Etudo, 1962) and further revised with additions in *Girls at War* (London: Heinemann, 1972).

7. See H. M. and Nora K. Chadwick, *The Growth of Literature*, vol. III (Cambridge, 1940; reprinted 1968), pp. 750-772 for a discussion of 'Heroic Narrative Poetry'.

8. See, for example J. P. Clark's poem, 'Ivbie' in the original version published in *The Horn* (Ibadan, 1958) and the review of it (also in *The Horn*) by Obi Wali. The poem is the closest in Clark's work to the Francophone African poets and novelists in their handling of the theme of white exploitation and cultural arrogance.

9. Written in prison in 1950, revised with a Dedication in 1961 and published by the author in Enugu in 1962.

10. Adrian Roscoe, *Mother is Gold* (Cambridge: Cambridge University Press, 1971), p. 131 and Moore, *The Chosen Tongue*, p. 194.

11. Roscoe, pp. 129-131.

12. In *Okike*, no. 10 (Enugu, Nigeria, 1971), pp. 6-20.

13. In *Sunday Nation*, Nairobi, 15 January 1967, p. 15; quoted in Hans M. Zell and Helen Silver, *A Reader's Guide to African Literature* (London: Heinemann, 1972), p. 119.

14. 'The African Writer and the Biafran Cause', *Conch*, I, no. 1 (March 1969,) p. 8.

15. *Africa Report* (July 1964), pp. 19, 20.

163

13

Wilson Harris and the 'Guyanese Quartet'

by

LOUIS JAMES

In 1972, while teaching a course at the University of Texas, Wilson
Harris was asked his opinion of black studies. He replied that 'it seems
to me, under the pressure of events . . . obviously there will emerge
this concentration on black literature; it is something which sprang
out of a whole situation in which areas were eclipsed. But I feel myself
that these studies should lie on the threshold of a far deeper exploration
of creative issues.' It should bring into the deepest psychic relationship
the traditional and the modern. It should avoid the dangers of formul-
ating the past. 'Will the study of black literature consolidate the
manner of the ghetto,' he asked, 'or alter the texture of the ghetto in
our imagination?'[1] The importance of black literature — and he writes
particularly with reference to the Caribbean—is in its potential for
change. For 'the very barrenness of the West Indian world reveals
the necessity to examine closely the starting point of human societies.'[2]
And, again, 'What in my view is remarkable about the West Indian
in depth is a sense of subtle links, a series of subtle and nebulous links
which are latent within him, the latent ground of old and new person-
alities.' This makes possible a 'revolution' in the Caribbean novel,
based on *'fulfilment* rather than *consolidation.'*[3]

Of itself, this position is not new. Aimé Césaire raised the potent
phallus of Négritude against the creaking structures of French colonialism, and wrote his *Cahier* in a new form to express his new vision.
Senghor sang of New York with its 'artificial hearts' and rusting
'steel articulations', 'I say to New York, let the black blood flow into
your blood . . . like an oil of life.'[4] What is unique is Harris's particular
imaginative world, and the exhaustive experimentation with which
he has pursued his search for a transfigured literature.

Wilson Harris was born in 1921 in New Amsterdam on the Guyanese
coastland. He was educated at Queens College in Georgetown and

164

became, with A. J. Seymour and the other contributors to *Kyk-over-al* (1945-1961) — the pioneer Georgetown literary magazine — in the vanguard of the creation of a Guyanese literature. In the 1940s he worked as a surveyor deep in the jungles of the interior, and later became Government Senior Surveyor. Isolated in the forests, a sensitive point between the 'civilization' of the densely populated coastal plain and the settlers and Amerindians of the heartland, Harris experienced the mystical awareness of both place and people that haunts his writing. At the heart of his novels are instants in which a place or an individual, in the words of another mystic, Martin Buber, steps 'out of the incomprehensibility that lies to hand ... and becomes a presence'.[5] Such moments have for Harris a revolutionary significance. They change the identity of the observer, bringing him into a new dimension of being. They also change his awareness of the world beyond him, and open possibilities for experience and action. For this reason Harris sees art as at once private and profoundly social. As he wrote in *Fossil and Psyche* (1974), 'that potential for dialogue, for change, for the miracle of roots, for new community, is real, I believe, *and it deepens and heightens the role of imaginative literature to wrestle with categories and to visualise the birth of community as other than the animism of fate.*'[6]

To find clues to new forms of writing, Harris ransacked such disparate areas as history and magic, anthropology and psychology. In Haitian *vodun*, for instance, 'one of the surviving primitive dances of human sacrifice', the initiate has a moment when 'one leg is drawn up into the womb of space', as the interior space of her trance overlaps with exterior reality, and she becomes a 'dramatic agent of the subconsciousness'.[7] Harris's novels constantly explore ways in which to 'dramatize' the interaction of dimensions of existence. On the other hand he has been influenced by an arcane Renaissance science such as Giordano Bruno's 'Art of Memory', in which by ordering all of creation into the form of a 'theatre' of being, the magician had power over the elements. It has clear affinities with Jung's theory of the 'collective unconscious' and with psychoanalysis. For Harris this becomes an expression of the way the individual, by ordering into a 'theatre' the deepest levels of his reality, discovers the magical transformation of experience and self. It is a recurring theme, in particular, in his novel *Tumatumari* (1968).[8]

Concerned with inward experience, his novels are liberated from 'clock' time and geographical space, and are free to weave between levels of reality in search of the deeper meaning that unites them. Similarly, his characters shift, alter and merge, explore psychological or mythical truths, within the total significance of the book. The changes are directed by a subtly controlled style, which can move from intense lyricism to earthy realism. At first this may be confusing to the reader. But the novels all have in fact a firmly located geographical and social world, and a distinctive imaginative perspective. Their concern to 'abstract' inner realities brings, them closer to poetry or modern painting than to the conventional novel. Indeed, I have never met a painter who found Harris 'difficult'.

To date, Harris has written some twelve novels, making him the most consistently creative writer in the Caribbean area. Because of limitations of space, I can here only examine his first four novels, the 'Guyanese Quartet', which still provide the most vivid introduction to his work. While each can be read separately, together they make a systematic exploration of various aspects of Guyanese life, an orchestration of what Dr. Michael Gilkes has called the 'Caribbean syzygy', the state of inner division brought about by its traumas of history, and the possibilities for integration.[9]

Palace of the Peacock (1960) leads us to the art of the colonialist era, and the crisis of community that it posed. Donne — his name suggesting the sixteenth century period of conquest — is a figure of the cruellest domination. He is hard and inhuman. But Harris also presents him as the inevitable product of his era — in a violent age 'one has to be a devil to survive'. At a deeper level, he expresses the inhumanity necessary to the maintenance of order. He is 'midwife, yes, doctor, yes, gaoler, judge, hangman, everything to the labouring people'. But colonialism is a dead end. Mariella, the peasant girl he has exploited and beaten, shoots Donne dead from his horse. The death, in a book freed from the usual limitations of time, is not the end but a beginning. The Elizabethan poet John Donne was a man of two worlds—the passionate worldly Donne of the love poems, and the saint and mystic who wrote the *Holy Sonnets*. *Palace* describes the unifying of the spiritual Donne—who becomes the narrator—with the wordly Donne. The shot awakes the idealist alter ego 'from heaven', and he takes his place beside Donne the exploiter. But idealism is equally inadequate in the hard, material world. Through a long, hard process the perspectives must be modified both into each other and into the wider community of the peoples of Guyana.

The image of their quest is a dangerous expedition upstream to find the legendary city of gold—El Dorado, the 'Palace of the Peacock'—and the aboriginal peoples of the interior. The image is a perfect one to express the ambivalence of the colonial adventure.

Harris has written elsewhere of the 'open myth of El Dorado', that 'an instinctive idealism associated with this adventure was overpowered by enormous greed, cruelty and exploitation'.[10] The first stage beyond the deadlock of exploitation is to see beyond the individual to the community. Into focus come the crew, embodying at once the mixed races of Guyana, and their particular contributions to the spirit of the community: Jennings, the tough 'republican' engineer, African; Vigilance, the spiritually watchful helmsman, Indian; Schomberg, half Arawak Indian, half German; Carroll, musician, African—and so forth.

As Donne's consciousness changes, so the object of his passion alters from Mariella as a peasant girl to Mariella a mission station, a settlement and a meeting point, up the river. The identities of dreamer and man of action begin to unite. The 'dreamer' has a vision in the morning light which merges a shifting log in the fire with a camp dog which stands over him. It becomes the 'nightmare' image of Donne's horse in the opening scene. Called on to take Donne's place 'I sat bolt upright in my hammock, shouting aloud that the devil himself must fondle and mount this muse of hell and this hag, sinking back instantly, a dead man in his bed come to an involuntary climax. The vaguest fire and warmth came like a bullet, flooding me . . .'. This extraordinary scene at once invokes the experience of Donne, with its power, violence and sex, and at the same time distances it in its lonely desolation. After this empathetic vision the dreamer understands 'for manhood's sake and estate I saw there must arise the devil of resistance and incredulity' to a fallen world. Donne the realist speaks of 'not being so beastly and involved in my own devil's schemes any more'. But neither can yet surmount the final barrier, 'fear of acknowledging the true substance of life.'

Moving up river they pass beyond the era of settlement to the aboriginal culture of the interior. In their boat appears an Arawak woman. Bearing the mysterious stillness of the primeval, she arouses in the crew an agony of self-evaluation and self-knowledge. This is expressed in the image of a frightful rapid, and, magically, Harris combines the Arawak woman with the raging water. 'Tiny embroideries resembling the handiwork on the Arawak woman's kerchief and the wrinkles on her brow turned to incredible and fast soundless breakers of foam. Her crumpled bosom and river grew agitated with desire, bottling and shaking every fear and inhibition and outcry.'

The rapids are 'the straits of memory', the turning point into recognition and fulfilment. And as the crew first came into focus in response to the quest for communal knowledge, now that the knowledge is

167

achieved, they can die into the totality of the reader's awareness. Carroll, expressing the harmony of the created world, is the first to go, to be heard again at the end filling the universe with his music. The story tells now of the seven days of re-creation into ultimate reality. The onward motion of the book is literally suspended—the travellers climb a vertical waterfall, an image reflecting the hanging moment at the beginning of Donne shot and about to fall in death. Only Donne and Vigilance are left. As they climb, the rocks become windows onto creation, the transfigured world of the mystic visionary. Donne is united completely with the dreamer, and he and the crew are also one.

This summary can do little to suggest the full impact and significance of the book; through its imaginative structure Harris literally changes our awareness of the realities he is describing. The opening sections are terse and epigrammatic. By the end the descriptions are in the forms of symbolist vision. The 'dense dreaming jungle and forest' becomes 'Tall trees with black marching boots were clad in the spurs and sharp wings of a butterfly.' Individuality disappears in 'the sacrament' of 'one undying soul'. It is a daring vision to set against the trauma of colonialism. Many would feel that it is too extreme to be socially relevant to an emergent nation.

As if in answer to this criticism, the following novel, *The Far Journey of Oudin* (1961), is low-key in subject and in style. Instead of the interior forests Harris focuses on the savannah, rice paddies and bush of the coastal strip, the four per cent of Guyana in which ninety per cent of its people live. The characters are of East Indian origin, the race making up some fifty per cent of the population. As V. S. Naipaul's *A House for Mr. Biswas* (1961) showed the disintegration of the Tulsi family in Trinidad away from the religious and cultural support of India, so Harris's novel plots the decay of a Muslim family, in particular the brothers Mahommed, Kaiser and Hassan, their cousin Rajah, and his daughter Beti. The erosion starts when the brothers plot to frustrate their father's will to leave his property to a love-child conceived out of wedlock. 'Something small and secure had been broken beyond repair. It was a unity of faith and family.' None of the brothers gain materially from the property. Mahommed in particular loses his power of will. The dissolution is both that of the family and that of a Guyana turning to modern ways with 'their partial neglect of the land . . . their disfiguring vulgar quest for new ways of making money, the new dreaming architecture and house, the acquisition of sordid power.'

The identity of the rejected love-child is deliberately kept uncertain. Harris characteristically keeps literal relationships indefinite in order to explore deeper psychic links. But spiritually, and perhaps by blood, this is Oudin, whom the beggar Mahommed takes on as a cowherd. Watching Oudin, Mahommed shivers. 'Certainly this was not *Oudin*. . . The man he beheld on the road, who looked like the spirit of Oudin— was his half-brother.'

Unknown to him, Oudin has been sent by Ram, capitalist and money-lender. Ram is the spirit of the new commercial Guyana, despoiling the peasants. Oudin is the exploited worker. Harris makes his story at once modern and traditional by identifying Oudin with the trickster god, Anancy, to whom the early slaves turned to defeat the brute force of their masters with the moral jujitsu of deceit. Now Anancy becomes Oudin (Houdini). Exploited, Oudin tricks not only Mahommed who had expropriated him, but Ram. He escapes into the forest with Beti, whom Ram seeks.

In these terms Harris has written an analysis of the Guyanese class struggle. But characteristically he searches deeper. Ram and Oudin are master and servant, in conflict with each other. They are also complementary, as necessary to each other as the Ego and the Id in the human psyche. Ram is a figure of the vitality Mahommed lost, with the drive essential to any progressing society. Harris introduces the debate about creative power when Oudin and Beti are fleeing through the forest, and come into a clearing beside a huge bull. 'The foaming black mouth had spattered the neck and the cheek with a saliva of snow. A ring was hanging from his nostrils with an exquisite, sens-itive look of silvery scorn, human and rich and malevolent.' It is at once dangerous — 'Is bad stone bull standing there', says its keeper— yet magnificent, and Beti instinctively reaches up her hand to stroke it. Like Europa in a different time and place, her psychic courage takes on a universal significance, for she becomes the image of creative wo-manhood for her society. Ram. as the name indicates, is also sexually dynamic, but his creative drive has been perverted into exploitation. His relationship with Oudin, which should be creative, is destructive, and when Oudin flees, Ram finds himself desolate and broken.

The form of the novel, as befits a story set in the cycles of the peasants year, is circular. Ram's awareness of need throws open the poss-ibility of spiritual rebirth, and when Oudin dies, Ram haunts his house to catch a psychic glimpse of him. The note of promise is rein-forced by Beti being pregnant with Oudin's child. Oudin's spirit watches. He 'knew it was still a dream, the dream of the heavenly cycle of the planting and reaping he now stood within—as within a circle—for the first time. He felt his heart stop where it had danced. It was the end of his labour of death.' These words come as the beginning of the book, which itself written in a continuous circle, the beginning following from the end, with an almost imperceptible transition from flashback to direct narrative towards the end of the first section.

The Whole Armour (1962) is set further back in the interior, and examines yet a different section of the Guyanese community — the river settlements and migrants, largely of African origin, that move into and from the bush. It is a hard, violent life, and the novel explores the meaning of violence and death. The heroine, Magda, is the 'toughest and best whore in the river district'. The hero, Cristo, is suspected of murder. Examining the nature of guilt, Harris gives the book a biblical substructure, as indicated by the names of the characters— Cristo (Christ), who spends forty days and nights in the wilderness; Magda (Mary Magdalene); Matthias (Matthew); Peet (Peter); Abram, the father figure; and Sharon, the rose of beauty and love.

The story contains a series of deaths. Abram dies in a confrontation with Cristo; Magda, his mother and Abram's lover, believing Cristo to have murdered Abram, in a violent scene forces Cristo to take on Abram's stinking clothes, and gives out that it is Cristo who is dead. She holds a nine-day wake for her son who, as Gerald Moore points out, has been forced to take on the body and death of Abram, as Jesus Christ took on the body of human death.[11] The wake is a rum-tranced orgy in which the villagers face the reincarnated spirit of the community. But they find only death, as, in a re-enactment of Abram's, Matthias dies accidentally confronting Peet.

The fear that underpins the novel is symbolized by the mythical tiger that lurks, never seen, in the corner of the villagers' eye, blamed for violent deaths, including that of Cristo (Abram). But the violence is not without, it is within. 'Mankind itself was the tiger'. It becomes identified with Cristo, who in the jungle literally takes on the skin and claws of a tiger. But by taking on the form of evil, he transforms it. He becomes the ambivalent tiger of Blake's poem, which Harris quotes, at once a symbol of fear and of divine energy. He has been accused of the murder of Sharon's lover: now he meets Sharon in the forest, and in a moonlit night of universal harmony he tells her how, himself of African origin, he found himself stripped of all 'civilized' clothing, dressed in the primeval soil and water of the jungle, and accepted as one of them by a primitive Carib tribe of the interior. Taking on himself the guilt of his history — 'every guilty body rolled into one' — he finds he is suddenly free to be himself, a vision that becomes political. 'Can't you see,' he asks Sharon, 'now what it all means. Nobody need carry a self-righteous political chip when the only slave-driver we've had has been ourselves.' He offers a new vision and hope for Guyana, a psychic redemption from violence. But the police, the representatives of society, come to take him to trial and probable death, leaving Sharon to wear the tiger-skin of redemption. It is the theme of Gabriel Okara's *The Voice*, with both the strengths and weaknesses of greater intricacy. The book, however, runs the danger of violating Harris's own code of creative exploration, and becoming trapped by the predictable formulae of its substructure of sacrificial death.

The Secret Ladder (1963) returns to the world of *Palace of the Peacock*. The theme is similar — an expedition up river, this time the Canje, 'one of the lowest rungs of the ladder of ascending purgatorial rivers, the blackest one could imagine', not to explore but survey. It centres on a meeting with the ancestors, the tribes that live in the interior. As did the journey from Mariella, the voyage and action takes seven days, the week of the creation of a world. Even the boat is called 'Palace of the Peacock'. But if *Palace* was mystical and poetic, *The Secret Ladder* is more prosaic, being concerned with the work and frustrations of a surveyor, in particular the control of a mixed and rebellious group of workers. The hero Fenwick, clearly semi-autobiographical, is, Harris has said, 'wholly related to a quest for authority and responsibility.'[12] The organization of the expedition becomes a microcosm of the problems of government in multi-racial Guyana.

The journey itself becomes political. For mapping the headwaters of the river — before undiscovered — would make possible the damming of the creek, thereby providing a constant flow for the rice-farmers of the coast, but flooding the precarious farmlands of the inland settlements. These settlers are represented by the ageless Poseidon, grandson of a runaway slave, 'the black king of history whose sovereignty over the past was a fluid crown of possession and dispossession'. As with the meeting between the crew and the Arawak woman in *Palace*, Harris makes Fenwick's meeting with Poseidon one of the great passages of ancestral meeting in Caribbean literature.

There was a faint hoarse sound of an approaching body swimming in the undergrowth. Fenwick adjusted his eyes. He could no longer evade a reality that had always escaped him. The strangest figure he had ever seen had appeared in the opening of the bush,

171

dressed in a flannel vest, flapping ragged fins of trousers on his legs. Fenwick could not help fastening his eyes greedily upon him as if he saw down a bottomless gauge and river of reflection. He wanted to laugh at the weird sensation but was unable to do so. The old man's hair was white as wool and his cheeks — covered with wild curling rings — looked like an unkempt sheep's back. The black wooden snake of skin peeping though its animal blanket was wrinkled and stitched together incredibly.[13]

The description exists simultaneously on three levels. It is the literal image of an old African, at once tattered and dignified in his poverty. But Poseidon is also associated with the processes of nature—his hair is like sheep, his skin like a black snake — and, beyond this, he has the aura of myth. His trousers flap like fins, his body swims through the undergrowth. As his name suggests, he is the water-god, the spirit of the inland rivers; like the Greek god, he is the son of time (Chronos) and nature (Rhea). Harris goes behind the Poseidon of classical literature to the primitive intimations of the Mediterranean islanders out of which the formal myth grew.

The relationships between the modern surveying expedition and the traditional black community are an image of the crisis of contemporary Guyana. Fenwick, who is profoundly implicated because he recognizes his own ancestry in Poseidon, writes to his mother, 'I wish I could truly grasp the importance of this meeting. If I do not—if my generation do not—leviathan will swallow us all.' Fenwick's ostensible duty is plain. He should assert the unfeeling processes of authority, assuming a stone mask 'petrified' by the example of his officer Jordan (Gorgon). But as a human being, Fenwick must break loose. In an interview Harris has pointed out that a compassionate breaking of the regulations — contravening rules about the issue of government property, Fenwick gives the gauge-reader his coat against the night air — starts a chain reaction by which the gauge-reader is struck down by two of Poseidon's followers in mistake for Fenwick. When the assailants flee into the interior to warn Poseidon that time is not on their side, they prevent a scheme of murder and save the lives of two others connected with the expedition, Bryant and Catalena. 'Fenwick is implicated in traumas of violence and terror as well as in the mystery of form, the mystery of salvation. A deeper content of authority is released.'[14]

The love of Catalena and Bryant — who so narrowly escape death from Poseidon's followers when Bryant attempts reconciliation but accidentally causes Poseidon's death — is again the result of 'a deeper content of authority'. Catalena is the wife of Perez, one of Fenwick's men, treated brutally by her husband and the men until Fenwick oversteps his official authority to free her from her husband. Unlike *Palace, The Secret Ladder* does not progress to any climactic resolution. The new birth of possibility comes through the depth of each experience. In words which Harris quotes from T.S. Eliot, in this novel

A people without history
Is not redeemed from time, for history is a pattern
of timeless moments.

Since the *Guyanese Quartet*, Harris has written some eight further novels. *Heartland* (1964) is an epilogue to the first four. His hero, Stevenson, returns to the country of *Palace of the Peacock* which has to some extent been opened up — a road now runs around the escarpment, and rest houses exist in the bush. The country is still ghosted by Donne's expedition, and one of them, the da Silva twin, still lives for part of the book to tell Stevenson, like Coleridge's Ancient Mariner, of what he has learnt through his suffering. In this world, Stevenson is helped to come to grips with his own life of failure and betrayal. Other novels explore totally new ground. Their theme varies from harnessing waterfalls for hydroelectric power, and reading the meaning of Guyanese history in the ancestral rocks (*Tumatumari*, 1968), to states of consciousness during an eye operation (*The Waiting Room*, 1967), or the adventures of a beggar and trickster in Edinburgh (*Black Marsden*, 1973). Each novel is different in content and technique, each is a new attempt at altering our mental dimensions.

Harris's work has a place in black literature alongside such diverse writers as Wole Soyinka, Christopher Okigbo, Amos Tutuola and Aimé Césaire. Each writer has in his own way used a heritage of cultural disruption by becoming a trickster — Eshu, Anancy, Palm-wine Drinkard or Oudin-Houdini — who magically transforms his cultural plunder into something new and amazing; who invokes, by the alchemy of the imagination, ancestral presences in order to disrupt and renew our awareness of the present.

1. 1. Munro and R. Sander, ed., *Kas-Kas. Interviews with Three Caribbean Writers* (Austin: University of Texas, 1972), pp. 47-48.
2. Harris, *Tradition, the Writer and Society* (Port of Spain and London: New Beacon Books, 1967), p. 14.
3. *Ibid.*, p. 28.
4. Senghor, *Selected Poems*, tr. John Reed and Clive Wake (London Oxford University Press, 1964), pp. 78-79.
5. Buber, *Between Man and Man* (London: Fontana Library, 1961), p. 40. Harris refers to Buber in *Tradition*, p. 29: 'the profound and unpredictable sense of person which Martin Buber, for example, evokes'.
6. Harris, *Fossil and Psyche* (Austin: University of Texas, 1974), p. 4, my italics.
7. Harris, *Tradition*, p. 51.
8. Harris writes on Frances A. Yates's *The Art of Memory* (London: Routledge and Kegan Paul, 1966) in *Tradition*, pp. 55-57, and refers significantly to Jung's 'archetype of the collective unconscious' in *Tradition*, p. 9.
9. Michael Gilkes, *A Caribbean Syzygy: the novels of Wilson Harris and Edgar Mittelholzer* (University of Kent at Canterbury, Ph.D. thesis, 1974).
10. *Tradition*, pp. 35-36.
11. Gerald Moore, *The Chosen Tongue* (London: Longman, 1969), p. 70. The whole of Moore's analysis, pp. 68-73, is worth reading. Moore connects the wake with African 'second burial' rites.
12. *Kas-Kas*, p. 53.
13. *The Whole Armour and The Secret Ladder* (London: Faber paperback, 1973), p. 155.
14. *Kas-Kas*, pp. 53–54.

14

Wole Soyinka: The Past And The Visionary Writer

by

KOLAWOLE OGUNGBESAN

Soyinka's persistent condemnation of the African writers' fascination with the past has tended to obscure his major theme, the spiritual interdependence between the past, the present and the future. The true African sensibility, he once told a group of African writers, establishes that the past exists in the present, 'it is co-existent in present awareness. It clarifies the present and explains the future'.[1] Soyinka's interest in African mythology, of which he has made a deeper use than any other African writer, reveals his awareness of the validity of the past, but he does not attempt to recreate the past for the purpose of enshrinement, nor does he merely stress cultural continuity. Unlike Achebe who is nostalgic about the past, Soyinka focuses more directly on the dilemmas of the living, to enable him to anticipate and safeguard the future, which he considers the primary concern of the writer. His major symbols—bridges, domes, circles, and the rainbow—show his concern with continuity, but it is the use of festivals as an organizing metaphor in his plays that reveals Soyinka's awareness of the dynamic relationship between the past and the present.

The festival is the dominant element in Soyinka's works. *A Dance of the Forests*, his first major play, was specially written for the Nigerian Independence in 1960. Its central action, the Gathering of the Tribes, is a kind of independence celebration. The action of the *Strong Breed* centres upon the Festival of the New Year. One of the themes of 'Idanre', his longest poem, is the gathering together and reconciliation of various cultures. The kernel of *The Road* is an event which happened at the last annual Drivers' Festival. The Festival of the New Yam brought *Kongi's Harvest* to its pessimistic denouement.

175

Soyinka's usual theatrical effects, both visual (dance and mime) and auditory (bells, drums, song, etc.) are those most commonly used during festivals among his people, the Yoruba, who are very conscious of their cultural past which they celebrate publicly and lavishly. As an expression of cultural continuity, the dead and the gods are understood to be present and to rejoice with the living. This interdependence between the past and the present is proclaimed by Adenebi, the pompous historian in *A Dance of the Forests* (1963):

> . . . . we must bring home the descendants of our great forebears. Find them. Find the scattered sons of our proud ancestors. The builders of empires. The descendants of our great nobility. Find them. Bring them here. If they are in hell, ransom them. Let them symbolise all that is noble in our nation. Let them be our historical link for the season of rejoicing. Warriors. Sages. Conquerors. Builders. Philosophers. Mystics. Let us assemble them around the totem of the nation and we will drink from their resurrected glory.

The writer as visionary of his people is greater than a historian or a cultural nationalist. A festival, Soyinka insists, is not an occasion to bask in unreal glories, or rejoice complacently; rather it should bring greater awareness by forcing us to confront ourselves as we are, and as we have always been. Instead of 'illustrious ancestors' for which they asked, the living in *A Dance of the Forests* are sent 'two spirits of the restless dead', the dead man who in his former life (eight centuries ago) was a captain in the army of Mata Kharibu and the dead woman his wife. But 'their choice was no accident. In previous life they were linked in violence and blood with four of the living generation.' The living not only provide continuity with the past, but have indeed chosen their appropriate dead.

Beyond the grim reminder that 'the pattern is unchanged', and that the present is intimately linked with the past, although the living would prefer to modify it for the sake of prestige, Soyinka insists that a festival is organized by the living, for the benefit of the living, to protect the future through present awareness. The main concern of *A Dance*, the problem to which the dramatist addresses himself, is how society can arrive at a truly new beginning. The living can only break the sordid pattern of their history through the awareness they gain by confronting their own past in all its ignominy. 'Let the future judge them by reversal of its path or by stubborn continuation.' The claims of the past prove too strong; the cycle of violence which has continued into the present is projected into the future. The self-proclaimed symbol of Posterity, the Third Triplet, a full body of a human being but fanged and bloody, struts on the stage with his clenched teeth and blood-spattered body, an image of that animalism which had plagued the past and which the Warrior had projected into the future eight centuries back. 'Unborn generations will be cannibals. Unborn generations will, as we have done, eat up one another.'

In an interview with Lewis Nkosi in Lagos in 1962, Soyinka confirmed the gloomy message he had sought to carry across at the Nigerian independence celebrations two years earlier: 'the main thing is my own personal conviction or observation that human beings are simply cannibals all over the world so that their main preoccupation seems to be eating up one another.'[2] This vision provides the background to all of Soyinka's plays written after 1960. Indeed his earlier plays can be seen as an exploration of this theme. The symbols from the animal world which permeate these plays point his theme. In *The Lion and the Jewel* (1963), the Bale, Baroka, is variously described in animalistic terms: the fox, the Lion, 'the panther of the trees' and 'the scourge of womanhood'. He cavorts with his wives in 'a rich bedroom covered in animal skins and rugs. Weapons round the wall.' The survival instincts of the animal which enabled him to defeat those who wanted to build a railway through his village also helped in completely routing both Sidi and Lakunle, the village school-master and apostle of a jejune modernism. The play celebrates the Bale's victory:

The Fox is said to be wise
So cunning that he stalks and dines on
New-hatched chickens.

The Swamp Dwellers (1963) also celebrates the victory of a predatory traditionalism. Prey to his twin brother, Awuchike, now living in the city and surviving by the law of the jungle, Igwezu returns to his home in the delta, and confronts a more elemental betrayal. The Kadiye, the priest of the Serpent of the Swamps, is the real serpent. 'Why are you so fat, Kadiye?' asks Igwezu. 'You lie upon the land, Kadiye, and choke it in the folds of a serpent.' Igwezu's apparent victory, which earns him the title of 'slayer of serpents' turns to defeat when he is forced to flee his home because he 'must not be here when the people call for blood'. In *The Trials of Brother Jero* (1963), the false prophet triumphs again. Jero, who has succeeded for so long in preying upon the credulity of his people succeeds in confining his assistant, Chume,

177

in an asylum in order to safeguard his trade. He is now allied to power, in the form of a newly recruited follower, a Member of Parliament, who he prophesies will be a Minister of War, the courier of an animalism which will infect his society.

The mood of *The Strong Breed* (1964), is perceptibly darker, reflecting the contemporary mood of crisis in Nigeria, and Africa as a whole, in the early sixties. An evil community which is not only hostile towards but preys on strangers by using them as carriers turns upon the Christ-like Eman, hunting him down like an animal. 'His pursuers come pouring down the passages in full cry.' He is finally hounded to death, caught in a trap. 'There is a sound of twigs breaking, of a sudden trembling in the branches. Then silence.' Soyinka said that *The Strong Breed* contrasts the 'idea of selfishness with sacrifice as opposed to the other general cannibalism of human beings'.[3]

The Road (1965) returns to this theme, using the Nigerian road as a pervasive symbol. Ogun, the god of iron and patron saint of drivers, preyed on his devotees, the champion drivers who all perished on the road: Zorro, Akanni the Lizard, Saidu-Say, Sigidi Ope, Sapele Joe, Indian Charlie, Cimarron Kid, and Sergeant Burma. These were heroes of the road, but ultimately its victims. To Ogun, their patron, they had sacrificed many dogs, and finally the 'heavier meat'—themselves. Life on the road was a constant war, and these veterans approached it in that manner. 'Like a battlefield they always say. Like a battlefield.'

Reflecting the artist's vision of the battlefield as the greatest theatre of animalism in nature, the key characters in *The Road* have been to the World War and returned to point out the absurd morality of war. 'It is peaceful to fight a war which one does not understand, to kill human beings who never seduced your wife or poisoned your water. Sapele to Burma—that was a long way for a quarrel.' Sergeant Burma had brought not only his name but also this absurd morality back to his own land; having been brutalized by four years of fighting and one year as a prisoner of war during which he was tortured, he was never moved by road accidents; rather he would first filch whatever he could before removing his dead comrades to the mortuary. 'Looting was after all the custom in the front. You killed your enemy and you robbed him. He couldn't break the habit.' Even those who did not go to the war have become beastly: politicians, touts, thugs, policemen prey on one another and on their society.

'Metaphysical quest', Soyinka wrote in 1965, 'is not of itself a static theme, not when it is integrated, by real proportions, into the individual or social patterns of life.'[4] Using the violence within his society, Soyinka explores the meaning of death. Professor's fascination with death is more than a compulsion; it is a spiritual quest, a journey leading towards a perhaps unattainable ideal. The very structure of a compulsion, the same act repeated over and over again, need not be seen only as a private hell; it may also be seen as a way of hoping, striving, living. Like all roads, however, it also leads to the grave. Professor pronounces stoically: 'The Word may be found companion not to life, but Death.' The romantic road may lead toward death, but we are shown how to accept life along the way; the destination is darkness, but hope, bravery and the will to continue illumine the way.

Soyinka's first novel, *The Interpreters* (1965), a complex but flawed work, re-examines the central dilemma of *A Dance of the Forests* within the changed circumstances of post-independence Nigeria. How much influence does the past exert on the present? And how much of the failings of the present can we attribute to the past? Unlike Achebe, Soyinka is not nostalgic about traditional society, nor does he think that we can look to it for solutions to present problems. The interpreters view the past with resentment because its platitudes have failed to set things morally right. Egbo asks: 'If the dead are not strong enough to be ever-present in our being, should they not be as they are, dead?' Sekoni replies that making such distinctions disrupts the dome of continuity, which is what life is. The past cannot be ignored, in spite of temptations to do so, for the present is no improvement. Yet, if we can no longer look to the past for guidance, where will morality come from? From the individual, is the unequivocal answer: 'A man's gift of life should be separate, an unrelated thing. All choice must come from within him, not from promptings of his past.'

Faced with the stench of contemporary Nigeria, Sagoe offers the Voidante Philosophy as a means of coping with a society blind to the truth that it leads a disgusting life; his aim is to force society to see its values realistically, even if this also means disgustingly and embarrassingly. 'To shit is human, to voidate divine'—sums up the plastic morality which society has created as an alternative to confronting the truth about itself. The interpreters refuse the easier and safer course of going with the tide. Egbo gently rebukes the female student who had stressed self-reliance: 'You have a gentle nature, but you are wrong. Who dares to be adequate?' But she replies firmly: 'One can be. It is necessary to be.' By posing courage and determination against the fear of non-conformity, Soyinka does not shut the door to hope for improvement in individuals—and therefore in society; because human values are not absolute, there is room for change and improvement.

179

In *Kongi's Harvest* (1967), Soyinka turns his satire on the contemporary political scene, attacking directly the politicians who have shaped the present direction of modern Africa. The play was inspired by a sentence which Soyinka once heard an African leader pronounce: 'I want him brought back, alive if possible . . .but if not . . . any other way.'[5] While it is true that many of the allusions in the play refer to Nkrumah (for whom Soyinka has a grudging respect) the real subject is much broader. Dictators rise and fall, but Kongism has never been dethroned in black Africa. Kongism is the dogma on whose altar human beings are sacrificed. Kongi preys on his subjects. He makes use of the Aweri and yet slowly starves them to death. 'Damn their greedy guts', he barks at their complaint. 'I eat nothing at all.' Instead of partaking of the feast of the new yam, Kongi is left alone on the dais with a human head on the salver, a cannibal, nourished on a diet different from that of other men.

The play makes a major statement on the spiritual interdependence between the past and the present, Soyinka's central tenet. Kongi already has the power, but wants the spirituality which is inherent in the obaship. With the Oba's surrender of the new yam, continuity would have been established between the new regime and its traditional predecessor. Kongism is presented as an intensification of the tyranny of the traditional regime. Oba Danlola's drummer sings:

> They say we took too much silk
> For the royal canopy
> But the dead will witness
> We never ate the silkworm.

But Kongism is also a decisive break with the past. Kongi's ascendancy spells the doom of tradition itself. His order 'to replace the old superstitious festival by a state ceremony governed by the principle of Enlightened Ritualism' means the destruction of what is authentically African. 'The period of isolated saws and wisdoms is over, superseded by a more systematic formulation of comprehensive philosophies.' No more the dance, but the life of the state will henceforth reflect the austere and joyless personality of its ruler. The frequent interruption of dancing and singing by the forces of modernism is a symbol of the danger to that ritualism which is at the heart of tradition. Oba Danlola finally gives voice to it:

This is the last
Our feet shall touch together
We thought the tune
Obeyed us to the soul
But the drums are newly shaped
And stiff arms strain
On stubborn crooks, so
Delve with the left foot
For ill-luck; with the left
Again for ill-luck; once more
With the left alone, for disaster
Is the only certainty we know.

Soyinka's pessimistic vision of the cycle of tyranny is evident in the denouement of *Kongi's Harvest* when Kongi triumphs over his enemies. The burst of gunshots which briefly interrupts the festival signifies not his end, but that of his enemies. 'Kongi relaxes gradually, swells with triumph. He begins to chuckle, from a low key his laughter mounts, louder and more maniacal. His eye fixed on Segi as a confident spider at a fly.' A greater degree of oppression is let loose on the people, yet there is no way out. The darkness at the end is completely stifling: 'the mixture of royal music and national anthem . . . comes to an abrupt halt as the iron grating descends and hits the ground with a loud final clang.'

Soyinka's first volume of poetry, *Idanre and Other Poems* (1967) is a harvest of poems written over eight years. Reflecting the gathering gloom in his society, the poet dropped from the collection such well-known light satirical pieces as 'Telephone Conversation', 'The Immigrant' and 'The Other Immigrant'. A highly organized volume, *Idanre* brought out in stark nakedness the poet's anguish in the face of society's general lack of awareness.

Do we not truly fear to bleed? We hunt
Pale tissues of the palm, fingers groping
Ever cautious on the crown.

Soyinka's awareness that pain is inextricably interwoven with fulfilment is part of a deeper awareness of death as an inevitable part of life. This volume comes to grips with the reality of everyday death. A group of poems entitled 'of birth and death', all on the death of infants, brings out two major beliefs of Soyinka's poetic idea, the idea of reincarnation (very prevalent among his people) and, ultimately linked to this, the cyclical pattern of existence. 'The ripest fruit was saddest', he wrote in 'Abiku', graphically conveying the idea that life, at its fullest, is closest to death. Abiku (literally 'the child born to die') keeps the cycle going endlessly; it prepares for death and rebirth simultaneously. When 'Abiku moans, shaping/Mounds from the yolk', it converts the egg-yolk, the universal symbol of regeneration, to burial mounds.

In 'Season' human beings are compared to reapers waiting for the fruits of life to ripen, so that they can gather them and move on to death, the fruit of life at its most mature. 'Rust is ripeness' the poem opens, in one of Soyinka's most economical statements, and concludes with what should be our attitude to this harvest of life:

> Now gatherers we
> Awaiting rust on tassels, draw
> Long shadows from the dusk, wreathe
> Dry thatch in wood-smoke. Laden stalks
> Ride the germ's decay—we await
> The promise of the rust.

Soyinka sees our fear of death as perhaps the most eloquent testimony of our fear to live fully. We should accept the fact of death, should indeed earn our death by confronting with passion the conundrum of life. We are responsible to life; it is a road we should negotiate as nobly as possible in order to deserve fully 'the promise of the rust'.

> let us love all things of grey; grey slabs
> grey scalpel, one grey sleep and form
> grey images.

Greyness is the dominant colour in *Idanre*, showing Soyinka's preoccupation with that transitional period between life and dissolution. A whole group of poems is entitled 'grey seasons', and details the poet's anguish at the wave of political violence that has engulfed his society. 'Of the road' re-examines death through the accidents on Nigerian roads. In the group of poems 'October '66' Soyinka shows his anguish at the massacre of the Ibos in Northern Nigeria. The poet has himself supplied the background to the poem:

Idanre lost its mystification early enough. As events gathered pace and unreason around me I recognized it as part of a pattern of awareness which began when I wrote *A Dance of the Forests*. In detail, in the human context of my society, *Idanre* has made abundant sense. (The town of Idanre itself was the first to cut its bridge, its only link with the rest of the region during the uprising of October 1965). And since then the bloody origin of Ogun's pilgrimage has been, in true cyclic manner, most bloodily re-enacted.

The bloody origin of the pilgrimage began when Ogun, against his will, was persuaded by the Elders of Ire to forsake his abode in the heights and lead their people in war. 'He descended and they crowned him king.' But 'drunk with wine and blinded by gore', Ogun devoured his own men. Soyinka the visionary anticipates the trend of violence in his society, and warns:

> To bring a god to supper is devout, yet
> A wise host keeps his distance till
> The Spirit One has dined his fill. What mortal
> Brands a platter with an awesome name,
> Or feeds him morsels choice without
> Gauntlets of iron. A human feast
> Is indifferent morsel to a god.

Soyinka delves into the mythical past of his people not only to state contemporary awareness but also to safeguard the future. *Idanre* contains a more urgent warning than *The Road* to the people of his country, who, by so casually unleashing violence on their land, had let loose a weapon which they would not be able to control. Ogun once roused cannot be stayed: at Ire when he finally stayed his own hand, the enormity of his wanton destruction struck the god himself; it was 'too late for joy' for the people of Ire:

> Too late came warning that a god
> Is still a god to men, and men are one
> When knowledge comes, of death.

Truth dawned too late also for the poet's own society, and his warning went unheeded. It is remarkable how Soyinka's vision of the inevitability of war proved prophetic. The Historian in Mata Kharibu's court assured the Emperor eight centuries ago: 'War is the only consistency that past ages afford us. It is the legacy which new nations seek to perpetuate. Patriots are grateful for wars. Soldiers have never questioned bloodshed. The cause is always the accident your majesty, and war is the Destiny.' The absurdity of wars is constantly declaimed upon: 'the magnificence of the destruction of a beautiful city' and the acts of wanton carnage which 'lifted mankind to the ranks of gods and demi-gods'. The Captain who refused to throw his men into a senseless war stood condemned by history. 'We were so near to the greatness of Troy and Greece,' the Historian mourned. 'I mean this is war as it should be fought . . . over nothing . . . do you not agree?'

When the Nigerian Civil War broke out in August 1967, Soyinka wrote in the newspapers pointing out its futility and went to see Ojukwu. He was arrested and detained for two years. *A Shuttle in the Crypt* (1972), the volume of poems which he wrote in jail, remains the most important artistic product of the Civil War. *The Man Died* (1971), his prose account of his sufferings, is a bitter book, marred by its uncontrolled anger and anguish to the point of shrillness. In *A Shuttle* the anger and the anguish are there, but have been disciplined by the requirements of art. Rather than his rage deadening his creativity, each poem reflects Soyinka's passionate intensity. Soyinka has abandoned his world of private mythology which makes the earlier poems so obscure. Instead there is a new directness, marked by a close naked expression shorn of all adornments. Brooding alone and at length in prison, Soyinka re-examines his major preoccupations, with a new urgency and at a greater depth. What is the poet's right approach as he confronts the violence of his society?

Through the symbol of Demoke's carving in *A Dance of the Forests* and Kola's pantheon in *The Interpreters*, Soyinka had brought out not only the focal position of the artist within his society but his function to unmask society's self-deception by revealing to it its own nature. In a 1965 essay entitled 'And After the Narcissist?' Soyinka had condemned the usual division between the poet (intellectual) and the politician (man of action). The essence of Ogun, the Yoruba god of war and the creative principle, best reflects the true essence of the poet as a man of action; the African poet *must* be a man of action to discharge his contemporary responsibility.

'Idanre' is a poetic embodiment of this statement, a record of Soyinka's own quest for the true poetic essence, with the poet following in the footsteps of Ogun who was the only god until Atunda his slave rolled a boulder on the godhead and 'shred the kernel to a million lights'. But the assertive act of Atunda is glorified as leading to the diversity which is the essence of living, rather than the uniformity of death; the celebration of Atunda for splitting the unified godhead lifts his action from betrayal to a divine creation: 'All hail Saint Atunda, First revolutionary/Grand iconoclast at genesis'. By exalting Atunda Soyinka exalts the individual who singly sets out to redeem his society. Analogous to Atunda, the former slave who becomes a god, the poet, the lonely visionary, ceases to be an outcast and becomes a divine, the conscience of his society.

> Let each seek wisdom where he can, life's
> Puppetry creaks round me hourly
> Trunks and motions in masquerades grotesques
> Post-mortem is for quacks and chroniclers
> Who failed at divination.

In his essay, 'The Writer in a Modern African State' in 1967, Soyinka stressed the redeeming function of the artist: 'It seems to me that the time has now come when the African writer must have the courage to determine what alone can be salvaged from the recurrent cycle of human stupidity.'[6] This is not new. Forest Head, the supreme deity, had recognized the present splendour of Demoke's carving, calling it 'the kind of action that redeems mankind', because it links the artist and his roots. 'It was the work of generations. I think your hands are very old. You have the fingers of the dead.' Soyinka believes that the artist can perform his redeeming function only if he asserts his direct and vitalizing connection with the long tradition of which he is inheritor. 'The artist has always functioned in African society as the record of the mores and experience of his society *and* as the voice of vision in his own time. It is time for him to respond to this essence of himself.'[7] The writer must not only be involved in everyday affairs of his society, he must be capable of looking beyond them:

> The writer is the visionary of his people, he recognises past and present not for the purpose of enshrinement but for the logical-creative impulse and statement of the ideal future. He anticipates, he warns. It is not always enough for the writer to be involved in the direct physical struggle of today, he often cannot help but envisage and seek to protect the future which is the declared aim of contemporary struggle.[8]

185

In *A Shuttle in the Crypt*, Soyinka examines four different stages of commitment, through the archetypes Joseph, Hamlet, Gulliver and Ulysses. He neither came to a definite conclusion, nor could he banish the question from his mind; it is this obsession which gives this volume its depth and poignancy. In 'Conversation at Night with a Cockroach' the cockroach attempts to justify the killing of the Ibos within the cycle of nature, the destruction that is an inevitable part of regeneration; but the anguished poet condemns the wanton destruction of human lives. Yet, it is the cockroach that triumphs at the end: 'All was well. All was even/As it was in the beginning'. The poet cannot see when the cyclic pattern of destruction will work itself out. This vision is taken a step further in 'When Seasons Change' where, by posing the seasonal variation against the prisoner's monotonous life and the permanence of history, the poet despondently admits that the great truths of life never change. This in itself is enough cause for grief: 'Shed your hard tears; it is an old earth/Striving to fresh touch of old pretensions'. Yet, although the poet's mind constantly 'soars in flight/Upon a dual flight of planes', between commitment and renunciation of will, he counsels against depair, basing his faith on the cyclic pattern of changes in nature:

> . . . this progression has been source
> For great truths in spite of stammering
> Planes for great building in spite
> Of crooked sights, for plastic strength
> Despite corrosive fumes of treachery
> And spirits grow despite the midwifery
> Of dwarfs; spires, rooted in quagmires
> Of the human mind rise to purer lights
> And wing aloft a salvaged essence
> Transcending death, legacy of seasons . . .

Soyinka's latest plays—*Madmen and Specialists* (1971) and *Jero's Metamorphosis* (1973)—complement their predecessors and reflect his response to the contemporary situation of his society. In *A Dance* he had portrayed a pattern of persistent animalism in human affairs, but probably because of the euphoria during the preparation for Independence when the play was written he also postulated through the action of Demoke the artist that it was possible to break the pattern and arrive at a new beginning. Even as late as 1965 Soyinka wrote in *Idanre:* 'Still awaited is that postcript image of dawn, contained in the beginning, the brief sun-led promise of earth's forgiveness.' But as events overwhelmed both the artist and his society he closed the door for all time. 'As Was the Beginning, As Is, Now, As Ever Shall Be, World Without.' The pessimism is complete.

The animalism which was prophesied eight hundred years ago in Mata Kharibu's empire has now pervaded the whole world. Soyinka does not use the artist figure, common in his earlier works; instead, the well-meaning individual who expresses a sensibility different from and opposed to the mass direction is labelled a madman and broken by a specialist appointed for the task. Yet, the new cannibals are forced to face the enormity of their crime against their fellowmen: 'Is there really much difference? All intelligent animals kill only for food, you know, and you are intelligent animals. Eat—eat—eat—eat—eat—Eat!' Power has its own mad logic, of which cannibalism is the first step. 'Power in its purest sense. The end of inhibitions. The conquest of the weakness of your too human flesh with all its sentiment.' Humanity, as the new catechism states explicitly, is the ultimate sacrifice to As. The former doctor now permanently wears khaki uniform and carries a swagger stick, a personification of the new spirit of militarism which in the play is an emblem of the total depravity of humanity. In Soyinka's own words, *Jero's Metamorphosis*, like *Madmen and Specialists*, deals with 'a problem in my own society, the betrayal of vocation for the attraction of power in one form or another.'⁹ Jero is now powerful, and consequently more dangerous to his society, because he is allied with the military and his sect takes on a military image. 'We shall manifest our united spiritual essence in the very form and shape of the rulers of the land. Nothing, you will agree, could be more respectable than that.' Both the body and the spirit have been shackled; the task is complete. The cycle of tyranny is restored.

How does Soyinka resolve his awareness of the cyclic pattern of Man's tragic fate with his belief that the artist only becomes complete by acting in the world? For the negative impulse towards pessimism inherent in an 'awareness of familiar, wearisomely familair patterns in history', contradicts the writer's belief in action as 'the ultimate expression of will, an assertion of the human intellect as instrument of choice, change, self-destination'.¹⁰ Soyinka explains only how he is able to function as a citizen when he says that expressions of pessimism in his works are simply a statement of truth derived from a particular situation, but they do not mean acceptance of that situation, nor do they preclude challenge. 'It is because I believe that the forces of history may be confronted that I believe in social and political action.'[11] As a corollary we can explain his creative efforts as performing a therapeutic function; he attempts to exorcize despair and obtain mental balance by externalizing his tragic awareness in his works of art:

Tragedy is merely a way of retrieving human unhappiness, of subsuming it and thus of justifying it in the form of necessity, wisdom or purification. The rejection of this process and the search for the technical means of avoiding the insidious trap it lays is a necessary undertaking today.[12]

NOTES

1. Wole Soyinka, 'The Writer in a Modern African State', Wastberg, ed. *The Writer in Modern Africa* (Uppsala: Scandinavian Institute of African Studies, 1968), p. 19.
2. Dennis Duerden and Cosmo Pieterse ed. *African Writers Talking* (London: Heinemann, 1972), p. 173.
3. *Ibid.*
4. 'And After the Narcissist?', *African Forum*, I: IV (1966) p. 55.
5. *Spear*, May 1966, p. 18.
6. Wastberg, p. 20.
7. *Ibid.*, p. 21.
8. 'The Choice and Use of Language', *Cultural Events in Africa*, LXXV (London, 1966), p. 3.
9. *New York Times*, 20 July 1970, p. 22.
10. *Transition*, VIII: 42 (1973) p. 62.
11. *Ibid.*, p. 63.
12. *The Man Died* (London: Rex Collings, 1971), p. 89.

15

Luís Bernardo Honwana's Place Among the Writers in Mozambique

by
GERALD M. MOSER

Overnight, a young black Mozambican journalist named Honwana won fame when he published a slender volume of seven stories in 1964. How is one to explain the rapid spread of his reputation on the basis of such a small output? Within three years, translations of some of the stories appeared in Nigeria, South Africa, Great Britain, France, the Soviet Union, and even the United States, where the usually parochial Sunday magazine section of the *New York Times* printed Honwana's 'The Hands of the Blacks' in Dorothy Guedes's English translation in April 1967. It had been recommended to the *Times* by the novelist Nadine Gordimer of South Africa, where it had been published three years earlier, in *The Classic* of Johannesburg. Honwana received wide recognition in spite of writing in Portuguese, a language studied by few and read by even fewer in their moments of leisure. His chances had been further reduced by the book having been published in Lourenço Marques, the Mozambican capital, a very calm backwater in the Euro-African cultural world. Was the notoriety due to political circumstances? To Honwana's arrest and imprisonment in 1966? Was he a freak in Mozambican society?

To be sure, the quality of his prose was high, unusually so for Portuguese Africa, where many dabble in writing occasionally but few are gifted and experienced. In Portugal, two well-known literary critics quickly recognized Honwana's excellence: José Régio, the respected co-founder of the *Presença* Movement of Coimbra, hailed Honwana's fiction as 'a genuine form of fresh, spontaneous realism'[1] while Amândio César, one of the rare intellectuals in Portugal proper to follow literary developments overseas with unflagging curiosity,[2] published an enthusiastic review article, 'Um escritor da costa do Índico' (A writer from the Indian Ocean coast), as early as 1964.[3] César welcomed the writer as 'the youngest revelation in Mozambican prose writing', pointing out his 'simplistic technique that lends a strange vivacity and authenticity to his testimony'. He asked his readers to watch this new star. But even the Portuguese were surprised at the appearance of Honwana's stories in Mozambique. Why should they have been?

In reality, Honwana's case is not unique. To understand it, one has to find out what stage of literary development had been reached in Mozambique when he appeared on the scene and to consider it within the larger picture of cultural activities in Africa south of the Sahara. Until the second half of the past century, no printed works worth mentioning were produced there. Then the earliest writings by black Africans and mulattos were published in the towns of the Portuguese and in the latter's language. Specifically they were printed in Angola or Portuguese West Africa and on the Cape Verdean Islands. Elsewhere, literature remained what it had been since time immemorial: the oral lore of the tribes. In the Portuguese territories, the traditional literature has continued to be cultivated, part of it having even been carried across the Atlantic to Brazil and to wherever else Africans were taken as slaves. However, the form in which the tales and songs were eventually recorded was accommodated to the moral and literary conventions of the urban West, particularly by the white missionaries who made the effort to learn the African languages, live among the villagers, and study their beliefs and customs seriously. Although some of these collectors respected African ways, such as Héli Chatelain in Angola, Marques de Barros in Guinea-Bissau, or the Junods, father and son, in Mozambique, none of them could avoid the impoverishment inherent in the writing and printing of oral recitations. In recent times, even the native-born African writer in those countries has lost direct, living contact with the patrimony of folklore, whenever he moved to the city and received his education there, as is the case of Mário António Fernandes de Oliveira, who went to Luanda (Angola), or of Luís Bernardo Honwana, who grew up in Lourenço Marques.

On the other hand, the African languages were rarely written in the Portuguese colonies, except in a very few periodicals started by Africans from the 1880s on and in the edifying publications of the mission stations. The native-born intellectual would tend to express himself in Portuguese, even and especially if he was an African nationalist.[4] In so doing, he would naturally follow western literary standards that reached him via Lisbon or Rio de Janeiro in their Portuguese version.

Honwana's literary apprenticeship, for example, followed two paths:

that of school, where Portuguese was taught through readings of anthologies of metropolitan Portuguese authors of the past, establishing in students' minds outmoded canons of style and grammar, and the path of working for a newspaper, which opened to him a circle of intellectuals in Lourenço Marques who gave him guidance to contemporary world literature and its innovations. In the preface to his stories, Honwana acknowledged his debt to three writers of the preceding generation with whom he became personally acquainted and who continue to play an important role in the cultural life of Mozambique: the critic Eugénio Lisboa and the poets Rui Knopfli and José Craveirinha. All of them were born there,[5] only Craveirinha had a black mother. Significantly, Honwana dedicated his first stories to Craveirinha.

Mozambique developed differently from the other regions under Portuguese domination. Only thus can the relative isolation of its writers, Honwana among them, be fully understood. In all those regions, a specifically regional literature has arisen, although it remains in the stage of infancy, prolonged by past police terror and civil war. Only Mozambique has not developed such a body of literature yet, as it has also lacked literary movements, although it is the most populous and, in its port cities, the most cosmopolitan. One reason for this state was its remoteness from Portugal, to the point of its being ruled for centuries by the Viceroy in Goa, India, without, however, sharing in the spiritual heritage of the Hindus. None of the Portuguese colonies in Africa was intended for European settlement originally, least of all Guinea and Mozambique. Transient soldiers, administrators and traders made up the European and Asiatic element of the population on the coast while the interior remained unsafe until the early decades of the twentieth century. Consequently, little mixing took place and even less cultural exchange, a situation well described by the Mozambican historian Alexandre Lobato.[6]

Mozambique did not spawn any of the 'Creole islands i.e',. small but tightly knit port communities of mixed families which provided the ground for the earliest African literature in Portuguese—towns such as São Vicente in the Cape Verdes or Luanda and Benguela in Angola. Europeans with a literary inclination felt like exiles in the cities of Mozambique, Beira or Lourenço Marques. Their writings, usually limited to lyrical poetry, were merely an extension of European literature, as if the authors were blind to the African environment. Such was the case during the monarchic age when outstanding poets, Luís de Camöens in the sixteenth century and Tomás Gonzaga in the beginning of the nineteenth, lived in the island town of Mozambique that gave its name to the whole vast territory. In general, the situation has remained the same to this day so that an American historian of Portuguese-African literature[7] found Mozambican writing moving on a higher aesthetic level than in other Portuguese territories but possessing scarcely a character of its own.

Attempts have been made before Honwana to break the stranglehold of the European model. Felisberto Ferreirinha, a Portuguese painter who lived in Mozambique for many years, was perhaps the first to produce poetry that aimed to convey the impressions made on him by Africa and the Africans. But he lacked inspiration to write more than picturesque idylls. Perhaps a search of early newspapers would lead to the first utterings of native Mozambicans, especially in *O Brado Africano*, founded in 1918 by the mestizo João Albasini and his brother José. The former published a volume of stories, *O livro da dor* (The Book of Sorrow) in 1925, the year of his death, which I have been unable to locate so far. In the judgement of one who read it, the Mozambican journalist Rodrigues Júnior, it is a work expressing the personal grief of an emotional, pensive, high-minded man who was a master of journalism. He also believed in assimilation.[8] João Albasini's stories must be presumed to represent a blind alley which later writers did not follow.

The earliest predecessor Honwana had was João Dias, a black African like Honwana. A. César was reminded of him when Honwana's stories appeared. Dias wrote stories that show the promise of a talented beginner; they are awkward and sketchy but one can find in them an unusual intensity of emotion as he gives literary utterance to the hurt feelings of an ambitious young man protesting openly and bitterly against condescension and prejudice. It was like a cry of agony. Shortly afterwards, in 1949, Dias died of tuberculosis in Portugal where he had gone for his studies. No doubt, he, like the poet Costa Alegre from the Island of São Tomé half a century before, had been moved to put his innermost thoughts on paper while far away from home. College friends, fellow Africans with European and Asiatic backgrounds, published the stories as an act of friendship and justice.

João Dias's outcry was repeated in Mozambique itself, but in a different manner, under the impact of the black consciousness movement originating in the Americas. Mozambicans of mixed parentage took it up in a romantic and simultaneously political fashion, to exalt Africanness in poetry. In the late 50s and early 60s a number of gifted poets published eloquent verse of this kind in simple language and

192

strong rhythms, defiantly proclaiming their dreams of black solidarity and the awakening of Mother Africa. Two of them became well-known: Noémia de Sousa and José Craveirinha. Craveirinha, whom Honwana admired as 'the true expression of Mozambican poetry',[9] was the more important of the two; he continues to write poems whereas Noémia, self-exiled in Europe, has long since fallen silent.

At least three types of prose stories had been cultivated in Mozambique before 1964, apart from J. Dias's little-known narratives: the traditional African folk–tale, the European settler's tale, and the missionary's tale. The tales spun by European hunters and the reminiscences of European soldiers may be considered at best as subspecies of the settler's tale, at worst as irrelevant, since they lack African roots.

The traditional tale of the Bantu peoples of Southern Africa has been collected by several generations of Europeans, chiefly by missionaries with some ethnological experience. In Mozambique, the Reverend Henri Alexandre Junod produced two collections, *Les chants et les contes des Ba-Ronga de la baie de Delagoa* (The songs and tales of the Ba-Ronga of Delagoa Bay, 1897), supplemented by *Nouveaux contes ronga* (New Ronga tales, 1898), and the classic on Ba-Tonga society, *The life of a South African tribe* (1912), which contained further tales and a general introduction to traditional Tonga literature. Animated by warm sympathy towards the Africans, he tried to make his readers understand and appreciate their great qualities, although as a Protestant missionary and a believer in natural science, he found it impossible to accept black magic and to condone practices he considered harmful. His work as a collector was merely a beginning as he himself confessed.[10] It is likely that other clans of the Ba-Tonga people know other stories and that their number could be multiplied by the dozen or so peoples inhabiting Mozambique, from the Makonde in the north to the Swazi in the south.

In connection with the development of prose writing, several of Junod's observations seem pertinent, especially since Honwana belongs to the Ba-Ronga people, known to South Africans as Shangana or Shangaans. Junod points out that the tales, while very old, are constantly transformed by the narrators and that 'the transformations go much further than is generally supposed'.[11] This means that a traditional tale can easily be adapted without shocking the audience.

Secondly, Junod attempts a classification, which, however, is unsystematic since he differentiates some types of tales according to their protagonists—animals, such as the tricksters Hare, Tortoise and Little Toad; weak but clever children; cruel ogres which are

193

invariably overcome—while defining others according to origin—stories based on actual occurrences and stories derived from foreign sources. A tale that strikes my western mind as exemplary tells of three sons whom their sick old father sends out to find the ogre that alone has the power to cure him, and how only the youngest has enough devotion and thus the courage to face the monster and carry it home to his father. Which leads us to the most interesting of Junod's observations: these tales, especially those of tricksters and of children, have an appeal for the common people, the women and the children, because by telling or hearing them they 'take their revenge in the Black man's usual way, i.e., by saying what they think (of the strong that dominate their lives) in a round-about manner. They do not try to upset the existing state of affairs. Far from it! But they take a malicious pleasure in telling of the clever tricks of the Hare and his associates'.[12] Junod's thought lends itself to generalization: the traditional tale in which the clever weakling triumphs may furnish, in Mozambique as elsewhere, a model for contemporary written literature.

The European settler's tale is identical with the tale about the European settler. It cannot but view Africa from the outside, no matter how sympathetically. The vast majority of writings in Mozambique belong to this category. Representative of it are the stories and novels by Rodrigues Júnior, descendant of a Portuguese family from Madeira, who has lived in Mozambique since early youth, considers it his true home, and has proved throughout a long career as a journalist that he writes out of a constant and serious urge. In his prose fiction, such as his earliest, *Sehura* (Lisbon, 1944), he does not rely on autobiographical experience but treats of the lives of typical small settlers and traders who went out into the 'bush' and acquired an African family, out of necessity, not out of inclination.

The missionary's tale has a moral purpose, as it shows the European missionary leading the pagan native to a different and, to the missionary's mind, higher and better life through religious, medical and vocational teachings. Its central figure is an African and not the missionary himself. Equally important is the direct knowledge of African village life on which it rests and which gives it its true interest. A good example of this type is the fictionalized biography of a black orphan from a Ba-Ronga village, *Chitlangou, Son of a Chief*, originally written in French by André Daniel Clerc, a Swiss Protestant missionary like Junod, and published in Neuchâtel, Switzerland, in 1946. It is almost the African lad's own story; 'Chitlangou' is quoted in chapter headings, and we are assured that 'this story was told to the author by Chitlangou himself'.[13] The account begins with the evocation of what must have been the typical upbringing of a village youngster, living in a hut with his widowed mother and close to his grandmother, who instil in him the pride and responsibility of being a chief's son, his further education by other boys with whom he herds goats and cows, and the formal schooling received in a variety of government and mission schools, including one in Lourenço Marques, the capital. There are some big events in the boy's life which, however, form part of the common experience, such as taking part in the clan's harvest feast and dance, visits to the Indian trader's store, consultation of a woman who can smell evil sorcerers, the terror of final examinations at school, the first bus ride to the city, his arrest there for failure to carry identification papers on him, the return of an elder brother from the South African mines, and his own conversion after a wild night in the village. These episodes are narrated with forceful directness. They gain significance if 'Chitlangou' is identified as Eduardo Mondlane (1920-1969), the slain Ba-Ronga leader of FRELIMO, the black Mozambican independence movement. According to Mondlane's own brief account in *The Struggle for Mozambique* (1969), he was born in a village in the Gaza district north of Lourenço Marques, 'herded the family livestock' with his brothers, and was sent to school, thanks to the insistence of his wise mother, who was his father's third and last wife. Mondlane remains silent on missionaries and their school to train 'agricultural evangelist-technicians' which figures prominently in Clerc's story.[14]

An earlier missionary's tale, also laid in Ba-Ronga country, was H. A. Junod's *Zighi*, which may have served Clerc as a model. A curious variation on their tales was written by a former Portuguese Governor of Mozambique, Brito Camacho, as one of three *Contos selvagens* (Wild tales, 1945). In the last part of his story, 'Evolução regressiva' (Regressive evolution), a Catholic mission wants to attract the son of a dead chief when he returns from Portugal with a European education. But there Armando has learned to hate the Christian churches and European civilization in general. He dreams of a future African renaissance and when he realizes that the frustrated missionaries are secretly trying to get rid of him he brings about their massacre. Tongue in cheek, the anti-clerical Portuguese author applied poetic justice: after his act of 'savagery', the young man is killed by a lion.

João Dias's stories belonged to a class of their own. Most of them were visibly autobiographical although he did not write them in the

195

first person. The exception to the rule is the last, 'Em terras do Norte' (In northern country), where he appears as a reporter going to northern Portugal and being gaped at by the natives as if he were a strange animal. At the same time, his stories may be placed in the category of the assimilated African's protest tale. Godido, the protagonist of several stories, named after a Vatua chief who has been defeated by the Portuguese, feels doubly a pariah: he is a young black in a European colony and he is the son of a peasant woman who has to hoe the fields of a white landlord whose bed she occasionally shares. While the mother, 'Black Charlotte of the Loose Life', is mocked at as the 'indolent woman who never reacted', her son Godido is characterized as an 'insurgent black' who considers his 'colour of coal' a tragedy and thinks that he is 'perhaps a dog, perhaps a human being'.

The nameless Negro who appears in the symbolic tale 'Génesis' is seen at dawn, 'bright as a coal on fire', just like Godido at the end of the first story. But the symbolic figure must carry a white man on his back until both of them sink into the muddy road. Then the white man cries out to him: 'My black brother!' To which Dias adds: 'The black man perhaps no longer thought that it was useless to rebel.'

Other tales by Dias present young people going to Portugal for their education as he had done and suffering from loneliness: the girls Olívia and Alice, the unsure, hypersensitive black students Josefo and Júlio, and young Portuguese who also miss true friends. A single tale has a different kind of protagonist but fits best into the category of the protest tale. 'Indivíduo preto' (Negro fellow) reads like a reportage of prejudice standing in the way of a black railway employee's advancement, which is only achieved because the top authorities felt that 'any injustice ... might be exploited by clever agitators'. Keeping the educated blacks, such as this employee, satisfied at a minimal cost is the policy expounded in Dias's story by no less than an archbishop. His fiction anticipated the sociological and political essays of the nationalists such as Dr. Mondlane.

When Honwana began to write he thus had several kinds of Mozambican prose fiction to draw upon. His collection of seven stories is his first and only book so far. Yet it does not appear to be the work of a beginner, unless the variety of approaches used in the stories is taken as the groping towards the technique that would be most suitable. It is probable that Honwana polished his stories for the first edition after they had (all of them?) appeared in the youth supplement of *Notícias*, a Lourenço Marques newspaper. It is a fact that the stories

196

were revised for the second edition (1972) as is indicated on the title page.

Which were the sources of Honwana's inspiration? What, if anything, did he owe to his Mozambican predecessors? The author informs us merely that he began to write stories when an unidentified 'group of journalists, painters and poets' in Lourenço Marques 'helped him read a lot of important books' at a time when he was still more interested in sports, that they took him to 'motion pictures that had to be seen' and 'shared some of their concerns with him'[15]. The subject matter of the stories, he assures us, is limited to what 'is happening around him', and he does no more than bear witness to 'situations and the ways in which things are being done that might be interesting to know'. Interesting to whom? Since the black Africans were intimately acquainted with those situations in the colonial territory, he could only refer to the white city dwellers or, more likely, to the outside world, the more so as the public which would read and buy books was minute in Mozambique. And to what situations was he alluding? It takes little reflection to identify them as how the blacks are at the bottom of the social ladder ('Nós matámos o Cão-Tinhoso'), how even a relatively well-off black family lives in the ghetto ('Inventário de imóveis e jacentes'), how the black farm labour is treated by the whites ('Dina'), how blacks are humiliated in the bars ('A velhota'), how a white man bullies his black neighbour before his children ('Papá, cobra e eu'), how black children are made to feel inferior in school ('As mãos dos pretos') and how the good farmland is taken away from the blacks ('Nhinguitimo'). Thus, every one of the stories centres on an unfair situation, and one is not surprised to learn that Honwana sympathized with FRELIMO, was arrested, condemned and jailed with others, among them Craveirinha, by a Portuguese military court in March 1966, and that he joined FRELIMO openly as soon as he managed to leave Portuguese territory, after having been deported to Portugal. And yet, the stories were written so well and so subtly, in the tradition of the 'round-about manner' observed by Junod, that they escaped censorship in 1964, the very year when FRELIMO started the armed insurrection in northern Mozambique. No wonder, then, that FRELIMO acknowledged Honwana's help in publicizing the plight of the African.[16]

The first thing to be said about Honwana's stories is that most are presented as personal experiences, above all 'Nós matámos o Cão-Tinhoso' (We killed Mangy-Dog), the first, longest and most dramatic, which gave its title to the entire collection. The narrator appears as a young African boy, so that the story develops as the recollection of a childhood experience, told from the viewpoint of a child and in the language of childhood. Four more stories are told in the same manner. While 'We killed Mangy-Dog' seems like a typical story about the pecking order and the games of a boys' gang, it turns into drama on several levels: the drama of a dog becoming an outcast among dogs, of the killing of the dog by the boys, and of a complex psychological conflict within the boy-narrator, who is bullied into leading the innocent, friendly but all the same obnoxious dog to its death and even firing the first shot, for fear of being cast out of the gang. A 'way of doing things' is suggested merely, the authoritarian way as applied to the victor-vanquished relationship in an African 'province': the youths are made partners in suppression; as the boy-narrator was pushed into participation, so the gang had been coaxed into it by its elders, people of real authority, a veterinarian, and a district officer. This story contrasts sharply with the vast majority of childhood stories and poems written in Portuguese Africa, where childhood represents a golden age of innocent, happy play and togetherness.[17] There is togetherness of a kind in Honwana's tale also. The gang includes Ginho the black youngster and a couple of East Indians. But the leader is Quim, a white Portuguese, and all of them boss Ginho.

Another peculiar feature in Honwana's story is the choice of a dog as a symbol. João Dias only used the comparison with a dog once and in passing. Honwana makes the almost human dog a central symbol, no doubt having in mind various connotations of the word cão, 'dog', which was not only the most common insult to which blacks were treated by angry whites but means 'Devil', here reinforced by tinhoso, 'mangy', which can have the same meaning. Using similes and other imagery very sparingly, Honwana restricted the human identification to a few realistic details in the description of the dog and its behaviour: its dull, tearful eyes 'looked at you like a person asking for something but not wanting to say,![18] walking, 'he bobbed his head up and down like an ox' and 'rocked so crazily that he seemed like an old tumbril'. The same simile of the tearful eyes is repeated so many times that it becomes a leitmotif. At one point it is also applied to Isaura, the one girl in the story, whom everyone at the school thinks is stupid but who is the one person to stroke, to feed and to protect the dog, though it is all in vain. When we are told that the district officer got angry at both the boy-narrator and the dog and spat at them, then and there deciding that the dog has got to be eliminated, no simile is used. When the decrepit dog's trembling is mentioned, the absence

198

of a simile is underscored: 'And I felt him trembling like I don't know what.' When the boy hears the explosion of his own gunshot it is followed by the dog's 'monstrous scream, a scream as of a person' and by moans, 'as of a child'. Then the boy wonders if scream and moans did not in fact emanate from a human being, the girl, who had stolen upon the scene and was clinging to the dog. Finally the boy reflects that this dog must have been wanting more than a home, or treatment for his sores, or food. But since we are not told what the dog's unexpressed wish was we feel invited to make our own guess. Did it perhaps want the right of the lowly, the repellent, the meek to live out their lives?

The technique of repetition might be the one device taken from the traditional tale. Honwana carried it so far that it slowed up the action of the 1963 version, the one included in the first edition of the book (1964). In the second edition (1972), he omitted several of the repeated sentences and tightened the narrative in other ways without any loss of its haunting quality. There is a bare hint at the indirect, Aesopian approach of the animal fable; Honwana does not give the dog any purely human traits. Its humanization occurs only in the minds of Ginho and the girl Isaura, the ones who feel for it. Thus, the author stays within the bounds of objective, psychological realism. Contemporary reality is also evoked through the diverse ways of speaking, depending on whether the speaker is a grown-up white, a child, or a black servant. Their talk is contained in a frame-work of unpretentious, factual narrative with a limited vocabulary, plausible as the account given by a young school boy. Picturesqueness is avoided. Regional expressions are held to a minimum, in contrast to the practice of many other writers. Emotionally charged expressions punctuate the matter-of-fact statements in the other stories, without ever disrupting the colloquial style, to suggest the moods of the characters: exasperation due to insomnia in a crowded home ('Inventário de imóveis e jacentes'), tension between the older black's passive endurance and the younger one's revulsion, ready to burst into open violence ('Dina'), bitterness of a mother who has to make up a story for her child to compensate for a teacher's nastiness ('As mãos dos pretos', a story adopting the manner of a folk–tale, the etiological story), etc. The combination of plain statement with emotional touches can be illustrated through the subheadings of 'Nhinguitimo', the final story (the italics are mine): 'The wild pigeon'; '*How could anybody forget that night, caramba?!*'; 'Storekeeper Rodrigues did *plenty of* polishing on the counter top'; 'Chief Goana's land was good enough for the people to *have plenty*'; 'Nhinguitimo'; 'That night *I swear I got mad*'.

It cannot be by chance that the first ('Nós matámos o Cão-Tinhoso') and the last story ('Nhinguitimo') deal with unjust acts that cause deaths—the death of a dog, the death of a small farmer. These two stories also share a symbolic meaning. The obvious symbolism of the dog's existence has been shown. 'Nhinguitimo' works with the symbol of the first gusts of wind announcing an approaching storm, for this is approximately the meaning behind the African term which designates the south wind sweeping down from the Libombo mountains to the accompaniment of lightning, thunder and rain. The storm leads the farmer of the story to say in an apocalyptic tone that 'come the nhinguitimo, everything will change'. The big plantations created by 'them' shall be destroyed, but 'our' little *mashambas* shall be protected by the big trees at the river—perhaps trees where the ancestors dwell. The tragic story, in which the farmer goes berserk when he loses his land, turning on his own people, ends with the words, which are the final ones of the book: 'Pâça, aquilo tinha que mudar!. . .' (Damn it, there had to be a change!) Ironically, they are uttered by an unaware visitor who had come to shoot pigeons and play cards. He is rudely awakened to reality and that causes him to be annoyed at himself: 'Caramba, como é possível haver tipos como eu?' (Caramba, how dense can a guy be?). The symbol of the storm introduces an active note, while the one of the dog had been passive. There had been another passive symbol in the central story, 'Dina', to indicate impotence. There, the old farm labourer had made the unconscious gesture of crushing an imaginary weed in his clutched fist, releasing it and then caressing its defoliated stalks.

On the basis of the information about earlier Mozambican writings, incomplete as it is, one can see that Luís Bernardo Honwana could have used various indigenous models for his stories but that he chose not to follow any. At most one detects faint echoes of traditional story telling, and the indignation expressed before by João Dias, in the Chitlangou tale and in the poems of the mixed-bloods, such as Craveirinha.

Some reviewers have perceived other influences at work on Honwana. Amândio César saw the influence of the American regionalist Erskine Caldwell in the story 'Dina'. But Caldwell is given to picturesqueness and sentimentality, neither of which we find in Honwana, while rural realism, the faithful rendering of untutored speech and sympathy for the downtrodden could have reached Honwana through the fiction of the Portuguese neo-Realists. Helena Riáuzova, a Russian critic, maintained that Honwana used the devices of the oral folk tradition, such as the personification of animals and inanimate objects.[19] We have seen that such devices are not prominent in the stories and that his controlled simplicity in the representation of human situations, perhaps regrettably, bears no resemblance to the magic, the terror and the farce characteristic of the folk-tale. She also found a similarity with the stories of the Angolan José Luandino Vieira, which treat episodes in the impoverished lives of Luanda's black slum dwellers. Honwana offers more variety; his experience is not confined to the city, nor does he attempt to stylize the simplified Portuguese, enriched with Bantu words, that the city folk speak.

The one thing Honwana has in common with many contemporary writers is his concentration on the 'here and now', a personally observed reality. He differs from most in achieving an effect of authenticity with a minimum of means. Emotions are communicated with skilful indirectness and at times with intentional ambiguity. All preaching is eschewed as superfluous. We are led onto a human level that is above any regionalism. In this sense, Honwana is a humanist and a classicist.

Does Honwana's single slender book signify a beginning or an end? Whither is Mozambican literature headed, now that Portuguese domination has faded out? When Honwana published the stories in 1964, he was unsure of himself. 'I don't know', he confessed, perhaps coyly, considering that he had been writing for journals, 'if I am really a writer.'[20] Many years of unbroken silence followed as the result of imprisonment in Mozambique, fixed residence in Portugal, voluntary exile in Switzerland in 1974 and only then his return to Africa, but not yet to a normal existence. Have those years been sterile? Honwana's opinion of his reputation is objective. He wonders if the general curiosity about the struggle in the Portuguese colonies was not responsible for the widespread interest in his stories. But in the same letter of 10 May 1974 in which he expressed this scepticism he saw in the interest a challenge and announced that he was working on a variety of literary projects.

A talent for writing such as Honwana's will be sorely needed in the new Mozambique. Perhaps it will be used up in the execution of too many immediate, time-consuming tasks. But given half a chance, Honwana will almost certainly create again, especially if the country remains united and the project of a national literature for Mozambique reunites the writers that once had encouraged each other, fine craftsmen such as Honwana, Craveirinha, Rui Knopfli, João Grabato Dias. Mozambican literature could then become like that of India: a multiplicity of literatures in the vernacular languages of the region, under the common roof of a literature in Portuguese, the idiom in which Honwana learnt his craft.

NOTES

1. José Régio's judgement on Honwana is quoted by the Mozambican critic Eugénio Lisboa, an admirer of Régio, in a lecture, 'Perspectiva sumária da literatura moçambicana', given in 1971 and printed in the monthly *Rádio Moçambique* (Lourenço Marques) no. 419 (January 1972), p. 59.
2. The others are the late José Osório de Oliveira, who pioneered as a critic of Portuguese overseas writing in Brazil and Africa; Manuel Ferreira, who has lived in the Cape Verde Islands and Angola and is married to a Cape Verdean; and Jorge de Sena, who has made several visits to Africa. Their interest was in the main limited to Cape Verde, the most creolized and least African of the regions exposed to Portuguese influence.
3. A. César included the article among the essays republished as *Parágrafos de literatura ultramarina* (Paragraphs of overseas literature) (Lisbon: Sociedade de Expansão Cultural, 1967), pp. 206-08.
4. The importance of Portuguese as a unifying language was stressed by Eduardo Mondlane, the leader of FRELIMO (Front for the Liberation of Mozambique). Thus it was given a central place in the FRELIMO school system. See E. Mondlane, *The Struggle for Mozambique* (Baltimore: Penguin Books, 1969), pp. 131, 148, 178.
5. Honwana was born in Lourenço Marques in 1942; Craveirinha was born in 1922, Lisboa in 1930, Knopfli in 1932.
6. 'There is no unified society (in Mozambique). How can there be a culture that expresses something that does not exist? (...) The European has not had time to penetrate below the skin of Africa. The size of the country, the easy acquisition of all that is necessary for living, and the paucity of settlers cause the ethnic groups to live isolated from each other. To a large degree, this condition is stimulated by the deleterious influence of the Anglo-Saxons and especially of the South Africans. Thank God that is attenuated by an equalitarian legislation and a sense of shame and of social solidarity'. Translated from Alexandre Lobato, *Sobre 'cultura moçambicana'* (Lisbon: privately printed, 1952), pp. 56-57.
7. Professor Russell Hamilton, of the University of Minnesota, in a forthcoming book on the literature of Portuguese Africa.
8. Rodrigues Júnior, 'João Albasini', in *Para uma cultura moçambicana* (Lisbon: privately printed, 1951), p. 399.
9. With the words 'a José Craveirinha, expressão verdadeira da poesia de Moçambique', Honwana dedicated the first edition of his book to the poet who had encouraged him. The book was also dedicated to a girl, 'a Dori, que é sensível à angústia dos cães' (to Dori, who is sensitive to the anguish of dogs.)

10. 'I am under the impression that having collected about fifty Thonga (*sic*) tales of different lengths, (...) I possess only a fifth, or perhaps a tenth part of the whole folklore of our tribe!' H. A. Junod, *The Life of a South Africa Tribe*, revised ed., II (London: Macmillan, 1927), p. 217. Junod counted as one story the fifty-six episodes of the cycle of the Hare which he had collected.

11. *Op. cit.*, vol. II, p. 218.

12. *Op. cit.*, vol. II, p. 224.

13. *Chitlangou, Son of a Chief*, translated into English by Margaret A. Bryan (London: United Society of Christian Literature, 1950), p. 4.

14. 'Chitlangou' was identified as E. Mondlane in the article on the latter in Janheinz Jahn, *Who's Who in African Literature* (Tuebingen: H. Erdmann, 1972).

15. 'Nota do autor à primeira edição', in L. B. Honwana, *Nós matámos o Cão-Tinhoso!* (Porto: Afrontamento, 1972), p. 5.

16. Honwana is prominently mentioned as one of the poets, painters and writers from all the Portuguese colonies who since the 1940s have analysed the colonial situation, in his case 'through a perceptive detailed analysis of human behaviour', E. Mondlane, *op. cit.*, p. 108.

17. Among the few exceptions to the sunny picture of childhood in Africa are a plaintive poem by the Angolan Geraldo Bessa Victor, 'O menino negro não entrou na roda' (The little black boy was left out of the circle) and a pathetic story by the Mozambican Ilídio Rocha, 'Quando a fome manda' (When hunger dictates). The usual commonplace of childhood as paradise appears, e.g., in the early chapters of *Chitlangou* and in poems, such as Nóemia de Sousa's 'Poema de infância distante' (Poem of a faraway childhood).

18. *Nós matámos o Cão-Tinhoso*, p. 9.

19. Helena A. Riáuzova, *Portugaloyazitshniye literaturi Afriki* (African Literatures in Portuguese) (Moscow: Fd. 'Nauka', 1972). She discusses Honwana's work on pp. 238-242 with great care and insight.

20. L. B. Honwana, Initial words of 'Nota do autor à primeira edição', *op. cit.*, p. 5.

16

Ngugi wa Thiong'o: The Novelist As Historian

by

IME IKIDDEH

In a general sense every writer and every artist is a historian of his time, the unconscious recorder of the events and the mood of his society. Even when the writer reaches out into the uncharted areas of experience, the ingredients of his dreams derive from the impact of events around him; thus, his view of the world however affected in the creative process represents at one level a confrontation with the reality of history, past or present.

There is a distinction, however, between the generality of writers who are in this way historians as a matter of course, and others like Ngugi wa Thiong'o for whom historical incidents provide at a conscious level the material from which the creative work is moulded. For that reason it is best to approach Ngugi's novels as explorations into history conducted through the medium and conventions of fiction. Although this might seem obvious, some readers of Ngugi still go for the polarities, that is, he is either a conventional novelist in the sense of a writer who creates a fictional world in prose out of an entirely imaginary situation, or he is a traditional historian seen as a recorder in whom one may look for an Agreeable factual account without the deviations of view and emphasis which are the privilege of the creative writer.

The examples of two recent commentators on this writer, W. H. Jordan and S. N. Ngubiah, illustrate these opposing tendencies, for while one regards the historical element in the novels as unartistic and objectionable interventions, the other complains that the writer is not always faithful to widely accepted historical 'fact'.[1] Many students of Ngugi may not go to these extremes. They take account of his most obvious historical references but often ignore that pervasive sense of history that is a marked feature of all his creative work. As far as the polarities are concerned it should be understood that the writer who merely reproduced commonly held opinions without an individual imaginative touch would hardly qualify as an interesting historian, let alone a novelist of any grade. On the other hand, if he writes creatively and his work consciously draws from discernible historical material and situations, then that historical content must compel our attention as an integral and vital part of the writer's work.

There are further reasons why in Ngugi's case one cannot ignore his attachment to history. Outside his creative work, particularly in the essays of *Homecoming* which he sees as elucidating the fictional world of the novels, he has strongly expressed his awareness of the unbroken inter-relatedness of the cultural side of man and the social reality around him in which politics and economics feature prominently. Making specific reference to the environment of his own writing he reminds his readers that it is wrong to think of culture as exclusive of these factors. Thus he writes:

> In the Kenya scene of the last sixty years you cannot separate economics and culture from politics. The three are interwoven. A cultural assertion was an integral part of the political and economic struggle.[2]

And what is history all about if not the way man through the ages influences and relates to changes in the political and economic conditions of society? History then is at the centre of Ngugi's cultural preoccupations. Besides, Ngugi's conviction that the story of Kenya has been deliberately distorted by European writers underlies the conscious historical perspective of his work. So does his belief that the past is important as a base for pondering on the present and the future.

The first obvious feature of Ngugi's interest in history is the chronological scheme of his novels: *The River Between, Weep Not Child* and *A Grain of Wheat* in that order, the sequence of treatment which I have referred to elsewhere as his thematic progression.[3] The novels cover the period in Kenya's history dating roughly from the first arrival of the Europeans in Kenya late in the last century to the achievement of independence in the sixties. They centre on what are among the most momentous events in Kenya's colonial history. These include the earliest co-ordinated attempt by the Gikuyu people to fight European colonialism on the political, economic and cultural fronts; the intensification of nationalist consciousness resulting in the Mau Mau war; the aftermath of the war and the victory of independence with its accompanying disappointments.

Accordingly, Ngugi's first novel, *The River Between*, is more than a story of cultural conflict, that fashionable subject of African writing of its time. It is Ngugi's recreation of an early crisis in Kenya's colonial experience. Historically, the epoch is the twenties and thirties following the formation of Harry Thuku's Young Gikuyu Association in 1921, and the more politically effective Gikuyu Central Association. It was the latter, with Jomo Kenyatta as secretary, which in 1925 submitted a petition to the colonial government asking for certain political and economic rights for the Gikuyu population.[4] An important resolution of the Association was the rejection of the Presbyterian mission's order banning Christians from practising the traditional rite of female circumcision. A bitter conflict of values resulted from the Presbyterian action, leading to the founding of several independent churches in Central Kenya, and schools mostly run by the Gikuyu Independent Schools Association. Of these institutions the most famous was the Kenya Teachers' Training College founded in 1938 which trained teachers for the independent schools. It may be recalled that Kenyatta's first duty on his return from Britain in 1946 was to help improve the standard of this college. The struggle between Church and tribe, the establishment of independent schools and the formation of the Kiama to discuss these and other pressing issues form the plot of *The River Between*.

The historical Waiyaki was a famous Gikuyu chief and warrior in Kiambu, Central Kenya, who successfully fought the British in the 1890s over the right to property in his area. He was betrayed by a paramount chief, arrested at Fort Smith and taken to the coast but died on the way, or as another version has it, was buried alive at Kibwezi in Eastern Kenya.[5]

Waiyaki the teacher, mediator and rejected 'Black Messiah' of *The River Between* is not the warrior of Kiambu, although the name is probably used in the novel for its historical importance. Rather, the hero of the novel is a fictional character compounded from pieces suggested by the lives of several leaders past and present. At least one scholar has seen in the description of his piercing, contemplative eyes the picture of Jomo Kenyatta who, like Waiyaki, descends from a family of seers.[6] But there the analogy must end. For in his historical scheme Ngugi intends here to portray the prototype of an earlier leader whose vision fails to grasp the true nature of his people's needs. When Kenyatta appears in *Weep Not Child*, although we only hear of him, the impression is of a leader with a consciousness different from Waiyaki's. So close is his message to the hearts of the people that when he is arrested a general rebellion sets in, followed by a state of emergency in the country and the Mau Mau War.

In general, Ngugi does not disguise the names and the roles of historical figures when he finds them essential for his purpose. The exploits of the legendary Waiyaki are briefly narrated in *A Grain of Wheat*. Kenyatta is referred to several times by name in that novel, Harry Thuku and other well-known names are mentioned, complete with dates of important historical events in a chapter which reviews the development of the nationalist movement in Kenya. The dust jacket of the novel prepares the reader for this by explaining that these names have been 'unavoidably mentioned as part of the history and institutions of our country'.

In relation to the history which it seeks to recreate, the preoccupation of *The River Between* is larger and more socially oriented than W. H. Jordan's assessment of it as a study in 'the rigidity of an ordered cosmos'. The commonly applauded cultural interest of the novel is not confined within what the same writer describes in bewildering metaphysical terms, nor does it consist in beautifully patterned imagery of 'ritualized geography' in isolation from its social import.[7] *The River Between* deals with a cultural problem within and related to a particular political and economic situation, with an immediacy that arises from the picture of a human predicament within that social context. It examines the disruptive tensions in Gikuyu society under the exploitation of foreign rule, the problems of leadership in the circumstance and its consequent failure to unite the people in a direction that responds to their frustrations and hopes. In this regard, the author's own statement of what the novel is about is misleading in that it emphasizes the theme of cultural reconciliation at the expense of other concerns which the novel both overtly and implicitly shows to be equally valid, even fundamental. Ngugi's statement on the novel has to be interpreted in the light of the question that had been put to him.[8]

The reconciliation of Christian doctrine with traditional beliefs as embodied positively in Waiyaki, Muthoni and Nyambura, and negatively in Joshua and Kabonyi, is central to the story of *The River Between* (and Lloyd Williams has done an interesting religion-centred study of this subject[9]) but so is the oppressive social and economic climate in which this consuming conflict of values takes place. Yet the trouble with this novel is that the author appears to take this climate for granted and fails to dramatize it in the lives of his characters to give the community he writes about sufficient sociological credibility.

207

We know some of the legends of the community and something of its geography; we see glimpses of Joshua's rigorous hand over his family and Waiyaki's frustrated efforts on education and leadership of the Kiama. But the picture does not include that side of everyday life under the trying conditions the people are reacting against.

Despite this, the evidence of several passages in the novel, in particular Waiyaki's failure at the end, leads to the conclusion that the political and economic theme is as important to Ngugi's message as any. There are references to political agitation all over the ridges following the increasing alienation of land and exploitation of labour. Kinuthia, a moderate, soft-spoken young man suddenly threatens rebellion against his father and against all that is 'harsh, unfair and unjust'. Siriana Mission which he accuses of exploitative collusion emerges not simply as a Christian institution at war with 'barbaric' traditional customs but, even more, as an active agent of colonial oppression. The Kiama is committed 'to keep the tribe pure' but it is equally determined 'to fight for the land which had now been taken by the settler, the missionary and the government'.[10] Indeed, Waiyaki's failure arises less from his inability to unite the people, and more from his lack of comprehension of what aspirations the unity would serve. And this explains why Kabonyi finds it so easy to rally the Kiama against him.

Waiyaki may be an ideal man, but he is far from being an ideal leader.[11] His passionate education drive becomes irrelevant because it does not cater for the milk-and-millet portion of the people's grievance. His admirable objective to unite the community on the principle of love and reconciliation is an ideal that has little chance of success in an unideal situation. As a religion it fails to satisfy the criterion which Lloyd Williams stipulates as fundamental to the success of all religions:

> religion must arise out of a people's total life situation; it must speak directly to those people within the context of their past history, their present experience, and their future destiny.[12]

Too late, Waiyaki himself comes to realize the short-comings of his mission. If he had another chance, he says, he would preach a more meaningful sermon: 'education for unity. Unity for political freedom'.

> And all at once Waiyaki realized what the ridges wanted. All at once he felt more forcefully. . .the shame of a people's land being taken away, the shame of being forced to work on the same lands, the humiliation of paying taxes for a government that you knew nothing about.[13]

That then is the political and economic message of the novel. It is the colonial history that lies behind and within *The River Between*.

That *The River Between* is overweighted on the side of Waiyaki the Messiah and his magnificent ideas on education and reconciliation highlights two major artistic weaknesses of the novel. The first is a structural one, for there is a certain imbalance between the powerful Waiyaki story and the thinly painted picture of the hostile historical forces which throw him up and combine to defeat him as a popular leader. As the novel shows in the end, the religious controversy is only one aspect of a larger conflict which Waiyaki's vision is ill-equipped to cope with.

But the organizational weakness of the novel is a reflection of the more fundamental problem of the author's ambivalent attitude towards his hero. The novel leaves little doubt that the author's approving sympathies lie with Waiyaki. Indeed, so fascinated is Ngugi by Waiyaki's prophetic role that he romanticizes his hero's life and mission to the extent that Waiyaki's rejection in the end is reluctantly effected. Accordingly, the reader tends to see Waiyaki's failure not in terms of his inadequacies but solely in relation to Kabonyi's sinister dealings and the people's fickle-mindedness.

Ngugi shares Waiyaki's idealism. The young undergraduate novelist, 'deeply Christian' in school, finds himself in this early work at the cross-roads of a Christian-inspired compromise solution which fights shy of confrontation, and an inability to accept that solution in the face of his experience of underlying injustices. The rejection of Waiyaki was to lead Ngugi in subsequent novels to a more realistic attitude to the colonial question in Kenya and a clearer picture of a people in pain contending with the harsh forces of history ringed around them. In this he has drawn as much from his developed sensibilities as from the changing events on which the novels are based. The interrelation between cultural issues and social dynamics is even more apparent in the two later novels and in the short stories which tell the agonizing story of the Mau Mau War and Kenya's rugged road to independence.[14]

The commentator who has complained of the 'oppressively secular historical setting' of *Weep Not Child*[15] is yet to accept Ngugi as a historical novelist. It is hardly open to question that this novel would collapse if it were stripped of its historical setting since much of its substance and its credibility draw from that source. The suggestion by the same writer that in this novel Ngugi has 'given in to the temptation to rise above the events' is utterly absurd. The prevailing picture of insecurity and frustrated hopes epitomized in Njoroge within the framework of a 'secular' historical setting is in fact autobiographical in emotion; and far from rising above the events the author is perhaps too involved in them.[16] Indeed, the painful sentimental realism which haunts the reader of *Weep Not Child* and conveys to so short a novel its most remarkable quality must owe something to his own shattering experience of the incident he is recreating with the aid of his acknowledged narrative ability. The return of Kenyatta from Britain and the upsurge of an active nationalist following, the complete control of commercial life in urban centres by Indian residents, the end of the Second World War and the return of the Boros with no means of livelihood and a military disposition, the further appropriation of the fertile highlands for newly arrived white settlers and the increasing deprivation of the African peasantry: these constitute the political and economic setting of *Weep Not Child;* they supply the material of the novel which continues the history where *The River Between* left off.

Historically, land as the source of man's life, the basis of any social community and the foundation of all human culture, remained the sensitive factor in the contention between Africans and Europeans in Kenya. From the attempt by Joseph Chamberlain in 1902 to found 'a national home for the Jewish race' on thousands of square miles of land in Kenya and the official appropriation for British ex-soldiers after the World War, to the open seizure and illegal speculation by white settler-farmers that went on all the time, the record of British usurpation of land in Kenya must be one of the most sordid scandals in colonial history.

The Crown Lands Ordinance of 1902 and subsequent laws in 1915 and after, far from controlling land dealings, led in fact to more profitable speculation by Europeans and greater loss to the African population. What individual settlers could own—and before 1902 they could have it for nothing—is illustrated by the case of Lord Delamere, the one-time indomitable leader of the Europeans in Kenya. In 1903 he applied for 156 square miles of leasehold at a half-penny an acre, to be held for 99 years with the right of purchasing it permanently at eight pence an acre. Delamere who already held large tracts of land was granted 100,000 acres on lease. Such was the rush to acquire land that the Land Commission reported in 1905 that 200 per cent of Masai grazing grounds had been applied for.[17] Forced labour which included the indiscriminate use of women and children went hand in hand with land, and so did increase in the taxes exacted from 'natives'. Commenting on the situation, W. McGregor Ross, a senior British civil servant in Kenya at the time, has written:

It may be restated that up to the year 1926 no native tribe in the country [Kenya] was given any legal or definitive right to any land . . . . In the years 1919-1921 the subjugation of the natives of East Africa was probably more complete than it ever will be again.[18]

Further Land Commissions were set up between 1928 and 1934, but the situation was not much better when Kenyatta returned to his country twenty years after Ross's comment. He had written pointedly in *Facing Mount Kenya:*

A culture has no meaning apart from the social organization of life on which it is built. When the European comes to the Gikuyu country and robs the people of their land, he is taking away not only their livelihood, but the material symbol that holds family and tribe together.[19]

It was primarily over land that the Mau Mau War was fought. No ideology could be as intelligible to Ngotho as his *shamba*, the patrimony he has lost to the big *muzungu* farmer Howlands, himself inseparably married to the land on which Ngotho now works as a *muhoi* on low wages. In the Ngotho-land-Howlands relationship Ngugi recreates an economic situation typical of colonial Kenya. Like Ngotho, Ngugi's own father had had to work in similar degrading circumstances. In a factual account the Danish Baroness Karen Blixen records a similar sensitive relationship between her and her Kenyan workers:

The squatters are natives, who with their families hold a few acres on a white man's farm, and in return have to work for him a certain number of days in a year. My squatters, I think, saw the relationship in a different light, for many of them were born on the farm, and their fathers before them, and they very likely regarded me as a sort of superior squatter on their estates.[20]

Seen in this historical context, the behaviour of Ngotho and Howlands over land and the Emergency becomes wholly credible. In the end the forces of 'law and order' close in on Ngotho and crush him, leaving Njoroge, his school education abruptly stopped, to fend for himself and the family.

With Ngugi's presentation of Kenya's bitter colonial experience goes his belief in the essential order and humanity of the African past. Like Chinua Achebe whom he fondly refers to as his 'wise elder brother', Ngugi is of the opinion that the true nature of the African past has been obscured and over-simplified, even distorted, through colonial subjugation. His comment in *Homecoming* that colonial education had taught the African that the black man did not exist or was asleep 'until the Livingstones and the Stanleys woke him into history' expresses the same idea as Achebe's statement:

> I would be quite satisfied if my novels . . . did no more than teach my readers that their past—with all its imperfections—was not one long night of savagery from which the first Europeans acting on God's behalf delivered them.[21]

Both agree that the African writer has a duty to re-tell the African story, animate the past and thus, in Ngugi's words, 'resume the broken dialogue with the gods of his people'. The African writer cannot do this, Achebe warns, 'unless he has a proper sense of history'.

It is of interest that the works of the two writers have followed a similar pattern in historical setting. Yet the two differ in method, for whereas Achebe disguises the historical content of his novels within a credible sociological framework and merely implies the economic aspect of the confrontation with Europe, Ngugi openly parades historical and economic data, using them all as props and material which he carefully places in a fictional but recognizable setting. Whatever names he gives to the location of his novels—Makuyu and Kameno, Kipanga or Thabai—the landscape remains that of the hilly country around Limuru, his own home.

The difference in creative approach between the two writers cannot be explained solely in terms of an assumed difference between any two writers: the historical situations which produced them are different. Undoubtedly there is a certain underlying unity of experience in all colonial situations, and a comparison of anti-colonial literature in Africa carries enough evidence. But there is little in Nigerian history before independence to compare with the protracted life-and-death struggle that marks the colonial history of Kenya. More than Achebe then, Ngugi, who grew up in the shadow of the Mau Mau War, is at pains to tell the story of an exploited peasantry and their heroic struggle.

The urge to do this does not arise only from his agonizing memory of the event. It is dictated also, as in many Kenyan writers, by the spate of European writing on Kenya which Ngugi sees as a falsification of the social and economic truth of the colonial situation and as involving a distortion of the African character in and outside the fight for independence European writing on Kenya in such diverse forms as history, travelogue, diary and fiction dates back to the last century. Many of Ngugi's essays in *Homecoming* contain references to this subject in which he discusses the attitudes displayed by such writers as Karen Blixen, Elspeth Huxley, Robert Ruark and Fred Majdalany. In creative terms, Ngugi's use of Gikuyu creation myths and prophetic legends in the novels is in part to leave no doubt regarding the timeless memory of the existence of Gikuyuland and the Gikuyu people. In this he has drawn inspiration from Kenyatta's *Facing Mount Kenya* which achieves the same purpose with anthropological evidence. When Ngugi creates the delicate relationship between Ngotho and Howlands in their passionate attachment to the land in *Weep Not Child*, he is using fiction to make a historical point: that Ngotho is in fact the rightful owner of the land, and that Howlands, despite the sympathy accorded him in the matter, is an intruder and exploiter whose devotion to the farm is an escape from the bitter memories of a European war. Ngotho may be helpless but he is a human being fully conscious of the injustice of his position. And that consciousness will move him, along with the taunts of his own son, to join the general strike.

If, however, Ngugi's purpose and abilities ended with the attempt to correct the colonial history of Kenya, he would probably go down in historical assessment as a petty, quibbling chronicler whose presentation of evidence was not always the most accurate. He could hardly escape Soyinka's indignant censure of those African writers who need 'an urgent release from the fascination of the past'. Ngugi is not simply recording and fictionalizing but recreating and re-interpreting history, building his experience, his imaginative presentation of reality, into a vision which seeks to probe 'what any political and economic arrangement does to the spirit governing human relationships'. For him that is what literature is about.[22] The depth of that vision of human relationships in a chosen historical situation is in greater evidence in the multidimensional drama of *A Grain of Wheat* than in the narrower worlds of his earlier novels.

A Grain of Wheat pulls together two related hallmarks of Kenyan history: the Mau Mau War and a long-awaited independence. It is a story of heroism on the one hand and of betrayal on several fronts on the other. The exploits of the young leader Kihika add to the spirit of the resistance, boosting the courage and heroism of many, including the women of Thabai who are forced to build a new village in the absence of their men.

Kihika is the legend invoked at every discussion about the approaching *uhuru*. His militancy is a far cry from the soft compromise of Waiyaki. He is the complement in action to the verbal political onslaught that Kenyatta had delivered before his arrest. In him the unrealized aspirations of Waiyaki, the anger of Boro and the juvenile dreams of Njoroge are crystallized in a fighting leadership, and the passages he underlines in his Bible reveal what the Scriptures have come to mean to him in relation to his people in bondage. Kihika is fictional, although he bears close resemblance in career and fate to the historical General Kimathi, the famous Mau Mau leader.

But unknown to anyone, Mugo, the noble slightly psychotic anti-hero of the novel who is being lionized, had betrayed Kihika to his death, while Karanja as an enemy-appointed chief has openly committed a similar crime against his people by his sycophancy. (Karanja is of course a latter-day development of the Jacobo strain.) The betrayal motif runs through the Gikonyo-Mumbi-Karanja relationship into John Thompson's tortured disillusionment with the British Crown, his wife's flighty sexual adventures at the most critical period in her husband's career, and the rape of Dr. Lynd with the collaboration of her trusted houseboy. These intensive explorations of human relationships in a period of crisis are placed in the novel in the larger context of a national betrayal in which the emergent black rulers feature as new oppressors of an aggrieved people 'who now see all that they fought for being put on one side'. Although the novel does not develop this political theme to give it the central significance it deserves, the indications are strong of its importance in Ngugi's message.

The intriguing narrative method of *A Grain of Wheat* must be seen not only as a reflection of the battered soul of a much mistreated community but also in the light of a significant aspect of Ngugi's conception of history which helps to determine the technique. Like some writers and thinkers before him, Ngugi sees history as a continuum in which the past, present and future are inextricably tied together, each helping to mirror, to justify or condemn the other. Thus he writes:

For what has been . . . is intimately bound up with what might be: our vision of the future, of diverse possibilities of life and human potential has roots in our experience of the past.[23]

214

What the novelist does then in *A Grain of Wheat*, in the interlocking of the past and the present, is to place seven years of the Mau Mau struggle on the unfolding scoreboard of *uhuru* and let individual lives, their relationships and the collective ethos reveal themselves in action. Not infrequently he reaches farther back to the childhood of characters, to past freedom fighters and the community's folklore, and confronts the present with the account in an attempt to compel it to come to terms with the past and with itself. The heroic martyrdom of Kihika, the plaintive chants of Thabai women, the countless indignities suffered by their men in detention camps, the broken homes, even the ignoble roles some are compelled to play in the long struggle for freedom—these are what the inheritors of *uhuru* must take account of or condemn themselves before history. For these events of the past must be the focus in re-ordering society to provide for Gikonyo and his alienated wife Mumbi, whose name suggests the legendary mother of the tribe and who at the end of the novel requests a new child from her husband, the baby that will consolidate their reconciliation and begin a new order in post-colonial Kenya.

In the larger context of the African scene and the black race, it is history seen against what Ngugi describes as 'the gory background of European imperialism and its changing manifestations' that must dictate for the present and future an equitable social and economic system for the masses of people. It is in the collective human values of the African past that the black race must seek the inspiration to build a new society.

NOTES

1. W. H. Jordan, 'Themes and Development in the novels of Ngugi' in *The Critical Evaluation of African Literature*, ed. Edgar Wright (London: Heinemann, 1973), pp. 95-119; S. N. Ngubiah, 'Ngugi's Early Writings' in *Standpoints in African Literature*, ed. Chris Wanjala (Nairobi: E. A. Literature Bureau, 1973), p. 63.
2. Ngugi wa Thiong'o, *Homecoming* (London: Heinemann, 1972), p. 26, also p. 11. See also Ngugi's 'Literature and Society', paper presented at the Conference of Literature Teachers, Nairobi, September 1974.
3. Ime Ikiddeh, 'James Ngugi as Novelist', *African Literature Today*, No. 2 (1969).
4. For an explanation of this variation in the spelling of Kikuyu, see Jomo Kenyatta, *Facing Mount Kenya* (London: Secker and Warburg, 1961) p. xv; first pub. 1938.
5. Kenyatta, *ibid.*, p. 46; personal information from Waiyaki's grandson, Nairobi, January 1974.

6. Micere Githae-Mugo, 'Visions of Africa', unpublished Ph.D. thesis, University of New Brunswick, 1973, p. 221.
7. W. H. Jordan, *op. cit.*
8. See James Ngugi: Interview by Alan Marcuson, *Union News*, Leeds University, 18 November 1966, p. 7.
9. Lloyd Williams, 'Religion and Life in James Ngugi's *The River Between*', *African Literature Today*, No. 5 (1971), pp. 54-65.
10. *The River Between* (London: Heinemann, 1966), p. 124.
11. This represents a modification not a retraction of my opinion in 'James Ngugi as Novelist', *op. cit.*
12. Lloyd Williams, *op. cit.*
13. *The River Between*, p. 164.
14. A collection of Ngugi's short stories, *Secret Lives*, is being published by Heinemann, London. Ngugi is also completing a new novel which deals with the contemporary scene.
15. W. H. Jordan, *op. cit.*
16. See Ime Ikiddeh, Introduction to *Weep Not Child*, School Edition (London: Heinemann, 1966).
17. For a fuller account see C. Ojwando Abuor, *White Highlands No More*, Vol. I, *Pan African Researchers* (Nairobi, 1970). Walter Rodney comments in *How Europe Underdeveloped Africa* (Dar es Salaam: Tanzania Publishing House, 1972), p. 165: 'While Lord Delamere controlled 100,000 acres of Kenya's land, the Kenyan had to carry a *Kipande* pass in his own country to beg for a wage of 15/- or 20/- per month.'
18. W. McGregor Ross, *Kenya From Within* (London: Allen and Unwin, 1972), pp. 76 and 103.
19. Jomo Kenyatta, *Facing Mount Kenya*, p. 317.
20. Karen Blixen, *Out of Africa* (London: Jonathan Cape, 1964), p. 9; first pub. 1938.
21. Chinua Achebe, 'The Novelist as Teacher', *African Writers on African Writing*, ed. G. D. Killam (London: Heinemann, 1973), p. 4; Ngugi wa Thiong'o, *Homecoming*, p. 41.
22. Ngugi wa Thiong'o, *ibid.*, p. xvi.
23. Ngugi wa Thiong'o, *ibid.*, p. 39.

17

Okot p'Bitek and The Rise of East African Writing

by

MICHAEL R. WARD

East African writers have used conventional forms of western literature, but some of the most dramatic successes (and failures) have been achieved on the borderline of what we normally conceive of as 'literature'. At independence, there were anthropological and historical works about East Africa (as well as some novels by settlers); there was also a tradition of oral literature which pre-dated colonialism. The experimental nature of East African writing has reflected attempts to refashion these traditions into a new and more appealing mode. In their attempts to experiment with form, East African writers have been preoccupied with the concept of a popular literature which either attempts to solve the crisis posed by the apparent and unfortunate contradiction between social commitment and artistic detachment, or which attempts to rescue oral literature from the ashen hand of social anthropology. It is not clear yet whether such attempts will continue. A vein of private protest has recently been established which does not seem to depend upon these early initiatives in East African writing.

A chronology of the rise of East African writing since the early sixties (the time of independence) records a steady growth in the output of literature from 1962 onwards. 1962 itself saw the appearance of the influential periodical, *Transition*, and the first production of Ngugi wa Thiong'o's play, *The Black Hermit*, the latter as part of the Ugandan independence celebrations. East African poems were included in the anthology, *Modern Poetry from Africa*, which followed in the next year. 1963 also saw the publication of J. Kariuki's account of his detention camp experiences, *Mau Mau Detainee*. The next two years were to see the appearance of Ngugi's early novels and short stories, as well as David Cook's anthology of student writings, *Origin East Africa*. It was the appearance in 1966 of *Song of Lawino* by Okot

217

p'Bitek which turned this small trickle into a flood. This particular book also marked the beginning of the publication of works of literature in East Africa: the effect of the East African Publishing House is significant. In 1967, another periodical, *Zuka*, was founded, the first anthology of East African poetry, *Drumbeat*, appeared and two Kenyan novelists, Ngugi and Godwin Wachira, produced full-scale novels on the Emergency years: *A Grain of Wheat* and *Ordeal in the Forest*. In addition, two non-fiction works appeared that shed new light on the development of the political struggle in East Africa: *Not Yet Uhuru* by O. Odinga and *Mau Mau General* by W. Itote. The following years saw the rise of the imitators of Okot p'Bitek (Okello Oculi and Joseph Buruga), as well as important collections of stories by writers like Taban lo Liyong and Leonard Kibera. 1969 saw the appearance of Zambia's first collection of stories, *A Point of No Return* by F. Mulikita. It is ironic that in these years of creativity, Taban lo Liyong's now famous article on the 'barrenness' of the East African literary scene was published in his book of criticism, *The Last Word*, the first full-scale critical work by an East African author.

Experimentation with literary forms characterized the works of this time. We see Kibera experimenting with form in *Potent Ash;* the same is true of Taban lo Liyong in *Fixions*. Attempts to develop traditional African forms proliferated, not only in the work of Okot p'Bitek, Oculi and Buruga, but in Taban lo Liyong's *Eating Chiefs*. The element of experimentation continued in the years which followed.

The year 1970 saw the publication of Kibera's novel, *Voices in the Dark*, and J. Angira's collection of poetry, *Juices*, both of which offered a private vision of events which offset the public voices of Okot p'Bitek and Taban lo Liyong. This tradition was strengthened in 1971 by R. Ntiru's collection of poems, *Tensions*. An experiment of a rather different kind emerged in the same year with the publication of A. Mazrui's 'novel of ideas', *The Trial of Christopher Okigbo*. Two novels also appeared from Zambia: *The Tongue of the Dumb* by D. Mulaisho and *Before Dawn* by A. Masiye. The same year also saw a new production by Okot p'Bitek, *Two Poems*, and Taban lo Liyong's first volume of poetry, *Frantz Fanon's Uneven Ribs*. Indeed, this particular year was a most prolific one and combined experimentation with density of output. 1972 saw a consolidation of some of these experiments with the publication of Ngugi's essays, *Homecoming*, and the appearance of new volumes of poetry from established poets such as Angira and Taban lo Liyong. However, innovation still appeared to be an important feature in 1973, the year in which an anonymous

218

Zambian writer published a collection of satirical anecdotes, *The Kapelwa Musonda File*.

The above survey gives some idea of the diversity of writing in East Africa and indicates the difficulties which face the critic who attempts to assess this development. But certain trends are obvious. For example, the renaissance in East African literature began in the year of Ugandan independence, growing slowly until Okot p'Bitek's *Song of Lawino*. It is also obvious that Okot p'Bitek's writing inspired many others to refer to traditional forms (by which we mean the forms that existed before colonialism). This became one of the strengths of East African writing. It is also clear that Okot p'Bitek's achievement raised many questions about the nature of East African writing in its relationship to western forms of literary expression. Before we discuss the centrality of this poet in the East African tradition, we need to look at the situation before he appeared.

In an interview with A. Abdullahi in 1964, the year in which *Weep Not Child* was published, Ngugi said that the African writer in Kenya

has got to be an observer, and at the same time a part of him is committed, committed to the situation. Let me put it this way: he must be wholly involved in the problems of Kenya; at the same time he mustn't allow the involvement in that particular social situation to impinge on his judgement or on his creative activities.[1]

Ngugi's own first-published novel was an attempt to write a story about the Mau Mau years without propagandizing about them. *Weep Not Child* succeeds in this because it manages to dramatize the conflict over land rights (the central issue in the Mau Mau struggle) in the developing relationship between two central characters, Ngotho, who owns the land by traditional right, and Howlands, the white man who has conquered the land. The tragedy of the detached observer is recorded in the story of Ngotho's son, Njoroge, who tries (and fails) to fulfil his calling for education. In this character, Ngugi is also dramatizing a social issue because, as we are told: 'Somehow the Gikuyu people always saw their deliverance as embodied in education'.[2] But the portrait of Ngotho who is at once a real man and an embodiment of the archetypical suffering figure of failed manhood (a figure which appears again in the character of Mugo in *A Grain of Wheat*) shows Ngugi successfully reaching a level of artistic detachment whilst telling the story of a highly politicized situation. Ngugi's analysis and attempts to deal with the central problem of commitment and artistic detachment have important ramifications for later writers.

Many of Leonard Kibera's stories in *Potent Ash* are set in the Emergency years. One of the most successful of these, 'The Stranger', deals with a blind shoemaker who defies Emergency regulations and is able to get away with it. Kibera tells this story through the sympathetic eyes of a young child who watches the activities of the shoemaker with awe and a certain admiration. The writer shows how the Emergency has become part and parcel of the lives of his characters; we are told: 'The sound of shooting down the valley had become our daily bread and one did not stop to think and feel afraid'.[3] Yet the story is told with detachment. The shoemaker is not a committed fighter: we sympathize with him because of his capacity to survive as a cripple in this context, and because his defiance provides a vision of freedom for the bondaged villagers.

Hence Kibera's stories, although firmly rooted in the realities of the Emergency years, do not depend on these realities for their major effect. The stories in the collection are concerned with people who are able to hold out against the public invasion of privacy caused by the Emergency and show how a universal love operated in the face of misunderstandings caused by the war years. It would be unfair to suggest that this is Kibera's only concern in *Potent Ash:* the urban environment is as much a brutalized context as the Emergency, as we see in 'The Tailor', a story which brings both settings together. A young boy applying for work is suspected of being a Mau Mau fighter by an Indian shopkeeper. The boy is taken off by the police, yet he is still able to feel pity for the pain of the Indian who, in his hasty pursuit of the boy, has been run over by a car and now lay surrounded by unfeeling people: 'An island of loneliness, he lay only encircled by a group of people with hard, urban faces which registered more curiosity than emotion'.[4]

Not all writers have been able to achieve the same level of detachment from the issues of Mau Mau as Ngugi and Kibera. Godwin Wachira's novel, *Ordeal in the Forest*, although an accurate account of the rise of the Mau Mau movement, fails ultimately to engage our attentions with the lives of the individual characters. The novel shows us how Nundi (one of a group of young people who, like the characters in *A Grain of Wheat*, find themselves drawn inexorably into the struggle) develops from a shy boy into a forest fighter engaged in superhuman feats of courage. But we are not really told how this development takes place in terms of the boy's individual psychology. Ngugi got round this problem in *Weep Not Child* by presenting Boro, the Mau Mau activist, as a man disillusioned by the carnage of the Second World War. Wachira, like Ngugi in his novels of the Emergency years, sets out to depict the struggle from the points-of-view of both sides, but he gradually loses interest in the settlers, and they disappear from the novel. *Ordeal in the Forest* comes the closest of all East African novels to reporting. The following passage gives an indication of the kind of problem that can crop up in a novel which steers close to actual events; the need for police posts is being described:

Home Guard groups were formed in the area under a Headman controlled by the Chief, and the members of a blissful European community were sure their security arrangements were becoming so stringent that nothing could harm them. As a matter of interest, the Government eventually did step into the breach and aided the settlers financially to build the outposts.[5]

Another book which appeared before 1966 and has a direct relation to the tradition of Mau Mau writing is Josiah Kariuki's *Mau Mau Detainee*. It deals with conditions in the detention camps in Kenya before Independence and gives an account of the way in which the detainees came to terms with the situation they found themselves in. Kariuki does not try to fantasize his experience and takes pains to present his immediate feelings at the time. The aspect of the book which is most relevant to our discussion is the way in which the author, whilst writing a book for outsiders, has his feet squarely in the experience of his own world. This is evident in his use of traditional proverbs to explain events to us, as in the following example which tells of the decision not to punish Homeguards after *Uhuru*:

We have a Kikuyu proverb, *Tutikuhe hiti keeri*, which is to say, 'Let us not give a hyena two meals'. When a man was killed in olden times his body was given to the hyenas. To kill his killer as well would help no one except the hyenas and so we did not do this. This decision by all those who suffered during the Emergency is the reason why peace has now returned to the Kikuyu people.[6]

Kariuki also documents how the vernacular language was used to defeat the ends of the white administration; Chapter Five shows the way the detainees improvised with the language to avoid having to say insulting things about their leaders. It is evident from the book that linguistic devices played an important part in the struggle itself. This is important to our discussion of writing in East Africa because it shows how traditional forms not only survived colonialism, but were in part responsible for its defeat. The work of Okot p'Bitek must be seen in this context because it represents the continuity of this tradition. *Mau Mau Detainee*, far from being a white book with a black cover,[7] helps to unravel the development of writing in this part of Africa.

Song of Lawino disturbed the quiet tenor of East African poetry which until then had shown little apprehension of the possible use of poetry as a public medium. Indeed, it is remarkable how few of the poems (or stories, for that matter), in David Cook's anthology, *Origin East Africa*, reveal any awareness of the issues of independence, or have any sense of identity as East African writing. There are exceptions, of course. David Rubadiri's poems show an awareness of the complexities of the colonial heritage, as do Ngugi's stories of village misfits. One should not, however, underestimate the private poetic tradition, as it is one that continues to grow in East Africa, and gathers strength.

East African critics have not done adequate justice to *Song of Lawino*. In his chapter on the poem, 'Lawino is Unedo', in *The Last Word*, Taban lo Liyong is able to discuss the poem from the point of view of the language in which it was originally written, Acoli. Yet the analysis sets out to show that Lawino is no more than a village simpleton, unable to understand the complexities of her worthy westernized husband, Ocol. This criticism is not relevant to Okot p'Bitek's intention. In addition, Taban lo Liyong's praise for the poem is at best grudging, and there is the suggestion that the work's only worth lies in the fact that East Africa has nothing else to offer: 'A popular event, yes. A great event? Yes. Since there is literary drought.'[8] Ngugi wa Thiong'o is fairer to the work in 'Okot p'Bitek and East African Writing' when he points out that the poem is a flowering of the tradition of 'orature'. But even here there are surprises: 'The poem is an incisive critique of bourgeois mannerisms and colonial education and values'.[9] *Song of Lawino* is of course critical of the features Ngugi mentions, but the poem is not phrased as a 'critique'. Its criticism of bourgeois values takes the form of a lamenting appeal, at the heart of which there is a profound concern for the maintenance of a traditional *status quo*.

The quality of lament which pervades *Song of Lawino* derives from Lawino's knowledge that her husband is lost to her. She is asking the

222

impossible when she pleads for him to be returned to her because she knows that Ocol is lost in the evil forest of his books:

> For all our young men
> Were finished in the forest,
> Their manhood was finished
> In the class-rooms,
> Their testicles were smashed
> With large books![10]

This judgement of *Song of Lawino* is confirmed by *Song of Ocol* which appeared in 1970 and is best considered as a sequel to the earlier poem. Ocol sets out to answer Lawino's criticisms of his western way of life mainly by holding up to ridicule the village traditions that Lawino has defended. This is how the unrepentant Ocol describes the kind of village beauty which Lawino has earlier praised:

> Her naked feet
> Digging the pathway,
> Nibbling away the earth,
> Her soles are thick
> Cracked like the earth
> In the dry season,
> The skin of her hands
> Are rough like concrete wall,
> There are stones
> Embedded in the skin,
> Her palms are worn out
> Like the soles
> Of old shoes.[11]

The contrast between the two poems is important to our understanding of Okot p'Bitek's work. The above passage views the villager from the outside. Ocol is proud of his acquired tradition and boasts of his new possessions:

> Beat the dust off your feet
> And jump into my Merc.,
> Let me take you for a ride
> And show you around my farm . . . .[12]

This example demonstrates, however, that Ocol's pride is not tempered with humility, as Lawino's pride in her tradition is. Lawino admits to her deficiencies:

> It is true
> I am ignorant of the dances of foreigners
> And how they dress
> I do not know.[13]

Ocol's voice is bitter and critical: it departs from the tradition of *Song of Lawino* which pleads for our understanding and sympathy. *Song of Lawino* sets out to engage the public sympathy while remonstrating; *Song of Ocol* simply remonstrates. This distinction has important reverberations, as we shall see when we come to consider this work alongside other aspects of East African writing.

Song of Lawino is an important achievement in East African writing because of its detailed reference to traditional forms. But the poet's purpose here is entirely unselfconscious: explanations do not obtrude into the poem and Acoli words do not stick out obviously from the English text. The success of the poem lies in the fact that Okot is able to use both languages with equal ease and in doing so has managed to effect a fusion of the two traditions. The following example will serve to illustrate this feature; Lawino, in defending her position refers to actual dances, ceremonies and traditional practices. This is one of them:

> Butter from cow's milk
> Or the fat from edible rats
> Is cooked together with *lakura*
> Or *atika;*
> You smear it on your body today
> And the aroma
> Lasts until the next day.[14]

Okot p'Bitek avoids the tone of anthropological description in a passage such as this by speaking directly to the audience (using the second person) and by using vernacular words in a way that does not upset the non-Acoli speaker's apprehension of the event itself. Indeed, the rhyming of '*lakura*' and 'rats' shows an attempt to integrate the two languages within the framework of the verse. The success of this kind of experiment demonstrates an East African ability to rescue oral literature from the grip of anthropologists and to combine this attempt with a sensitive handling of the English language tradition.

Not all East African writers have been as successful as Okot p'Bitek in translating the experience of African tradition. But the poet has had many imitators, including Oculi, Buruga and Taban lo Liyong. Joseph Buruga's *The Abandoned Hut* in particular seems to rely heavily upon Okot p'Bitek's achievement. Buruga's poem, in which the hut is a symbol of tradition, deals with the lament of a man whose wife has deserted the tribe. The poet makes a similar selection of detail to that of Okot p'Bitek: the strangely shaped water tap, for instance, is chosen for observation, as it is in *Song of Lawino*, as is the practice of hair-stretching. The passage from *The Abandoned Hut* which speaks of the western practice of dancing quietly and in darkness 'like a wizard'[15] reminds us strongly of the passage in *Song of Lawino:*

> Dancing without a song
> Dancing silent like wizards
> Without respect, drunk . . . .[16]

It is important to notice that Okot p'Bitek's work has encouraged people to experiment with the use of form. One of the most interesting, and at the same time baffling, of these experiments is Okello Oculi's *Prostitute*, another lament, but written in the form of a novel. Oculi draws upon the technique of the direct appeal after the fashion of *Song of Lawino*, as is illustrated by the following passage which laments the influence of money: 'Metals, metals, metals. These metals are killing us. These ones they call money are driving us mad'.[17] The novel ends on a note of appeal when Rosa, the prostitute, pleads for her death not to be noticed. Oculi also uses the kind of appeal phrases that are typical of Okot p'Bitek's writing, as in Chapter Six which begins with the phrase: 'Bisi! Bisi! My man Bisi . . . '. *Prostitute* attempts to combine the lament tradition in poetry with the form of the modern novel. This leads to difficulties. The novel begins simply enough with the story of a young village girl who is dragged off to town by a Minister in a Mercedes. But from here on, it is difficult to detect a 'plot' as such. The narrative strays from the third person to the first person. The element of drama is lacking. *Prostitute* is perhaps one of the most experimental works to have appeared in East Africa in the sense that it attempts to unite the tradition of the lament with the western novel form. Oculi tries to do too much, but in doing so he perhaps opens a new road for writers in East Africa.

In view of Okot p'Bitek's influence on other East African writers, we need to look at Taban lo Liyong's *Eating Chiefs*. In his review of

Song of Lawino, Taban lo Liyong suggested that Okot p'Bitek ought to have included footnotes to explain parts of the work to outsiders. Taban lo Liyong's own folk-epic uses footnotes, after the style of the anthropologist, even though the writer's avowed intent is to 'induce creative writers to take off from where the anthropologists have stopped'. How successfully does he achieve this? *Eating Chiefs* is a collection of folk-myths arranged in several parts. The early section deals with creation myths, and from there, Taban lo Liyong moves to more up-to-date tales. An example from one of the early stories shows us the kind of problem that can crop up in this sort of endeavour; in the following passage the writer is employing an old-fashioned form of English to convey the story of tribal ancestors. We are told:

> Lwo's son was Labongo
> Labongo brought forth Kijok, Tereo and Tika.[18]

Whether one successfully updates African myths by the use of archaic English forms, or whether one is thus committing them to an even greater obscurity, is difficult to judge. At all events, it is clear that Taban lo Liyong has trouble in breaking free from the influence of some anthropologists. Consider this passage from a later story:

> The Pari are five to six feet tall
> And of slight build as befits their mode of life.
> They pay greater attention to the location of work for women
> Than any other tribe I have met.[19]

Here we have an example of a superfluous verse pattern imposed on an otherwise unmetrical piece of prose. It is evident from these examples that the fullest sympathies of the true interpreter are absent in this work.

Not all poetry in East Africa has fallen under the influence of Okot p'Bitek. The poetry of Taban lo Liyong, for example, demonstrates an author who has assumed the platform of public concern in a particularly individualistic way, as is demonstrated in his poem 'Student's Lament' from his first collection, *Frantz Fanon's Uneven Ribs, with Poems More and More*,[20] the title of which helps to suggest the prolific nature of Taban lo Liyong's output. His second collection, *Another Nigger Dead*,[21] has more restraint and shows a shared concern with those poets in East Africa who, unlike Okot p'Bitek, protest against social evils in a quiet vein. One is thinking here of the poetry of J.

Angira and R. Ntiru. The work of these poets goes a long way towards establishing an alternative tradition of poetry to that offered by Okot p'Bitek, and does not depend on his work for effect. It is passionate and deeply felt, and reveals with anger the feeling of frustration in the younger generation of poets. Ntiru's verse is unromantic about men in the public eye. This is revealed in his poem 'Chorus of Public Men', from *Tensions*, a title which sums up Ntiru's view of the atmosphere of public affairs in East Africa, and in the poem from the same collection 'The Masqueraders', which says:

In this unsung and songless age,
We wear our masks during the day,
We wear our selves inside out,
To avoid the prying rays of the sun
That focus our actions into question marks.[22]

This kind of poetry indicates a retreat away from nationalistic euphoria and shares a similar viewpoint with new novels like Kibera's *Voices in the Dark*.[23]

East African literature has been highly experimental. Some of these experiments have not always met with success, and some of them are hard to classify in terms of western concepts of 'literature'. Ali Mazrui's novel, *The Trial of Christopher Okigbo*,[24] takes place in an imaginary African after-life and is, according to the author, a 'novel of ideas'. Like other East African novels which deal closely with actual events, Mazrui's work is critically weakened by failures in characterization and by a tendency for both narrative and dialogue to stray into the direct reporting of events in retelling the drama of the Nigerian war.

Zambian writing is difficult to fit into our classifications of East African writing and seems to operate from a different, and as yet unexplained, tradition of writing. Of all the fictional works by Zambian authors, Fwanyanga Mulikita's collection of stories, *A Point of No Return*[25] (the title is significant), indicates an awareness of changes taking place within the nation. Andreya Masiye's novel, *Before Dawn*[26] (again, a title which clearly bears a reference to the independence issue), attempts to reassert the importance of a return to the values of traditional village life, but does not clear up the issue of how the central character, Kavumba, is able to succeed as a villager where other characters in the novel so dramatically fail. Masiye does not idealize village life and presents us with sensitive insights into the complexities of villagers coming to terms with the colonial experience.

227

But Kavumba is a shadowy figure: the success of his return to the soil is more a matter of luck than anything else.

Perhaps the most interesting experimental piece of writing to emerge from Zambia is a collection of anonymous satirical anecdotes entitled *The Kapelwa Musonda File*, which deals with the issues of modern Zambia with a directness and humour that is unrivalled in the writing of East Africa. 'Kapelwa Musonda' delves like a lie-detector beneath the fabric of modern Zambian society to reveal the complexities and paradoxes of public life and public men. *The Kapelwa Musonda File* is at once honest and cruel, and draws its strength from the kind of knowledge about public events that newspaper reporters possess. As an experiment in satire, this work is unrivalled in East Africa. 'Kapelwa Musonda' is cynical, but beyond the cynicism is a deep understanding of the conflicts that develop in the establishment of a national unity.

In the following passage, the story tells of how misunderstanding generates further misunderstanding. A Congolese national who is having difficulty speaking English finds himself being accused of belonging to an opposition party. The man himself simply wants 'no trouble':

'Me Congoleece. Want peace, no trouble.'

'I don't give a damn whether you are Congress,' exclaimed the Zambian. 'I can teach you such a lesson that you will never know where you put your Congress cards.'

'He is Congress, is he?' joined another from the next table.

'I heard him say so,' replied another patron from the furthest end of the room. 'These Congress people are the cause of all the trouble by bringing politics into these drinking places.'[27]

We can say at this juncture that there are two distinctive features in East African writing. First of all, there is the work of men like Ngugi, Kibera and Kariuki who display an awareness of and a concern for the events of the Emergency years. None of these authors is in any way confined by these events, yet they draw their strength from the test of political commitment offered by the Emergency. Their work is in sharp contrast to writers in other parts of East Africa, such as D. Mulaisho and A. Masiye, the two Zambian novelists whose work does not show the same kind of awareness of political strife. It may be that this reflects the nature of the Zambian independence struggle, which, as some commentators have pointed out, was less dramatic than the events in Kenya. But the important thing to note here is that the Kenyan writers are reflecting on the nature of public events which affected all men and women, whether directly or indirectly, and which took the form of a national crisis. Naturally, fiction which deals with events of this kind risks the hazard of veering too close to actual events, as we saw was the case with *Ordeal in the Forest*. Such a crisis, however, ensures that writers who deal with this topic do so in the knowledge that it is a widely shared experience. This, of course, is no guarantee of success; nor does it give the writer an occasion for complacency. Indeed, as Ngugi has pointed out, writers in this kind of situation need to be particularly careful that the appeal of their work on the level of commitment accords with its value in terms of artistic excellence.

This brings me, secondly, to a final consideration of the work of men like Okot p'Bitek which depends for its effect on a reassertion of values which existed before the crisis in East Africa. The work of such writers also makes an appeal to public sentiments, but it does so in a different way. Okot assumes the platform of public concern by way of an open appeal. Lawino's particular crisis is not simply presented (as Ngugi or Kibera might have presented it) as a private tragedy. It is true that ultimately Lawino is only a village woman whose husband has gone wrong; but she is also an archetypal national figure who aims to speak for all people on an issue of national concern:

O, my clansmen,
Let us all cry together![28]

Ngugi, in contrast, cannot claim or aspire to express national sentiment simply and directly through his characters—the form he uses, the carefully constructed world of fiction, makes this impossible. Okot p'Bitek's writing, though it may have been widely attacked by critics, does speak with a united voice. This provides an explanation for the popularity of p'Bitek's work, and its influence on other writers in East Africa.

In my analysis of important trends in the rise of East African writing, I have tried to do justice to the qualities of the literature which recommend themselves to us as the expression of a national feeling. Current trends in the new poetry and some new novels, however, indicate a direction away from the sort of national panegyric which draws its strength from the reassertion of traditional forms. But for the moment it seems safe to say that Okot p'Bitek stands out as the central voice in this tradition of writing. His is a loud voice, and a strong one.

NOTES

1. 'Ngugi wa Thiong'o', *African Writers Talking*, ed. Duerden and Pieterse (London: Heinemann Educational Books, 1972), p. 128.
2. James Ngugi, *Weep Not, Child* (London: Heinemann Educational Books, 1964), p. 119.
3. Leonard Kibera and Samuel Kahiga, *Potent Ash* (Nairobi: East African Publishing House, 1968), p. 51.
4. *Ibid.*, p. 120.
5. Godwin Wachira, *Ordeal in the Forest* (Nairobi: East African Publishing House, 1968), p. 125.
6. Josiah Kariuki, *Mau Mau Detainee* (London: Penguin Books, 1964), p. 66.
7. See Lalage Bown, 'The Development of African Prose Writing in English: A Perspective', *Perspectives on African Literature*, ed. Heywood (London: Heinemann Educational Books, 1971), pp. 39-40.
8. Taban lo Liyong, *The Last Word* (Nairobi: East African Publishing House, 1969), p. 141.
9. Ngugi wa Thiong'o, *Homecoming* (London: Heinemann Educational Books, 1972), p. 75.
10. Okot p'Bitek, *Song of Lawino* (Nairobi: East African Publishing House, 1966), p. 208.
11. Okot p'Bitek, *Song of Ocol* (Nairobi: East African Publishing House, 1970), p. 35.
12. *Ibid.*, p. 60.
13. *Song of Lawino*, p. 31.
14. *Ibid.*, p. 56.
15. Joseph Buruga, *The Abandoned Hut* (Nairobi: East African Publishing House, 1969), p. 25.
16. *Song of Lawino*, p. 41.
17. Okello Oculi, *Prostitute* (Nairobi: East African Publishing House, 1968), p. 79.
18. Taban lo Liyong, *Eating Chiefs* (London: Heinemann Educational Books, 1970), p. 10.
19. *Ibid.*, p. 81.
20. Taban lo Liyong, *Frantz Fanon's Uneven Ribs, with Poems More and More* (London: Heinemann Educational Books, 1971).
21. Taban lo Liyong, *Another Nigger Dead* (London: Heinemann Educational Books, 1972).
22. Richard Ntiru, *Tensions* (Nairobi: East African Publishing House, 1971), p. 15.
23. Leonard Kibera, *Voices in the Dark* (Nairobi: East African Publishing House, 1970).
24. Ali A. Mazrui, *The Trial of Christopher Okigbo* (London: Heinemann Educational Books, 1971).

25. Fwanyanga M. Mulikita, *A Point of No Return* (Lusaka: National Education Company of Zambia, 1968).
26. Andreya S. Masiye, *Before Dawn* (Lusaka: National Education Company of Zambia, 1971).
27. *The Kapelwa Musonda File*, (Lusaka: National Education Company of Zambia, 1973).
28. *Song of Lawino*, p. 207.

18

Ayi Kwei Armah and the 'I' of the Beholder

by

D. S. IZEVBAYE

How often the unconnected eye finds beauty in death—the
women looked at . . . whiteness, saw famine where the men
saw beauty, and grew frightened for our people.

Two Thousand Seasons

The theme of beauty and the 'I' of the beholder is central to Armah's
fiction.[1] It is the starting point for his social ideas about old Africa
and contemporary Africa. In his treatment of the theme he makes a
distinction between two kinds of beauty—an active, external beauty
whose power makes the beholder's eye a mere receiver of impressions,
and a passive ideal beauty hidden in nature and thus challenging the
beholder to test his ability to penetrate the object to the beauty beyond.
The eye of the beholder thus becomes a moral organ and an index to
his moral integrity, since 'the perception of beauty is so dependent
on the soul's seeing'.[2] This view of beauty has strongly affected the
conception of plot and incident in Armah's fiction. Just as the strong
moral tone in his writing gives his plot and incident a ritual movement,
so is the text flooded with images of seeing and hearing. Even the
characters are generally not whole persons but active and passive senses,
like the watchers and listeners, the seers and hearers listed in the paragraphs which introduce the characters in *Two Thousand Seasons*.

This preoccupation does not, however, limit Armah to a philosophical interest in the question of beauty and the subjective character
of seeing. It is his contribution to the debate on black aesthetics.
It therefore has a political relevance for the celebration of black civilizations which has now become a major twentieth-century theme. Both
the philosophical statement and its political relevance for contemporary
Africa are embodied in 'An African Fable',[3] a story constructed after
the theme of a knight's quest for an ideal which later appears to him
in the form of grail or lady. In this complex little tale an inexperienced

232

warrior mistakes the uncontrolled throb of his own heart for a woman's cry of distress and, because of an imperfection in his vision, becomes a betrayer where he should have been a liberator. This tale contains the philosophical kernel of themes to bloom later in Armah's fiction: post-independence disillusionment in Africa, the sense of the beautiful as a shibboleth for leaders and liberators, and the theme of Pan-Africanism.

In the warrior's rape of the woman we have the theme of the strong taking advantage of the weak, as a conqueror exploits a people he claims to have saved from oppression. This retold tale of disillusionment has been preceded by various versions presented in a more explicit form, from Peter Abrahams's *A Wreath for Udomo* through *Kongi's Harvest* and *A Man of the People*, until we arrive at its contemporary, *Bound to Violence*. In the new philosophical context in which Armah places it, the story of the new African ruler betraying the people he should help is given its specific political meaning through the use of a symbolic but nevertheless identifiable landscape which the warrior traverses as he wanders south through desert, scrub and forest, to arrive at the sea-shore goal where he displaces an older warrior whom he finds raping the woman. The comparable sexual licence of the conquerors and kings in *Two Thousand Seasons* becomes a figure for the rulers' exploitation of land and people, and the way they perceive beauty becomes a kind of moral test, as it is also in *The Beautyful Ones Are Not Yet Born* and *Fragments*.

The two types of beauty which Armah distinguishes in 'An African Fable' give us an insight into the psychological impotence of the hero of *The Beautyful Ones*. While 'the man's' awareness of true beauty stimulates a powerful revulsion against the corrupt path to wealth taken by the new middle class, his power of perception is nevertheless too inactive to resist the impressions of beauty which it receives from the shiny trinkets from Europe:

> There were things here . . . with a beauty of their own that forced the admiration of even the unwilling . . . He could have asked if anything was supposed to have changed after all, from the days of chiefs selling their people for the trinkets of Europe. But he thought again of the power of the new trinkets and of their usefulness, and of the irresistible desire they brought. . . the thought ran round and round inside his head that it would never be possible to look at such comfortable things and feel a real contempt for them.[4]

What poses the social problem in *The Beautyful Ones* is, however, not the inability to purchase foreign trinkets but the ordinary question of daily bread. The economic gap between Koomson, the minister, and 'the man'—between ruler and ruled, that is—prepares the way for the class conflict prescribed by Marxists as a solution to social inequality. But the language in which the plight of the poor is described suggests their capacity for endurance and hope rather than their readiness for confrontation. It is still a few days to the end of the month when the novel opens, and the author sees it through the eyes of his characters as Passion Week when life is 'not as satisfactory as in the swollen days after pay day'. In spite of the figure of religious suffering used here, the image of pregnancy suggests a capacity for hope on the part of the author and his characters. The beauty of the flower in the last chapter has an indirect link with the Passion Week of the first chapter, and the flower is also presented enclosed in an oval shape—an egg or ovary—awaiting the birth of beauty as the workers' Passion Week preceded the birth of the day of comfort. Armah's art is thus too ambiguous for us to see a simplified Marxist solution in it, and his critique of socialism in 'African Socialism: Utopian or Scientific?'[5] is a criticism of theories built on simple Marxist oppositions. The importance of African family connexions in the plot of his first two novels is an acknowledgement that there are ways in which African family interests can act against African socialism. The artless dishonesty of Koomson the minister and the passivity of 'the man' in *The Beautyful Ones* can both be traced to family demands on the individual. Because of his loyalty to family 'the man' identifies too closely with Koomson's motives, if not with the means he adopts, for him to have been intended as a class representative in an impending struggle. Perhaps it is this sympathy for Koomson's motives which moves 'the man' to help Koomson out of a tight spot during the coup.

Fragments is essentially a representation of the themes of *The Beautyful Ones*, using the benefit of the author's personal experience of the extended family. It contains basically the same cast of characters and roles that we find in *The Beautyful Ones*. 'The man' is now named Baako Onipa ('Onipa' is Akan for 'man'), and Brempong (i.e. 'an important person') is mainly Koomson re-christened, although he now trails a larger retinue of relatives and hangers-on, and is a 'been-to'. His initials, 'H.R.H.', foreshadow Armah's denunciation of all forms of African royalty in *Two Thousand Seasons*. Although the first two novels are similar in plot and characterization, the opposition of characters takes place at a higher social level in *Fragments*. In *The*

Beautyful Ones Koomson was once an uncouth dockhand now risen to be minister, while 'the man' is a secondary school leaver denied university education by lack of opportunity. In *Fragments* on the other hand, the two protagonists are equipped by their education to join the new middle class, and are equal, at least theoretically. Baako is denied entry into this class because of his refusal even to begin to accept their behaviour patterns. He discovers for himself what it is to be socially isolated when the asylum walls rise around him. And his mother's confession now comes like a belated lesson:

> 'We come to walls in life, all the time. If we try to break them down we destroy ourselves. I was wanting you to break down and see the world here, before I saw you yourself were a wall.'[6]

Refused entry by his own professional kind and denied emotional support by his kin, he is only let through the gates of madness.

The situations developed by Armah in his novels appear to close some of the main social options for Africa. We might summarize these situations into a statement of this kind: on the one hand the alliance between the privileged class and the poor is arranged by the extended family who ensure the flow of material benefits from rich to poor relations; this reduces the chances of a class confrontation. But then family demands for a share in the rewards of individual ability and training discourage maximum fulfilment for the average gifted individual. This is a very crude summary of what happens to Brempong and Baako in *Fragments*. We may ignore two bits of evidence in order to develop this theme: first, there are hints within the novel that Baako had neurotic tendencies before his return to Ghana, and second, there is the important fact that to give a character in a ritual-oriented society a first name like Baako or 'lonely one' is to encourage us to see his malady as a congenital one rather than a means devised by the author to make a social comment. Whatever the case, Baako's progress to full madness is intensified by the family's general lack of real regard for individual feeling. Brempong is sturdy and crafty enough to bear the weight of family demands. But an individual as sensitive and intelligent as Baako can see in these demands only his own death and the sacrifice of his personal talents. Although Juana, his Puerto Rican friend, cannot understand what Baako's grandmother means when she tells her that the family 'tried to kill' Baako, the essay draft in which Baako uses the Melanesian Cargo Cult as a model for interpreting the Ghanaian extended family institution clarifies for Baako and for the reader the ritual meaning of family expectations. The ritual death of travelling out to return with cargo for the community is successfully enacted by Brempong and Araba's child (who, unlike Brempong, suffers actual death). The plot also provides instances when the ritual proves abortive, in the stories of Skido, the driver who brings cargo but dies in spite of fulfilling the symbolic death of travelling out, and Baako, who dies symbolically by travelling out but is rejected because he brings no cargo.

This rejection by society is also ritually performed in *The Beautyful Ones*. Koomson the corrupt minister ritually repeats the public crimes he has committed by eating and vomiting what he has eaten. His subsequent escape through the latrine hole and by sea is the national penalty for his failure to distribute cargo to a wider group than his immediate relations. In other words, he is punished for an anti-social act rather than the sin itself. The ritual movement of the last three chapters defines the area of social taint. Before Koomson's expulsion the necessity for social purification is made evident by excremental symbolism. The symbolism works with a logic that is Freudian: eating is impure, excretion a form of purification. The result of this attitude to food and latrines is the hero's recoil from all forms of sensuality, which gives the novel its impression of a horrifying passivity:

> The thought of food now brought with it a picture of its eating and its spewing out, of its beginnings and endings, so that no desire arose asking to be controlled. . . Sometimes it is understandable, the doomed attempt to purify the self by adding to the disease outside... The nostrils, incredibly, are joined in a way that is most horrifyingly direct to the throat itself and to the entrails right through to their end.[7]

The man's oversensitive sense of smell is similar to the reaction of Soyinka's Sagoe, another character who uses the latrine as a haven to which one may retreat from an oppressive social order. The eyes and the nostrils of Armah's hero are really moral organs, however. 'The man' functions as the artistic conscience of the work, although he is not exclusively so. His obsession with corruption is obliquely commented on through various parables like those of Rama Krishna, the recluse who would escape corruption but rots before he dies, and the picture of the man-child brought to school by Aboliga the Frog. Translated into political terms, the parable of the man-child preaches cultural relativism by its insistence on the universality of corruption.

Corruption is in the nature of things, and the degree of corruption is relative to the time it takes to bridge the space between the beginning of growth and its end. The insanity of the man's recoil from contact appears most effectively in the scene where his wife's Caesarean scar prevents him from making love to her. He is not therefore to be expected to read the more subtle lessons of inescapable decay and perpetual renewal written even in water:

> the water escaping through a gap made by the little dam and the far side of the ditch had a cleanness which had nothing to do with the thing it came from. . . . Far out, toward the mouth of the small stream and the sea, he could see the water already aging into the mud of its beginning.[8]

In spite of these comments on the *involvement* of ripeness in rottenness, the man's reaction is not wholly subjective. The smell of physical corruption which Koomson brings to the man's house on his second visit is noticed—significantly—by a child, but not by an adult—the watchman who 'did not seem to notice the smell'. Although community is not offered as the place of salvation and well-being for the individual in *The Beautyful Ones*, we must see the man's return to community, however reluctantly he returns, as an acceptance of responsibility to his family.

In *Fragments*, individualism is not accepted as an alternative to a corrupt community, even though the talented individual who suffers in this work may not look to the group for his salvation. Of the chapter titles (which are used as comments on the action within each chapter), two—'Gyefo' and 'Osagyefo' ('Saviour' and 'Saviour in war')—support the idea tentatively offered in the novel that such individuals may look for support only in the bond between one individual and another. But the idea is rejected, not developed. When Juana says that 'salvation is such an empty thing when you are alone', back comes Teacher Ocran's reply that one would not find it in the market place. However, Baako's madness is the author's ironic comment on the chances of individualism. For in *Fragments*, as in *The Beautyful Ones*, the question of value is tied to the problem of seeing. The individual is imperfect, a fragment from the whole. His vision is thus subjective; it is not, however, a distortion of truth. It is a reflection of social imperfection, a mirror of that which is not beautiful. Its reflection is justified in so far as it does not invite an adjustment of the seeing lens. But its true value is not in the accuracy of the lens but in its diagnosis of the presence of rot and the need for a cure. This problem gets its sharpest focus in that scene where the stranger Juana describes Baako's isolation as 'going against a general current' and receives as reply Baako's ambiguously chosen substitute: 'as a matter of fact it's beginning to look like a cataract to me'.

The cataract which caused the partial blindness of Naana, Baako's grandmother, has the same source in the historical experience which brought the malady of madness to people like Baako. It also suggests that the extended family practice was never a 'current' even in the past, because the cargo mentality caused the ancestors to sell their own people to any white slaver who came along. In spite of her physical blindness, however, Naana's seeing is the nearest thing to completeness in the novel because she sees not the surface gleam of trinkets, but the higher Platonic beauty described in 'An African Fable'. She is not an isolated individual like Baako because she can relate to 'Nananom'—the community of ancestors living underground. Her vision is complete and inclusive because it *contains* both the wholeness of the past and the fragments of the present:

> The larger meaning which lent sense to every small thing and every momentary happening years and years ago has shattered into a thousand and thirty useless pieces.[9]

Because Naana's values belong to a community of the past her voice is merely the voice of the singular person left over from the past, as her name, Naana, is the singular form of Nananom.

Armah's criticism of honoured African institutions like the extended family and his frequent suggestion that the initiative for the slave trade came from Africans themselves are best seen against his argument in favour of a realistic appraisal of the African past and the future of Africa. Such realism is the topic of the conversation between Baako and his boss Asante-Smith. Asante-Smith's objection to the allusions to slavery in Baako's film script is countered by Baako's retort that slavery has everything to do with the African past. Behind Baako's anger is the knowledge of a suffering community of slaves betrayed by their rulers.

The true test of Armah's attitude to the African past is his depiction of suffering as a communal experience, especially in *Two Thousand Seasons*. Although his first two novels deal with suffering as the experience of individuals, his heroes are individuals only because they are set against their community. Even as individuals they stand for

238

something larger than themselves in the sense that not only does the author vest some of his themes and values in them, he also makes them the representatives of other suffering individuals in society. Moreover, the centrality of the first person narrator in the first two novels is mainly an instrument for sounding the depths of social discord, even though the nature of the seeing by either hero is done in a very personal manner. But whatever resonances of group suffering the author manages to strike by giving his characters generic names and developing their problems through his use of social institutions, suffering is most effectively conveyed in the novels through the individual experience, as when on-coming madness is seen through Baako's eyes. The irony in the author's treatment of character and experience in the novels prevents us from interpreting too simply the later argument in *Two Thousand Seasons* that the individual is nothing, the group everything. What the argument does is to reinforce the horror of isolation which marks Armah's works.

It is only in *The Beautyful Ones* that we are clearly shown how close the relationship between individual suffering and a communal experience of it can be. But an author is a chameleon figure endowed with the power to assume the colour of his characters' emotions. When Armah claims and uses this privilege, he successfully focuses on the group while using the experience of the individual. He achieves this simply by leaving things unsaid and refusing to identify the actual sufferer among the group of three boys who flee from the dogs of the white man whose garden they have just raided. The outlines of the incident are clearly enough sketched to be an individual experience although it is an experience with which many African children can identify.

> Such a lot of mangoes and such big almonds to have to leave behind, and the hole is far too small and the thorns are cruelly sharp, coming through the khaki all the painful way into the flesh. The backward glance brings terror in the shape of two dogs, and they look much larger than any angry father. . . . Can a dog also roll a child over and leave it feeling thoroughly beaten by life?[10]

The suffering here is given wider relevance because its recall by the listening man is stimulated by the speaking teacher's account of a parallel experience. Here we can at best only try to explain the method by seeing it as the experience of either three boys coalesced into one, or of one boy made to serve for three. A slightly different version of the method occurs in that scene in *Fragments* where Baako and Juana roll down the sandy beach to dry their skin. The incident is done through Juana's eyes alone and we feel the tactile sensation more fully than we do the group frenzy of the worshippers who roll down the beach in chapter two, although as far as actual sensations go, Juana's experience should be far less intense than that of the group. The group frenzy is seen—can only be seen—mainly from the outside, and it becomes less meaningful because it invites less sympathy.

In *Two Thousand Seasons*, as in the sixth chapter of *The Beautyful Ones*, Armah opts for a narrator in the plural, in contrast to the personalized narrators who dominate his first two novels in the manner of the conventional novel. The plural voice is suitable for the theme of an oppressed community which he develops in the fourth novel. But it demands that the author surrender his chameleon privilege to enter into and identify with the individual when the suffering of the group is being portrayed. Here is Armah's re-creation of a slave-branding scene:

> The askaris brought another captive forward and burned the mark into her flesh. When we had all been burnt the slave driver took the calabash and the horn from the woman . . . . Then walking up to each of us he dipped a piece of cloth in it and rubbed our raw wounds with the mixture.[11]

One cannot help noticing the hiatus in this report. The swift transition from the third person singular, 'burned . . . her flesh', to the first person plural, 'when we had all been burnt', leads us to see in the deliberate suppression of the first person singular a reluctance to identify with the individual, or perhaps even to acknowledge his existence.

The reason for this is made clear not only by the chosen narrative focus but also by the credo announced at the book's close: 'There is no beauty but in relationships. Nothing cut off by itself is beautiful . . . . The group that knows this . . . [is] itself a work of beauty.' Armah is consistent in his portrait of the migrant blacks in this novel. Individualism is not allowed. Even Anoa, the prophetess whose utterance defined the path to the people's salvation, is not any one individual because 'she was not even the first to bear that name'.[12]

If the suffering of a community is often less intense in this work than the suffering of individuals in the first two novels, it is nevertheless consistent with the function of Armah's novel in showing that suffering

240

is less unbearable when shared. In fact, in 'African Socialism: Utopian or Scientific?', we come upon Armah's definition of community as 'shared suffering and shared hopes'. This is the foundation for his attitude towards individualism on the one hand, and socialism on the other. Placed against this unambiguous preference for the group rather than the individual in this novel, the intensity of the focus on flawed individuals in his first two novels shows up as a call for social reform rather than a distorted vision of society. This applies to the criticism of Nkrumah's Ghana in both the first two novels and the essay, where the satirical emphasis falls on the gap between word and deed. The definition of socialism in the popular language of the latrine graffiti in *The Beautyful Ones* is both a criticism and a reminder: 'socialism chop make I chop'.

The emphasis shifts from satire in *The Beautyful Ones* to patriotic history and exhortation in *Two Thousand Seasons*. It is easy to draw a parallel between the career of a committed writer and the emphases in his writing. We would not therefore learn much from pointing out that *Why Are We So Blest*, a novel in which Armah develops the theme of human isolation and pessimism first sketched in 'Contact',[13] was published when he was in the United States as a visiting lecturer. But there must be an extra-literary significance in the East African publication of *Two Thousand Seasons*, a work which urges the return to true socialism on the part of all Africans, now that Armah is living in Tanzania, the land where Nyerere's practical experiment with African socialism has been launched.

This does not necessarily imply agreement with the policy which preceded the experiment, for Nyerere was as much a target of Armah's criticism in the socialism essay as Nkrumah was. Published in the Year of Ujamaa, the essay is critical of the Tanzanian programme for being 'rich in sacerdotal sanctimonious piety as it is poor in political realism'. But the Arusha declaration has at least one realistic feature worth mentioning here: the insistence that socialism must have a local, even rural, base. This view is extended to Nyerere's stand on Pan-Africanism, an issue on which he disagrees with Nkrumah, when he insists that African political leaders must first deal with local realities as a prelude to continental unity.[14]

The issues of socialism, Pan-Africanism and local realities are important in Armah's work. The satire in the first two novels begins from the confrontation of African socialist theories with the reality of national life. Theories are after all only fictions, as we infer from 'African Socialism: Utopian or Scientific?':

the socialist tradition itself [is] ... *a mytho-poetic system.* The greatest source of power and influence available to the socialist tradition is *its acceptance and imaginative use of the archetypal dream* of total liberation, ... the thoroughgoing negation of the repressive facts of real life.[15]

But it is as if Armah had set his sights too low when he dealt with national problems in his first two novels, for he later adjusts the focus in *Two Thousand Seasons* by developing the Pan-African theme implied in 'An African Fable' along the lines of earlier Pan-African novels, from Casely-Hayford's *Ethiopia Unbound* and William Conton's *The African* to Ouologuem's *Bound to Violence.* To realize the full importance of this, his fourth novel, it is important to see it ultimately as fiction, a mytho-poetic system accepting and making use of the archetypal dream of total liberation. And like the socialist tradition which Armah analyses in his essay it is constructed after a Marxist mytho-poetic model: it locates an imaginary African Eden, the Way of Reciprocity, in the pre-migrations past of the Africans in the novel, and projects a socialist heaven too, in its hope for the recovery of the Way. Although Armah did not approve of the name 'Kenya's Bible' given to the Kenyan document on socialism,[16] *Two Thousand Seasons* is manifestly intended as 'Africa's Bible' because of the explicitness of its moral exhortation and the Pan-African manner in which it draws its characters' names from all over the continent. The very thinly disguised names and the historical framework it adopts imply a denial that this work is primarily fiction, while its grave relevance for the present commits us to an ethical goal that is irresistible. But we recall that in citing the Kenyan document in support of his criticism of African socialist theories, Armah argues that socialist intellectuals are so busy condemning religion that they do not see how they are themselves creating a religious system.

As the author distrusts formal religion, *Two Thousand Seasons* is offered as a kind of ethical manifesto rather than a bible for blacks. Nevertheless its combination of poetic form and social theory brings us close to a magical view of art. But it is the method rather than the message which tells us how to place the novel. The style is probably its most important achievement. In this work Armah develops what promises to be one of the major literary styles in Africa, finding its base in the same tradition that encouraged Aidoo's dramatic style. The writing is not merely oral, but oracular. Its imagery shows a preference for that which is fundamental and unchanging. The poetic effect of the prose is sustained without verbal inflation and dead metaphor. The essential simplicity of the style is sustained by calling an object by its name, not its praise name. Thus Armah avoids the convention which enables an orator to wrap his truths and untruths in mere words. Here kings are surrounded by 'flatterers', not 'counsellors', and the recollection of the past is a 'remembrance' rather than 'history'. 'Remembrance' suggests that memory fails, that only what is relevant is remembered for the present and for posterity, while 'history' implies inclusiveness, accuracy and objectivity. The novel is similarly stocked with folklore elements and motifs which, with the theme of black diaspora, give pattern and direction to the work. Within the large tidal movement marked out by the theme of migrations we find the tinier waves of rhythm achieved through the use of structural parallelism, formal repetition and the repeated return to the motif of flowing water:

> Springwater flowing to the desert, where you flow there is no regeneration. The desert takes. The desert knows no giving . . . .
> Hau, people headed after the setting sun, in that direction even the possibility of regeneration is dead . . . .
> Woe the headwater needing to give, giving only to floodwater flowing desertward. Woe the link from spring to stream. Woe the link receiving springwater only to pass it on in a stream flowing to waste . . . . [17]

The literary model is the traditional dirge of Ghana. The function of the dirge, according to Professor Nketia, is to involve the group in the suffering of the individual, and to lessen individual grief by channelling it into collective grooves.[18] The result is artistic pleasure, rather than pain, an experience of beauty which every hearer and every beholder should find in Armah's peepshow into Africa's past and present.

NOTES

1. Armah has written four novels so far: _The Beautyful Ones Are Not Yet Born_ (London: Heinemann, 1969, first published in 1968); _Fragments_ (Boston: Houghton Mifflin Co., 1970); _Why Are We So Blest?_ (New York: Doubleday, 1971); _Two Thousand Seasons_ (Nairobi: East African Publishing House, 1973). All quotations are from these editions.
2. _Two Thousand Seasons_, p. 285.
3. _Présence Africaine_ (Paris), no. 68 (1968), pp. 192-196.
4. _The Beautyful Ones_, pp. 170, 175, 177 passim.

5. 'African Socialism: Utopian or Scientific?', *Présence Africaine* (Paris), no. 64 (1967), pp. 6-30.
6. *Fragments*, p. 253.
7. *The Beautyful Ones*, pp. 28, 47-48 *passim*.
8. *Ibid.*, p. 27.
9. *Fragments*, p. 280.
10. *The Beautyful Ones*, pp. 79-80.
11. *Two Thousand Seasons*, pp. 184-185.
12. The Ghanaian legend of Anoa has been re-interpreted by another Ghanaian writer, Ama Ata Aidoo in *Anowa* (London: Longman, 1970).
13. *The New African* (London), vol. IV, no 10 (Dec. 1965), pp. 244-246, 248.
14. See interview with Nyerere in *Africa* (London & Paris), ed. Raph. Uwechue, no. 21 (May 1973), p. 13.
15. 'African Socialism: Utopian or Scientific?', p. 8, italics mine.
16. 'Kenya's Bible' is Kenyatta's description of Sessional Paper no. 10, 4 May 1965: *African Socialism and its Application to Planning in Kenya*, as Armah notes in his essay.
17. *Two Thousand Seasons*, p. ix.
18. J. H. Nketia, *Funeral Dirges of the Akan People* (Achimota: 1955), p. 8: ' "One mourns one's relation during the funeral of another person" ... , says the Akan maxim ... Grief and sorrow may be personal and private, nevertheless Akan society expects that on the occasion of a funeral they should be expressed publicly through the singing of the dirge.'

19

The Development of Sierra Leone Writing

by

EUSTACE PALMER

It has been one of the mysteries of the African literary scene that although Sierra Leone led the field in education and literacy from as far back as the early nineteenth century, her literary output has lagged far behind those of other West African countries such as Nigeria, Ghana, Guinea and Senegal. The reasons for this literary lethargy probably lie deeply imbedded in Sierra Leone's unique historical, social and educational situation. Up to the very recent past, the educated classes who should have provided the crop of budding writers largely consisted of Creoles, the descendants of liberated Africans, freed slaves from Nova Scotia and the Caribbean, and the 'Black Poor' from London. These people were settled by the British in Freetown and its environs towards the end of the eighteenth century and the early nineteenth century. Unlike the indigenous inhabitants of the interior, the settlers had become largely detribalized and thus alienated from the rich source of African tradition which has been one of the props of African creative writing. With largely western names, customs, and dress, the Creole community could not perhaps have been expected to demonstrate that African consciousness which lies at the heart of the greatest African creative writing.

This, however, cannot be a conclusive explanation since the same historical and cultural situation obtained in the West Indian islands which have nevertheless produced a vital literature. Perhaps one ought to consider whether those forces which gave such a great impetus to African creative writing in the fifties were absent from Sierra Leone. The foremost of these was surely the awareness amongst Africa's educated elite of the traumatic effects of the contact between their societies and alien western imperialist civilizations. The flowering of

245

creative activity was the cultural manifestation of that wave of national-
lism which swept through Africa in the fifties, and which was never
very strongly felt in Sierra Leone. The Creoles were the nearest, in
Anglophone Africa, to the 'assimilés' that French policy produced in
Francophone territories, but among them there was never that reaction,
that process of rediscovery of a lost identity, which led to the Négritude
movement. Most Sierra Leonean intellectuals continued to regard
Britain with respect or even affection. The intellectual elite thus lacked
that awareness of the damage done by an alien civilization to indigenous institutions and that concern for the dignity of African traditions
which motivated the works of writers such as Achebe, Laye and
Senghor.

Furthermore, Sierra Leone society paid little attention to the arts.
There was, and still is, no comparable magazine to *Black Orpheus*
which did so much to stimulate creative writing in Nigeria. Writing
was a spare-time activity indulged in by the most distinguished men
in the community, almost as a public service or duty, in the same way
as they would participate actively in church matters or in the Boy Scout
movement. It is significant that almost all of Sierra Leone's leading
writers in the fifties and early sixties were professional men who were
members of the establishment.

However, Sierra Leone can still boast of a literature even if she has
not yet produced a classic; and it is a literature going much further back
than most people seem to be aware. Like most African countries,
she possesses a very rich and vital oral literature. Ruth Finnegan's
classic work *Limba stories and story-telling* has popularized the artistry
of the oral literature of merely one of a number of tribes, each of
whom can boast a rich oral lore.[1] Even the detribalized Creoles of the
coastal areas have a considerable body of folk-tales, most of them
of the Anantsi variety, which are being actively studied at present.

The pioneers of Sierra Leone written literature—Adelaide Casely-
Hayford, Crispin George, Jacob Stanley Davies and Gladys Casely-
Hayford—were all writing well before the upsurge of literary activity
in Africa in the fifties. Adelaide Casely-Hayford was actually born in
Ghana, but moved with her husband to Sierra Leone. She was the
author of several stories, the most interesting of which is 'Mista
Courifer',[2] and an autobiographical novel *Reminiscences* (1953).
Both are well written portraits of Creole society. They are also remarkable in that their author, though a privileged member of the Creole elite,
devotes a great deal of energy towards the exposure of those who imitate
the European way of life. Both works are shot through with the

author's awareness of herself as being first and foremost an African.

Crispin George and Jacob Stanley Davies were early Sierra Leonean poets, with a very limited conception of what poetry is supposed to be. The most cursory glance at their poetry suggests the dominant influence of the hymnal and the Book of Common Prayer. Both were great churchmen, Crispin George being in fact a chorister for several years. In 1952 he published privately a collection of poems entitled *Precious Gems Unearthed By An African*.[3] Crispin George is at his best on the rare occasions when he writes in blank verse, liberated from the constricting effects of rhyme. 'Help Deferred' and 'Ingratitude' are two of his best poems, each a *tour de force* of declamatory grandeur, with well chosen images and analogies reinforcing the effortless flow of thought:

The basest forms of vices that we know
Seem chaste, compared with base Ingratitude,
That freakish, misbegotten child of pride
Seduced by basest treachery, void of all
extenuating pleas adduced by vice.[4]

Crispin George emerges from his poetry as a profoundly religious moralist with great faith in a divinely and justly ordered universe. In this he adequately reflected the attitudes of his generation and his milieu. He sees the realities of life as a revelation of God's love and an assurance of heaven; he advocates the virtues of tolerance, patience, love, honesty, humility, justice and gratitude. Even in poems such as 'Homage to Mother Africa' where he is asserting his pride in and love for the continent, he contrives somehow to bring in the religious theme. Modern readers might find his optimism a bit facile and bordering at times on sentimentality, but his work, taken as a whole, is a not unimpressive expression of the corporate attitudes of his class and generation.

Jacob Stanley Davies was less prolific and versatile than Crispin George. Davies never published his poems, which were written primarily for the satisfaction of members of his family and circulated among them. But individual poems have been reproduced in anthologies.[5] 'A Negro's Prayer' exudes the religious aura we have noticed in Crispin George's work and similarly shows the influence of the hymnal and Prayer Book. The metrical scheme is similarly conventional and the diction archaic. Nevertheless there is little awkwardness and the sentiment, though commonplace, is dignified. Davies, like George, reveals tremendous pride in and concern for the moral purity of his race.

Racial matters also form the theme of 'Even There' which must surely rank as one of the most brilliant satirical poems written in Africa before Soyinka's 'Telephone Conversation'. Using the community of ghosts, angels, devils and skeletons in the other world, Davies creates a perfect imaginative medium for exposing the absurdity of racial discrimination. There is consternation when the white skeletons refuse to mingle with the black ones, the white angels with the black angels, the white ghosts with the black ghosts and the white devils with the black devils:

> There was a great commotion in the cemet'ry last night
> Skeletons in altercation!, twas a grisly sight!
> Said one, 'I'll have you know, Sir, though in this lev'lin' place,
> You're not my equal here, Sir, you're of a different race.
> Prevent your Nigger worms man, from capering round my bones
> I'll never fester with you here, man, our skins were different tones.'
>
> . . . .
>
> There was a great dissension 'midst t' angels up in heaven
> Because an equal brand of crown had to them all been given.
> The white ones said, 'By right of race we should have crowns
> of gold
> While crowns for natives all should be quite of a different mould.
> They shall be made to doff their crowns when one of us goes by
> And if they don't we'll take our crowns and dot them in the eye.'

The choice of words is exact, the tone is beautifully modulated and controlled, the metre is well chosen and the whole perfectly structured. The satirical detachment suggests precisely that unsentimentality and toughness which one misses in Crispin George.

Gladys Casely-Hayford, daughter of Adelaide, was, like her mother, largely educated in the British tradition and was a member of the privileged Creole elite; yet her work is also notable for its demonstration of the beauty and dignity of the black race. In 'Rejoice' she calls rousingly to her fellow Africans to rejoice in their blackness. The poem is infused with a rather naive religious optimism, and she gets her metaphors hopelessly mixed in the middle, but the sense of rejoicing is accurately captured by the rhythm. In 'Nativity' she sees the birth of Christ in purely black terms. The Christ child is a black babe born in a native hut to a black mother and father; he is wrapped in 'blue lappah' and laid on his father's 'deerskin hide'. 'Freetown' is an accomplished poem showing that although Gladys Casely-Hayford shared the naive optimism and sentimentality of Crispin George and, to a limited extent, of Jacob Stanley Davies, she was capable of greater metrical sophistication:

> Freetown, when God made thee, He made thy soil alone
> Then threw the rich remainder in the sea.
> Small inlets cradled He, in jet black stone.
> Small bays of transient blue he lulled to sleep
> Within jet rocks, filled from the Atlantic deep.[6]

These four pioneer writers lived in an age of comparative peace and stability; the placid surface of their work is understandably unruffled by the undercurrents of tribalism, tribal consciousness, African nationalism and all those other turbulent forces characteristic of Africa in the fifties and sixties. These forces begin to be reflected in the work of the succeeding generation of writers.

Both artistically and thematically Delphine King acts as a convenient bridge between these two generations. Her collection *Dreams of Twilight* was published privately in Nigeria and aptly described in a foreword by Chinua Achebe as 'intensely personal without being private'.[7] Some of the early poems convey a naive sentimentality couched in archaic rhymes and diction. But she soon permits herself greater freedom and fluency in poems such as 'Reunion Sweet', 'What is this thing called love?' and 'Destiny', culminating in the brilliance of 'Lost Innocence', one of the most intensely personal of her poems. The poem, which is about loss of virginity, communicates tremendous depth of feeling. It powerfully recreates the actuality of the experience by means of realistic images and diction, and the headlong rhythm:

> Suddenly without a sign, a hint
> It struck
> Its cruel pointed horns
> It dug, dug deep
> Until the blood
> Fresh red blood
> Did stream mercilessly, ceaselessly
> From the vicious wound, dug deep
> So deep, its horns, pierced right through
> Into the vital organs, the heart, too.[8]

This poem and others such as 'Emotion' and 'Magic' show that even when she is describing powerful feeling and is liberated from the constricting regularity of rhyme and metrical form, Delphine King still exercises perfect control. Her themes are varied; there are poems about betrayal, the failure of love, despair, isolation and restless unfulfilled searching. But there are also poems about acceptance, resignation, recovery, faith and optimism, courage, determination and boundless aspiration.

A great many of her poems, like 'The Child', are about pride in blackness, the hypocrisy of Africans trying to behave like white men, Pan-Africanism and misguided nationalism. Some, like 'The Elite' and 'It Seems', are social satire directed against snobbery, social climbers and corruption. It is her African consciousness and social conscience, together with the fluency, freedom and lyricism she eventually achieves, that lead logically to the same effects in Abioseh Nicol, thus linking her with the middle generation of Sierra Leone writers.

The four figures whom I regard as comprising the middle generation—Abioseh Nicol, Sarif Easmon, Robert Wellesley-Cole and William Conton—have several factors in common. They are all brilliant, highly qualified professional men. These men, who were roughly the literary contemporaries of Achebe, Laye and Ekwensi, were not merely, like these latter, members of the intelligentsia; they were the cream of the intelligentsia—highly competent men, each with a number of publications in his field to his credit. They were also the cream of the social elite. Unlike their Nigerian counterparts, they had all spent their undergraduate and post-graduate days in Britain and were perfectly at home in British culture. They could not, in any sense of the phrase, be called men of the people, and could not, perhaps, be expected to convey in their writings the feelings of ordinary men and women. With the possible exception of Abioseh Nicol, their work does not reflect that cultural conflict, that sense of individuals and societies torn between acceptance of alien values and loyalty to their own traditions which was the mainspring of African writing in the fifties and sixties. Their background and training led them to regard British values and standards as perfectly acceptable and this acceptance is reflected in their work.

Possibly because they were away from Sierra Leone for considerably longer than the others and therefore had more reason to feel alienated, Abioseh Nicol and Wellesley-Cole show some African consciousness. And yet it woud be too simple to say that Abioseh Nicol's poetry reveals that glorification of Africa one finds in the poems of the Négritude school. The glorification is partly present in 'The Continent That Lies Within Us', but only as part of the rose-tinted picture of Africa held by the idealistic African student in Britain who is fed up with the monotony, artificiality and mechanization of the life he sees around him. The second half of the poem presents a picture of the real Africa that confronts the young graduate on his return. And the portrait is far from flattering:

Is this all you are?
This long, uneven red road, this occasional succession
Of huddled heaps of four mud walls
And thatched falling grass roofs.[9]

The contrast between the imagined splendour and the actual drabness is effectively enacted in the poem. 'African Easter' gets down to the theme of cultural conflict, dramatizing the dilemma of the African intellectual torn between the traditional religion he has abandoned and the white man's brand of Christianity he has accepted. In a number of stories with a distinctly sociological bias such as 'The Truly Married Woman', and 'Love's Own Tears', Nicol gives penetrating accounts of life in Freetown Creole society.[10] In others such as 'The Leopard Hunt' and 'The Devil at Yolahun Bridge' he gives equally penetrating accounts of the relations between the colonial administrators and their Sierra Leonean subordinates. All the stories are wittily and graciously written with good characterization and accurate observation.

With Robert Wellesley-Cole we turn to the novel form. Sierra Leoneans have always shown a greater capacity for non-fictional than for fictional works. It is therefore not surprising that the novel form started in Sierra Leone as autobiography with Adelaide Casely-Hayford's *Reminiscences*. The trend continues in Wellesley-Cole's *Kossoh Town Boy*.[11] In fact, of the five Sierra Leonean novels or pseudo-novels so far written, only one–Sarif Easmon's *Burnt Out Marriage*—does not seem to be wholly or partly biographical in form. Although they are not concerned with the cultural–sociological questions which interested other African novelists, they attempt to present as detailed a picture as possible of various aspects of Sierra Leone society. *Kossoh Town Boy*'s main claim to attention is that it is a picture of an African society, an unaffected portrait of life in the East End of Freetown in the early twentieth century, seen through the eyes of a growing boy. William Conton's *The African* partly records Conton's own impressions as a student in Britain and partly the imaginary career of a poor but clever Sierra Leonean boy (Sierra Leone is referred to in the novel as Songhai) who gains a scholarship to pursue a university course in Britain. He returns home to teach, establishes a political party and becomes his country's Prime Minister. This fairly straightforward stereotyped story of the rise of the successful African politician is given added interest by the hero's brief affair with a South African girl, which ends in the girl's murder and the hero's rather stupid decision at the end to give up his political career and travel overland, incognito, to South Africa, ostensibly to help the freedom fighters, but in reality to seek out the girl's murderer. This is obviously a sociologist's, historian's, or anthropologist's novel, full of reflections and reminiscences and giving the author an opportunity to express his ideas on various topics. The sociological material is not so much presented as talked about, and it is clear that views which are at times presented as the young boy's, or the student Kisimi's, are Conton's. Conton makes no concession to the fact that he is writing about an African setting; he does not see that in order to reflect the authenticity of the setting he needs to modify the language, which remains formal, mannered or ornate. The point of view is often embarrassingly western as when his hero rhapsodizes on the architecture of Durham Cathedral or the grandeur of Bach's 'St. Matthew Passion'. Although the hero becomes a successful politician canvassing for the people's votes, neither he nor his creator is able to enter into the people's feelings, even when Kisimi is a young boy in a rural environment.

In many ways Sarif Easmon's attitudes are rather similar to Conton's. The Creoles, who had adopted a pseudo-English way of life, came to regard the interior as rather uncivilized and most provincial peoples as inferior. The provincial peoples resented this in their turn, and came to regard the Creoles with great hostility, particularly when power passed into their hands with the political advances of the fifties. Even amongst the Creoles themselves there were interesting though not openly acknowledged social divisions; some families saw themselves as forming a kind of aristocracy. Sarif Easmon's ancestry was partly Creole and partly Susu, a tribe which also had its own social divisions. He was therefore well placed to make a study of all these forces. His first play, *Dear Parent and Ogre*, deals with class consciousness, social snobbery and tribalism. On the surface Easmon seems to be suggesting that the Africa of the future will be dominated by a meritocracy, not by an effete aristocracy. But the message is undermined by his inability to develop his themes thoroughly and logically. In the play, Easmon seems to throw his weight behind the values of the Susu-Creole arist-ocracy. Easmon and his major characters are attracted to the values of the aristocracy—luxurious cars, champagne, a nostalgia for Paris and New York, the music of Wagner and the poetry of Byron—all adding up to a kind of life which is not only foreign but impossible to most Africans.[12]

Easmon's second play, *The New Patriots*, is steeped in the social and political situation of Sierra Leone in the sixties and sets out to attack corruption, tribalism and political incompetence.[13] The play achieved great popularity, since for most people Easmon seemed to have accurately reflected the existing situation. And yet Easmon's moral judgement is just as warped here as it is in *Dear Parent and Ogre*. He suggests that the Mende Chief Byeloh is a rabid tribalist, but fails to demonstrate his reputed pathological hatred of the Creoles. Easmon does his best to put Byeloh in the wrong because he wants to endorse once more the values of the pseudo-western Creole aristocracy. All the Creoles turn out to be sterling characters, and most of the provincials turn out to be villains. The good ones among them are reclaimed for Creoledom.

In the novel *The Burnt Out Marriage*[14] the same pattern emerges. Sarif Easmon intended to demonstrate the destructive potential of tribalism, but because of a lack of thoroughness in the development of his themes he seems to end up throwing his weight behind an equally repulsive form of tribalism. The progressive Mende Chief Briwa and his first wife, Mah Mahtoe, who remain faithful to their traditional customs, are denigrated and, in the Chief's case, brought to a ghastly end, while Makallay, the Susu-Creole wife who is highly conscious of her social and cultural superiority, is rescued to live happily ever after with her Creole lover. When Sarif Easmon talks about culture he clearly means western culture and all his cultured men adhere to western values—to champagne, western music, western literature and western clothes. Where other African writers have idealized traditional village life, Sarif Easmon seems to have no time for rural culture or for the villager unless he or she comes under the influence of a city-bred person for 'improvement'.

It is with the work of the younger generation of Sierra Leone writers, most of them still in their twenties and early thirties, that Sierra Leone literature begins to fall within the mainstream of African literature. In poetry the fluency and clarity of Abioseh Nicol gives way to the almost deliberate obscurity, concentration of thought and personal symbolism of Syl Cheyney Coker, Lemuel Johnson, Muctarr Mustapha and Gaston Bart-Williams. In the novel the melodramatic romanticism and sentimentality of Conton and Easmon make way for the earthy realism of Pat Maddy; and in drama Easmon's theatrical innocence and reliance on melodrama are replaced by Maddy's more professional knowledge of the stage and his greater awareness of the interaction of characters and setting.

These younger writers are all Creoles and all spent considerable periods of their young manhood in Britain, the United States or Germany, as free-lance writers or undergraduates, where they were exposed to the rigours of racial discrimination and where the inevitable detachment enabled them to re-examine the implications of their Creole ancestry, the role of the black race in general and the plight of the developing countries. They share with other modern African writers that sense of cultural alienation which is largely absent from the work of the middle generation.

Pat Maddy, who now writes under the name Yulisa Amadu Maddy, is the exact antithesis of Sarif Easmon. He belongs neither to the intellectual nor the social elite. To a certain extent his novel *No Past, No Present, No Future* is an autobiographical account of his own experiences as a drama student in Britain.[15] Where Sarif Easmon idealizes the Creole aristocracy, Maddy spares no pains in his novel to expose their snobbery, their contempt for the provincial peoples, their religious hypocrisy, their sterile striving after respectability and their regard for English culture. Maddy takes his characters from low life—the drop-outs from school, the underprivileged orphans, the prostitutes and the pimps—and he sets his scenes in brothels or amidst the corruption of a railway goods shed. Their language is earthy, realistic and almost crude; they have no hesitation in using four-letter words and quite often make use of Krio as it would be spoken in the fleshpots of Freetown. Where Sarif Easmon's characters play the piano and sing Byron's songs, Maddy's recreate an almost obscene song-and-dance sequence, of the kind that would be relished by Freetown's street corner boys, for the entertainment of their English friends.

In his treatment of the theme of tribalism however, Maddy shows just as great a lack of proportion as Easmon, though he errs in the opposite direction. He attributes the breakdown of the friendship of the three heroes, Joe, Ade and Santigie, to the Creole boy Ade's snobbery, a fact which is not by any means clearly demonstrated and which ignores the shortcomings of the other boys. Similarly, in his desire to attribute some of the boys' suffering to the narrow-mindedness of Freetown society, he relates their various acts of rebellion with great gusto and conducts them on a rake's progress of drinking, whoring, promiscuity and corruption, blinding himself to their responsibility for their own catastrophe. Like Easmon he allows his anger and prejudice to cloud his objectivity in the analysis of such complex social issues. His plays, which thrive on social satire and incorporate traditional songs and dancing, are technically more sophisticated than Easmon's and reveal him once more as a man from the people.[16] A typical one is *Allah Gbah* which concentrates on a condemned man's last twenty-four hours and is about freedom from the restrictions of the laws and conventions of a hypocritical Creole society.

Of all the poets in this younger generation the work of Gaston Bart-Williams is distinguished by its lack of pretentiousness and affectation; his images are clear, crisp and effective. He generally concentrates on the predicament of the black race. 'God Bless Us' is not just about the destructiveness of war, but about the absurdity of black men, oppressed themselves in Harlem, teaming up with white Americans to kill other coloured peoples—the so-called communist Viet-Cong. The tragedy of the black predicament is intensified by the speaker's own indifference to it all. 'Despondence Blues', cleverly modelled on Negro gospel blues, is a black man's cry against oppression in a world supposedly ruled by a benevolent, omnipotent God.[17]

Syl Cheyney-Coker is probably the most interesting of the younger generation of poets. Unlike Easmon who sees membership of the Creole group as a cause for congratulation, Cheyney-Coker sees it as a cause for regret, since it reminds him of the Creole history of slavery, suggesting degradation of the black race and alienation from one's roots. The preface to his collection of poems subsumes his major themes—his sense of frustration and disillusionment, his rejection of institutionalized religion, the betrayal of his love, his disgust with himself, and his awareness of the erosion of his original black personality.[18] A dominant motif in his poetry, which he claims is largely influenced by the Congolese poet Tchicaya U Tam'si, is the figure of the Argentinian woman with whom he fell disastrously in love. Since he sees the history and present predicament of Sierra Leone and Argentina as being basically similar, he had hoped, through his love, to bring the two continents together in a common cause. The woman therefore becomes the symbol of betrayal of love, personal despair and loss of hope for the regeneration of an ailing third world.

In poems such as 'Hydropathy', 'Freetown', 'Absurdity' and 'Masochist', Cheyney-Coker presents what he feels is the tragedy of his Creole ancestry:

> I think of Sierra Leone
> and my madness torments me
> all my strange traditions
> the plantation blood in my veins
> my foul genealogy!
> I laugh at this Creole ancestry
> which gave me my negralised head
> all my polluted streams . . . .

His ancestry is one of the devastating effects of the slave trade and he sees himself as the polluted product of a violent and filthy rape. The consequence is a feeling of disgust with himself; he becomes 'the running image' and 'the foul progeny' of his race; the rot of his country, and even the vultures will be afraid of his corpse. But the meaning of their ancestry is lost on some of his countrymen who 'plaster their skins with white cosmetics to look whiter than the snows of Europe' and who plead:

> make us Black Englishmen decorated
> Afro-Saxons
> Creole masters leading native races.

Several poems present his disgust with the Christian religion. He often refers to Christ as the Eunuch who lied to him at Calvary. In 'Obelisk' he says:

> I was myself the light in the dark
> I branded Jesus on the chests of millions
> but Christ you lied to me at Calvary
> you did not die to save the world
> but to make it a plantation where my people sweat.

The 'Misery of the Converts' and 'I throw myself to the Crocodiles' similarly present a Christianity that has taken sides with the oppressor against the down-trodden. Other poems, like 'Toilers', consist of social comment pointing to the neglect of the toiling masses by the powers that be, and contrasting the opulence of the latter with the squalor of the former.

The work of this new generation of writers suggests that Sierra Leone literature is at last beginning to flourish. Future development is likely to follow largely along the lines they have mapped. Moreover, the growing popularity of plays in Krio suggests a future flowering of vernacular literature. The writers who have so far achieved publication all come from the Creole group, but there are signs that the not-too-distant future will see a number of writers from the other tribes making effective use of their rich stores of traditional lore and experience for the general enrichment of our literature.

NOTES

1. Ruth Finnegan, *Limba Stories and Story Telling* (London and New York: Oxford University Press, 1967).
2. Adelaide Casely-Hayford, 'Mista Courifer', in *An African Treasury*, ed. L. Hughes (New York: Crown Publishers, 1960), pp. 134-143.
3. Crispin George, *Precious Gems Unearthed By An African* (Ilfracombe: Arthur H. Stockwell, 1952).
4. *Ibid.*, p. 34.
5. Two of them—'A Negro's Prayer' and 'Even There'—are to be found in *Our Poets Speak*, ed. D. St. John-Parsons (London: London University Press, 1966), p. 34 and pp. 36-7 respectively.
6. Gladys Casely-Hayford, 'Freetown', in *West African Verse*, ed. D. Nwoga (London: Longmans, 1967), p. 6.
7. Delphine King, *Dreams of Twilight* (Apapa: Nigerian National Press, 1962).
8. *Ibid.*, p. 24.
9. Abioseh Nicol, 'The Continent That Lies Within Us', in *The African Assertion*, ed. Austin Shelton (New York: The Odyssey Press, 1968), p. 58.
10. Abioseh Nicol, '*The Truly Married Woman and Other Stories* (London and New York: Oxford University Press, 1965).
11. Robert Wellesley-Cole, *Kossoh Town Boy* (London and New York: Cambridge University Press, 1960).
12. R. Sarif Easmon, *Dear Parent and Ogre* (London: Oxford University Press, 1964).
13. R. Sarif Easmon, *The New Patriots* (London: Longmans, 1965).
14. R. Sarif Easmon, *The Burnt-out Marriage* (London: Thomas Nelson and Sons, 1973).
15. Yulisa Amadu Maddy, *No Past, No Present, No Future* (London: Heinemann Educational Books, 1973).
16. Yulisa Amadu Maddy, *Obassai and Other Plays* (London: Heinemann Educational Books, 1971).
17. Gaston Bart-Williams, 'Despondence Blues' in *New Voices From The Commonwealth*, ed. Howard Sergeant (London: Evans Brothers, 1968), pp. 168-9.
18. Syl Cheyney-Coker, *Concerto For an Exile* (London: Heinemann Educational Books, 1973).

Notes on Contributors

Martin T. Bestman, a Nigerian, teaches French in the Department of Modern Languages, University of Ife. He has written on various aspects of Sembène Ousmane, and is finishing a book on *Les Bouts de bois de Dieu.*

T. J. Couzens, lectures in the Department of English, University of the Witwatersrand. A regular contributor of Introduction and Bibliography of South African Literature in the *Journal of Commonwealth Studies,* he has published articles on Sol Plaatje and H. I. E. Dhlomo, and is working on an edition of the latter's works.

J. Michael Dash, a Trinidadian, lectures in French at Abdullahi Bayero College, Kano. He is finishing a book on Haitian poetry.

M. J. C. Echeruo is Professor of English Literature at the University of Ibadan. He has published a book of poetry *Mortality,* a critical study *Joyce Cary and the Novel of Africa,* and co-edited with E. N. Obiechina *Igbo Traditional Literature and Art.*

Willfried F. Feuser, Professor and Head of the Department of Modern Languages at the University of Ife, was born in Germany. His publications include *Aspectos da literatura do mondo negro* and (with O. R. Dathorne) *Africa in Prose.*

Ime Ikiddeh, teaches English at the University of Ife. His publications include *Drum Beats: An Anthology of African Narrative Prose* and a play *Blind Cyclos.* He was Visiting Fellow in Literature at the University of Nairobi.

P. S. Izevbaye received his doctorate degree from the University of Ibadan where he is now a Senior Lecturer in English. He has contributed articles on African literature to many books and journals.

Louis James earned his Ph.D. at Oxford, is British by birth but was brought up in Africa. He has taught in the West Indies, Africa, the United States and now lectures at the University of Kent at Canterbury. Founder-member of Caribbean Arts movement, he has published *Fiction for the Working Man,* and edited *Islands that lie Between.*

Bridget Jones is 'British in origin and Jamaican by marriage'. She has written articles on Orlando Patterson and Léon Damas. She teaches French at the University of the West Indies, Jamaica.

Adele King is Reader in French, Ahmadu Bello University. She has published books on Camus and Proust.

Bruce King, an American, is Professor of English at Ahmadu Bello University. He has published a book on John Dryden's plays and edited several Collections of essays including *Introduction to Nigerian Literature* and *Literatures of the World in English.*

Lloyd King, a Trinidadian, is Senior Lecturer in the Department of French and Spanish, University of the West Indies, St. Augustine, Trinidad. He has published articles on Spanish literature and on West Indian drama.

Vere W. Knight is Head of the Department of French and Spanish at The University of the West Indies in St. Augustine, Trinidad. He has written articles on Césaire, Fanon and West Indian literature in general. He is a Barbadian and has taught in Nigeria.

258

Gerard M. Moser is Professor of Spanish and Portuguese at Pennsylvania State University. His many publications include *Essays in Portuguese African Literature* and *A tentative Portuguese-African bibliography.*

Kolawole Ogungbesan earned his Ph.D. at the University of Ibadan and is Senior Lecturer in the department of English at Ahmadu Bello University. He has published articles on Armah, Achebe, and Conrad. His book on Peter Abrahams will be published soon.

Eustace Palmer, Senior Lecturer in English, Fourah Bay College, University of Sierra Leone, has published *An Introduction to the African Novel* and articles on Béti, Sembène Ousmane, and Elechi Amadi. A Sierra Leonean, he has also contributed to the *African Encyclopaedia.*

John Reed, formerly Professor of English at the University of Zambia, has published, in collaboration with Clive Wake, *A Book of African Verse, French African Poetry,* and editions of Senghor and Rabéarivelo. He has translated two of Oyono's novels.

Helen Pyne Timothy, a Jamaican, is a lecturer in English at the University of the West Indies, St. Augustine, Trinidad.

Clive Wake is Senior Lecturer in French at the University of Kent at Canterbury. His publications include *The Novels of Pierre Loti* and *An Anthology of African and Malagasy Poetry in French.* He has translated works by Seydou Badian, Sembène Ousmane and Mohmoud Fall. He has edited, in collaboration with John Reed, anthologies of Senghor, Rabéarivelo, and *French African Poetry.*

Michael R. Ward, British, has lived and worked in Africa for fifteen years. He formerly lectured at the University of Zambia and has published articles on East African literature.